A
DRUID'S HERBAL
OF
SACRED
TREE
MEDICINE

A DRUID'S HERBAL
OF
SACRED TREE MEDICINE

Ellen Evert Hopman

Destiny Books
Rochester, Vermont

Destiny Books
One Park Street
Rochester, Vermont 05767
www.DestinyBooks.com

Destiny Books is a division of Inner Traditions International

The Library of Congress Cataloging-in-Publication Data
Hopman, Ellen Evert.
 A Druid's herbal of sacred tree medicine / Ellen Evert Hopman.
    p. cm.
 Includes bibliographical references and index.
 ISBN 978-1-59477-230-6 (pbk.)
 1. Trees—Religious aspects. 2. Druids and Druidism—Miscellanea. 3. Celtiberian alphabet—Miscellanea. 4. Trees—Therapeutic use. I. Title.
 BL444.H65 2008
 299'.161212—dc22

                                                                    2008008140

Printed and bound in the United States

10 9 8 7

Text design and layout by Carol Ruzicka
This book was typeset in Garamond Premier Pro, with Charlemagne and Barbara Svelte as display typefaces

For the Druids of the past, the Druids of the present,

and the Druids of the future. In Gratitude.

Many thanks to Alexei Kondratiev for help with the Gaelic

and to Dr. Jane Sibley for advice on

ancient divination techniques.

Contents

INTRODUCTION 1

Part One
THE OGHAM TREE ALPHABET

BIRCH • *BEITH* 17

ROWAN • *LUIS* 23

ALDER • *FEARN* 29

WILLOW • *SAILLE* 33

ASH • *NION* 41

HAWTHORN • *HUATH* 48

OAK • *DAIR* 55

HOLLY • *TINNE* 62

HAZEL • *COLL* 67

APPLE • *QUERT* 73

VINE • *MUIN* 79

IVY • *GORT* 85

REED • *NGETAL* 90

BLACKTHORN • *STRAIF* 96

ELDER • *RUIS* 102

SILVER FIR • *AILM* 112

FURZE • *ONN* 118

HEATHER • *ÚR* 122

ASPEN • *EDAD* 128

YEW • *IDAD* 136

Part Two
THE DRUIDIC ARTS

DRUID MAGIC 144

MAGICAL TOOLS OF THE DRUIDS 147

THE MAGICAL ARTS OF THE FOREST DRUIDS—
A PRACTICAL GUIDE 150

CELEBRATE THE CELTIC FIRE FESTIVALS 165

OGHAM DIVINATION 199

DIVINATORY MEANINGS 203

APPENDICES

SELECTED GAELIC PRONUNCIATION GUIDE 212

PRONUNCIATION GUIDE FOR THE WORD OGHAMS 222

NOTES 226

BIBLIOGRAPHY 236

ABOUT THE AUTHOR 239

INDEX 240

Introduction

When I visited Ireland a few years ago, I was privileged to meet followers of the Irish Druid tradition. They called themselves "Forest Druids" and, upon hearing of my Druid studies, my work with the trees, and my book *Tree Medicine, Tree Magic,* they told me that I was one of them. Forest Druids are working to reconstruct the ancient woods wisdom of Ireland and hand it down to the future.

The Forest Druids told me the story of their past, and why it is so important to keep their woods wisdom alive today. According to them, until the Elizabethan era most of Ireland was covered with a vast oak forest. The native peoples depended upon trees for fuel, shelter, medicine, furniture, household implements, weapons, and food. The trees were also a focus for spiritual teachings and rituals. The Forest Druids were the wisdom-keepers of the tribes (as opposed to the ancient aristocratic Druids who served courts and kings). The Forest Druids kept the ancient tree wisdom and lore in their heads, and passed it down through the generations.

Queen Elizabeth I (1533–1603) began sending troops into Ireland at the start of her reign in 1558, with orders to cut down the trees. She was terrified that the Irish would ally with Catholic Spain and attack England, and she knew that by removing the trees the English would have a military advantage because they would be able to see any troops that were massing. The English used the wood to build ships to face the Spanish armada, and once the trees were gone they parceled out the cleared lands to English lords so they could establish "plantations," large farms and estates so named for the "planting" of British citizens on Irish soil. The process of forcing English laws and social customs on the Irish and the cutting of native trees that began at the start of Elizabeth's reign continued until 1603, with particular violence from the 1560s to the 1580s.

Suddenly many of the native people had nowhere to live or hunt for food, and if they did so on the newly privatized land they were declared "poachers." A bounty was put on the head of any poacher, who could be legally shot while seeking food. Almost half of the native people of that time were still Pagan, living by their wits and the ancient woods wisdom.[1]

The chaos of this period marked the beginning of the end of old tribal families and relationships that had existed for millennia. It was also the beginning of the end for ancient tree medicines, lore, and stories. The alphabet that is covered in this text still has some of the old traditions associated with it, particularly via the "Word Oghams," or poetic descriptions of the individual trees. The work of piecing together these lost fragments of tree magic and healing continues, and this book is but a small contribution to the ongoing reconstruction. It has been my distinct honor to contribute to this effort.

I was in County Cork attending a summer solstice ritual, part of which called for everyone to "jump the flames." (Tradition states that it is very lucky to jump over a sacred fire on one of the holy days of the Celts.) A Forest Druid who was present fell into the fire, and an ember became embedded in the flesh of his knee. He was badly burned.

I had a jar of my tree salve with me, made from horse chestnuts, walnut hulls, comfrey, calendula, lavender, beeswax, and olive oil. I told him to apply it to the burn. He later wrote to tell me that the burn healed in a week and he never saw a doctor.[2]

THE OGHAM LEGACY

The "Tree Alphabet" is a vital bit of tree lore that has been handed down through the centuries. The ancient Scots, Irish, and other Celtic peoples did not use the alphabet that we use today (A, B, C, and so forth). They had their own script, called Ogham, which was both a type of sign language and a written alphabet. Ogham writing appears to be as old as the second or third centuries CE, but written descriptions of it do not appear until medieval times when literacy became widespread courtesy of the Christian scriptoria. Before that, knowledge of Ogham was part of the oral tradition.

Ogham was not used to write books; it was used on commemorative stones such as burial markers. It was also used for magic: an Ogham spell could be written on a scrap of tree bark and placed in the way of an approaching army, which would stop them in their tracks. The Druids and ancient Irish knew other alphabets, such as the Greek alphabet, which they used to tally merchants' goods and for other mundane functions. But they preferred to keep truly sacred things in the oral tradition, to preserve them.[3]

Oghams typically had four or five groups of letter symbols, of five letters each. The oldest Ogham seems to be four sets of five letters.* According to the Ogam Tract in the late fourteenth century Book of Ballymote, there were other ogham alphabets besides the tree alphabet. For example, in the *mucogam* the characters were named for five different kinds of pigs of different color. In Ogham *usceach,* each ogham group lists wells, rivers, rivulets, and weirs. *Conogam* lists groups of dogs: watchdogs, greyhounds, herding dogs, and lapdogs. *Damogam* is a list of bulls, oxen, bullocks, and steers. *Boogam* is a list of milk cows, strippers, three-year-old heifers, and yearling heifers. There were other Oghams, including ones that consisted of whole phrases and musical

---

*In the medieval period an extra five characters were added to the tree ogham. I have not discussed the extra characters because they are not part of the original set of letters.

notations.[4] I will be focusing on the Tree Ogham (*crannogam*) and "plant" or wood ogham (*fidogam*) here.

Most Ogham is found on standing stones in Ireland, Scotland, the Isle of Man, and Wales, dating from the fourth to the seventh centuries CE.[5] The best collection of Ogham stone boundary markers and grave markers is housed at the University of Cork, Ireland. For those interested in this subject, the collection is well worth a visit. But that does not mean that Ogham was only written on stones. As we will see, Ogham was also written on rowan, birch, and yew, as well as other woods, according to traditional stories.*

THE MAGICAL USES OF OGHAM

Ogham was carved not only on stones but onto wood and possibly other media; but, being perishable, these have not come down to us, except in verbal accounts and stories. The stories show that the Ogham alphabet was a secret language known only to the Druids, since a Druid had to be found to interpret the message. Ogham was used in the practice of magic and also as a divination tool.

The *Táin Bó Cúailnge* (*The Cattle Raid of Cooley*) tells us how Cúchulainn (the greatest warrior hero of northern Ireland) wrote Ogham letters on a hoop and placed it on a stone in the path of an approaching army. The letters were mysterious to the warriors and had to be shown to a Druid for interpretation. A similar magical challenge was written on a tree fork.[6] The purpose of these spells was to halt the advance of the warriors.

In *Tochmarc Etaíne* (*The Wooing of Etaíne*) the Druid Dálán inscribed Ogham letters on four sticks of yew and cast them to divine the hiding place of Etaíne.[7] In the same story, Etaíne's rival Fúamnach used a magic wand made of rowan to turn Etaíne into a pool of water.[8]

---

*Readers may already be familiar with the "Tree Calendar" that has become popular in neo-Pagan tradition. However, there is no evidence that the Celts ever used the Tree Ogham as a calendar. The tree calendar was the invention of the English poet Robert Graves, who claimed to have intuited the evidence for it.

In the story *Baile in Scáil* (The Phantom's Frenzy), a young woman who personifies the sovereignty of Ireland is preparing to serve ale at a feast. The giant Scál tells her to wait until the poet Cesarn can recite the names of every ruler of Ireland, to the end of time. Cesarn has difficulty doing this until he consults four sticks of yew upon which Oghams are inscribed.[9]

In the *Book of Leinster,* Corc, son of Lugaid, rejects his stepmother's amorous advances. She then accuses him of attempted rape, and Corc flees to the territory of King Feradach in Scotland, bearing a shield with a mysterious Ogham inscription. Feradach's seer interprets the inscription, which says that Feradach will kill Corc by beheading him. But Corc had once rescued the seer from slavery, so the seer interprets the shield differently to King Feradach, saying that it advises Feradach to give Corc his daughter in marriage. This seems to provide evidence that Ogham was only for the initiated Druids, poets and seers.[10]

In the *Sanas Cormaic* (Cormac's Glossary), there is a story of how Finn mac Cumhaill (the greatest warrior hero of southern Ireland) was initiated into the secrets of Ogham. Finn's jester cuts Oghams onto a four-sided wand, and Finn has to use all of his wits to interpret the message, which reveals his wife's infidelity.[11]

We have these stories and many others, but we really have no idea how the ancient Druidic soothsaying system worked. The Druids wrote nothing down, preferring to keep in their memories things that were sacred and important. Divination systems that readers may know, such as Ogham card decks, were created by modern neo-Pagans, and will not be discussed here.

DECODING ANCIENT SECRETS

When addressing the subject of Druids the byword is "caution," because so little is known about what the ancient Druids actually believed and practiced. The earliest accounts of their teachings come to us from foreigners and military occupiers—not the most reliable informants for learning spiritual mysteries. Later, the Christian monks, who had prejudices of their own, reported on Druid beliefs and activities. Bards and poets kept some truths alive but hidden, and folklore preserved the rest, embedded in stories and traditions.

That said, I have chosen to tackle the subject of the Tree Ogham Alphabet from my own perspective as a practicing Druid priestess and professional herbalist of the early twenty-first century. I have turned my herbalist's eye to the word phrases and descriptions of the Tree Alphabet found in the Word Oghams. Word Oghams are short phrases used to describe a letter. For example *beith* (birch) becomes "faded trunk and fair hair" and *luis* (rowan) becomes "delight of eye." These poetic phrases are an invaluable aid to deciphering the mystical meaning of the trees.

The oldest written account that we have of the Ogham letters is from the fourteenth century, which is fairly late in terms of ancient Druid traditions. The only obvious tree names that we have in the ogham lists are *beith* (birch), *fearn* (alder), *saille* (willow), *dair* (oak), and *coll* (hazel), yet even these have been called into question by some scholars. According to German linguist and Celtic scholar Rudolf Thurneysen (1857–1940) for example, *beithi* or *beith,* the first letter of the Tree Ogham Alphabet, may be an imitation of the Hebrew *beth*.[12] He also asserts that *ailm* may have been inserted in imitation of the Greek *alpha* by medieval scholars.[13] To make matters worse *ailm* has been translated as "elm" and also as "silver fir."

Quert is often translated as apple, yet the actual word for apple is *aball*. *Quert* may originally have been something like *cert* or *ceirt,* which means "rag."[14] Some scholars have translated *quert* as *quillenn,* or holly.

The *t* sound is often listed as *tinne,* holly, or *teithe,* furze. *Onn* is often translated as "furze," "ash," or "wheel" (as in the wheels of a chariot).[15] *Muin* is sometimes translated as vine but may also be a corruption of *midiuiti* or "unsimple."[16] There was no *ng* sound in Irish, so the word "*ngetal,*" which is often translated as "reed," may be a corruption of *cétal,* or "charm."[17]

Scholars have translated *straif* as blackthorn or as a corruption of *sraiph,* that is, "sulphur," a tool of alchemy.[18] And *úr,* heather, has been translated both as "humus" (as in "earth") and as "moisture or rain."[19] There are many other translations for the purported "trees" in the alphabet.

I do not claim to possess the ultimate truth on this subject, nor can anyone else. Scholars can't even agree that there ever was a "tree alphabet" (because they have decided that some of the Word Oghams do not refer to trees or even plants) and much confusion reigns as to the kennings and meanings of the Ogham symbols. I feel that the way into the meanings is to remember that the Word Oghams were written by poets. They are bardic allusions to well-known trees and herbs of ancient times. With that in mind, I present in this book what my own *imbas* (poetic inspiration) has shown me.

I have chosen to omit the *forfeda,* a group of five symbols that seem to have been grafted onto the tree alphabet at a later date, preferring to stick to what may be an older, purely Pagan symbol system.

Some have claimed that the Tree Ogham derives from or is related to the Germanic Runes. I prefer to think that the original four *aicme* ("tribes") of five letters each represent a pictorial description of an ancient sign language that was spoken with the five fingers against the nose, palm, or shin (see the introduction to part 1 for more details on the use of Ogham in signing).

How to Use This Book

For me, the Tree Ogham is a practical tool for passing down tree lore to future generations. It can serve the same function as did the ancient tales of the *senachie* (traditional storyteller) before literacy was widespread. Until a century or two ago, few humans could go to a bookshelf to look up the herbal uses of a tree or herb. The lore was passed down by word of mouth and practical experience.

The first section of this book gives details about the letters of the tree alphabet. A chapter is devoted to each tree and letter, including the poetic meanings of the Word Oghams, herbal uses of tree berries, leaves, bark, wood, and roots, and spiritual aspects of each tree. The Herbal Basics section at the end of this chapter describes methods for preparing tree medicines and proper dosages.

I have included Native American plant lore and healing uses because of the unbroken tradition that still exists regarding their use of trees as medicine—a boon to reconstructing the herbal tree medicine of the past.

In the second part of the book, I include magical practices and suggestions for ritual and prayer using trees, as well as a guide to the ancient fire festivals of the Forest Druids and instruction on Ogham divination methods and meanings.

Because we have no genuine accounts of how Druids used the Oghams for divination, I have consulted with a traditional Norse soothsayer who uses rune sticks in her divinations. We know that Vikings and traders from Scandinavia were plying the coasts of Celtic Europe for millennia; therefore, I have adapted some of her methods, and also offer some techniques of my own.

HERBAL BASICS

Please note: In the event of a medical situation, readers are advised to seek the assistance of a competent health professional. Some of the remedies described in this book are from herbal tradition and have not necessarily been empirically tested. Persons on medications prescribed by a health professional should seek advice before ingesting herbal preparations.

A Note about Dosages
The dosages mentioned herein are for an adult weighing approximately one hundred and fifty pounds. Amounts should be halved for a child who weighs seventy-five pounds, and quartered for a child of thirty

pounds. Infants can get the benefits of the herbal remedies mother's breast milk.

Preparation

The general rules are that roots, barks, and berries are "decocted" (simmered, not boiled) and leaves and flowers are "infused" (steeped in freshly boiled water, removed from the stove) using two tablespoons of plant matter per cup of water for about twenty minutes. Please use only nonaluminum cookware, and be sure you have a tight lid on your pot to avoid losing the volatile oils via the steam.

Herbal teas can be safely stored in the refrigerator for up to a week in a tightly capped glass jar. Unless otherwise stated, the usual dose is one-quarter cup, four times a day, not with meals.

See instructions for making salves on pages 161–62 in The Magical Arts of the Forest Druids—A Practical Guide chapter.

To make a poultice, soak a clean cloth in a strong tea and apply, or put tree parts into a blender with enough water to make a slush. Pour into a bowl. Add buckwheat flour (not wheat, as many people are allergic to it) or powdered slippery elm bark and knead with your fingers until you have a "pie dough" consistency. Roll out on a clean cloth using a rolling pin. Apply to a wound or burn for one hour and discard.

A Bit about Gathering Medicinal Parts from Trees

Never gird a tree by removing bark from the main trunk, as this will kill the tree. Bark should only be taken from a twig or from the root or trunk of a tree that has fallen or been cut down. The medicinal parts are found just under the outer bark, in the thin living layer of tissue called the cambium. Leaves should be collected *before* Summer Solstice (after that they will contain too many natural insecticides and be too harsh for human consumption), and berries are gathered in the fall.

Part One

The Ogham Tree Alphabet

The Alphabet and the Ogham Trees

B ├ Beith • Birch

L ├ Luis • Rowan

F ├ Fearn • Alder

S ├ Saille • Willow

N ├ Nion • Ash

H ┤ Huath • Hawthorn

D ┤ Dair • Oak

T ┤ Tinne • Holly

C ┤ Coll • Hazel

Q ┤ Quert • Apple

M ⅄ Muin • Vine

G ⅄ Gort • Ivy

P or Ng ⅄ Ngetal • Reed

Ss ⅄ Straif • Blackthorn

R ⅄ Ruis • Elder

A ┼ Ailm • Silver Fir

O ╪ Onn • Furze (Gorse or Whin)

U ╪ Úr • Heather

E ╪ Edad • Aspen

I ╪ Idad • Yew

hen Ogham was carved onto a stone, only the edge of the stone was chiseled. The edge of the stone became the "stem line" for the shorter lines that denoted the different letters. These short lines were carved to the right, the left, diagonally across, or straight across the implied stem line. The position and number of short marks identified the letter. The carving began at the bottom left of the stone and was read in an upward direction, bottom to top. If the message was too long for one side of the stone it continued around, either down or up the right side of the stone.[1] Sometimes the Ogham was written in a horizontal line.[2]

The letters were grouped into four sets of five letters, each set called an aicme, or "tribe." Each aicme is named after the first letter in its group. *Aicme beith,* the birch group, includes beith, luis, fearn, saille, and nuin; *aicme huatha,* the hawthorn group, includes huath, dur, tinne, coll, and quert; *aicme muine,* the vine group, includes muin, gort, ngetal, straif, and ruis; and *aicme ailme* (the silver fir group, includes ailim, onn, ur, edad, and idad.

The letters seem to be paired phonetically—that is, letters with related sounds appear adjacent to one another—and these pairings also reflect similar uses and growing conditions, or similar poetic meanings, for the corresponding trees. For example, alder and willow (F and S) are paired; both are trees that like to have their feet wet and grow near water. Oak and holly (D and T) are paired; both are trees that have hard wood and make a very hot fire. Hazel and apple (C and Q) are paired; both are trees that are used for food and both have strong associations with the otherworld. Ash and heather (O and U) are paired. Both are associated with fertility and water. And aspen and yew (E and I) are paired; both trees have funerary associations.[3]

The letter *f* was probably pronounced like *v. Str* (as in "straif") was probably pronounced like *z.* The letters *h* and *str* have only been found on Pictish (Scottish) stones. N and *g* each have their own Ogham letters, as does *ng* (as in Ngetal). *S*, *t*, and *r* each have their own letter, as does *str*.[4]

Ogham must have been used by Druids, bards, and poets to communicate with each other in secret—the average person did not memorize these extensive word lists, such as dog Ogham, cow Ogham, pig Ogham, and so on. The medieval Book of Ballymote gives a description of how Ogham was also used as sign language; the person signing could use his or her fingers against the shinbone, the ridge of the nose, or the palm to make the characters.[5] To make the signs, the fingers were placed to the right of the shinbone for the letters in the B aicme, to the left for the H aicme, athwart the shin for the M aicme, and straight across for the A aicme. One finger was used for the first letter, two for the second letter, three for the third, and so on. For nose Ogham, the fingers went to the right, left, oblique to, or across the nose, and for the palm Ogham, the side of the upturned palm was used as the baseline.

OGHAM AND THE BREHON LAWS

The ancient Irish law text on farming called *Bretha Comaithchesa* groups trees according to their status. There are eight "chieftain" trees, eight "peasant" trees, and eight "shrub" trees. The chieftain trees are alder, oak, hazel, vine, ivy, sloe, furze, and heath. The peasant trees are birch, quicken, willow, ash, whitethorn, whin, and apple, according to the *Auraicept na N-Eces* (The Scholars' Primer). All other shrubs are peasant trees.[6] The trees are divided this way according to the penalty for illegally felling them and due to their value as crops. These laws are valuable in helping us to understand the uses and value of trees in the Ogham alphabet.

Ogham was also a feature of the Brehon Laws (early Irish laws). The use of Ogham as a form of legal notice predates the coming of Christianity. One such use was to mark tribal territories or farm boundaries. The process of claiming a piece of land to which one was legally entitled but which was being held by another group or person is outlined in the Brehon Laws. Legal entry of the disputed property, or *tellach,* involved a number of formal procedures that had to be done in the presence of witnesses. The first step was for the claimant to enter the contested land accompanied by witnesses and two horses, crossing the boundary mound of the property. The person occupying the land could challenge the entry in court after five days. If the occupant did not issue a legal challenge, the claimant could enter again, ten days after he or she first laid claim to the land. This time he had to bring two witnesses and four horses, and the horses were set free to graze on the property. The occupant could challenge the entry in court after three days.

Twenty days after the first entry the claimant could enter the property again, with three witnesses and eight horses. At this point the claimant could feed and stable the horses on the land. If no legal challenge was forthcoming, the claimant now had legal ownership. Ownership was formally declared by the new owner spending the night on the land, lighting a fire, and tending his or her animals.[7]

The next step in formalizing the claim was to erect or identify a permanent boundary marker. Twelve kinds of boundary markers were acceptable, including a rock, a ditch, a tree, a body of water such as a creek or river, a road or lane, a venerated old tree, a great oak, a mound with a tree on it, or the stump of a large tree.[8]

A large natural rock or stone might be used, or a stone placed by the occupants such as a gravestone or a standing stone with Ogham markings. The Brehon Laws state: "The Ogham in the standing stone . . . is like a witness [of ownership]."[9]

Ogham was also used to mark the graves of dead nobles. The Book of Ballymote describes the death of Fiachra, brother of Niall of the Nine Hostages:

Maidhi Meascorach wounded Fiachra mortally in the battle. . . . Then Fiachra carried away fifty hostages out of Munster, together with his tribute in full, and set forth on his march to Temar. Now when he had reached Forraidh in Uibh Maccuais in West Meath, Fiachra died there of his wound. His grave was made, and his mound was raised and his *cluiche cainte* (funeral rites including games and dirges) were ignited, and his Ogam name was written, and the hostages which had been brought from the south were buried alive around Fiachra's grave.[10]

The *Leabhar na h-Uidhre* (*Book of the Dun Cow*), an eleventh- or twelfth-century manuscript of which only fragments remain, describes the grave of Fothadh Airgthech, a ruler of Ireland, who was killed by Cailte, foster son of Finn mac Cumhaill, in the Battle of Ollarba (285 CE).

The *ulaidh* (cairn) of Fothadh Airgthech will be found at a short distance to the east of it [the iron head of a spear buried in the earth]. There is a chest of stone about him in the earth. There are his two rings of silver, and his two *bunne doat* [bracelets?], and his torque of silver on his chest; and there is a pillar stone at his cairn; and an *Ogham* is [inscribed] on the end of the pillar stone which is in the earth. And what is in it is, Eochaid Airgthech here.[11]

Airgthech means "robber" or "plunderer," and it is unusual that the Ogham was cut so as to be hidden under the ground. Perhaps Fothadh Airgthech disgraced himself in some way.

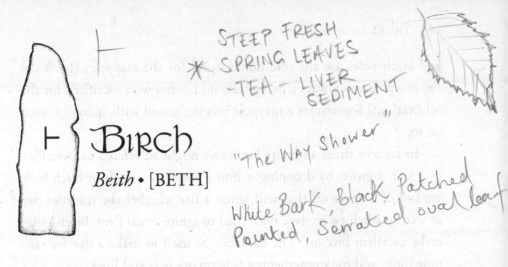

STEEP FRESH SPRING LEAVES — TEA — LIVER SEDIMENT

Birch

Beith • [BETH]

"The Way Shower"

White Bark, black Patched Pointed, Serrated oval leaf

ccording to tradition the Ogham alphabet was invented by Ogma, god of eloquence and fair speech. The first message he wrote in the alphabet was a message on a birch rod, consisting of seven strokes. For this reason, birch is the first letter of the Ogham alphabet.[1]

The poets give beautiful and evocative descriptions of the birch tree in their ancient Word Oghams. In the *Word Ogham of Morainn mic Móin, feocus foltchain* is described as "withered foot and fine hair." The *Word Ogham of Mic ind Oic* lists *glasium cnis,* "most silvery of skin."[2] We also have *maise malach* "beauty of eyebrow" (from *Briatharogam Con Culainn*).[3]

It is fitting that birch is the first of the Ogham trees. Birches are among the very first trees to make an appearance after ground has been disturbed. They were also one of the first trees to take hold after the ice retreated ten thousand years ago. Mystically, the birch is a tree of new beginnings.

Birch is also "the way shower." Try visiting a mature forest on a night when the moon is full. The white birch blazes forth gloriously, shining in the starlight.

In Siberian cultures the shamans use birch as a sky ladder, traveling in drumbeat trance up her branches and out to the Sky World. Native American women fashion prayer baskets from her wood. Birch is a wood of choice in Scandinavia for carving rune sets for divination,

17

and birch poles are the traditional wood for the maypole. (In Wales the maypole was always a living tree; no birches were sacrificed for the celebration!) Sometimes a maypole was decorated with sprays of birch on top.[4]

In ancient times an entire birch tree might be offered as a sacrifice in a sacred grove, by dropping it into a votive pit. Coils of birch bark are full of a dense oil that will ignite a fire whether the tinder is dry or wet, so birch twigs were once used to ignite ritual fires. Birch twigs make excellent brooms. The bark can be used to make a dye for tanning hides and for strengthening fisherman's nets and lines.

Birch wood was used to make cradles in Wales, thus bringing the protective power of the Goddess into the nursery. In the Western isles of Scotland, birch was hung over the cradle as protection. Rituals celebrating Imbolc in Scotland featured a "bride doll," a straw effigy of the goddess Brigid, who held a birch *slachdan,* or magical wand, symbolic of her ability to transform the weather. Striking a cow with a birch twig was said to promote calving.[5]

Throughout Europe, birch wood was used on New Year's or at Winter Solstice to "beat the bounds" of the local district. Birch torches were believed to purify the land and expel evil spirits. Birch was said to repel ill-intentioned fairies. One could place a wreath of birch under the milk pail to prevent the milk from being spoiled. A Scottish story tells of a man who protected himself from "Headless Hugh," a nasty headless horse-riding spirit, by clinging to a birch tree.[6]

HERBAL USES

In ancient Scandinavia after a long, hard snowbound winter, everyone went to the sauna for a purifying sweat. During the sweat they would beat themselves with bundles of fragrant birch twigs, to increase circulation.

Birch leaves can be picked in very early spring to make a laxative tea. Used as a gargle, the tea heals mouth sores. Taken internally, the tea helps to purge kidney and bladder sediment and benefits gout and rheumatism. The tea is also slightly sedative and helps sore muscles.[7]

CAUTION

If you are going to chew leaves or use them in tea, please collect them before the Summer Solstice. After that they will contain too many plant alkaloids.

Make a strong tea using the leaves, twigs, and bark, and add it to the bath or use it as a wash for eczema, psoriasis, and other moist, oozing skin conditions.

All birches are valuable as medicine. *Betula alba,* white birch, has no real flavor and should be avoided as a beverage tea, but the leaves can be used in an herbal brew. Native American herbalists and medicine people have used a yellow fungus that grows on birch for millennia to heal tumors. Known as *chaga,* it boosts the immune system. Modern medicine has only recently discovered that birch sap contains betulinic acid, a potent antitumor cancer treatment.[8]

White birch is used by the Cree for skin conditions, by boiling the powdered wood and applying it to the skin. The Ojibwa use the roots, cooked with maple syrup, for stomach cramps.[9]

Betula lenta (cherry birch) is used by the Cherokee as an antidiarrheal and for treating colds. They make a tea of the leaves or chew them.

The Chippewa use the bark tea for diarrhea. The Iroquois use the bark as a decoction for fevers, menstrual cramps, and exhaustion. The Mohegan use the bark in spring tonics. The bark can be used to make dwellings; it makes a beautiful waterproof covering.[10]

Betula lutea (yellow birch) is used by the Delaware as a cathartic—the tea of the bark is emetic (it makes you vomit). The Iroquois used it as a wash for itching skin. The Potawatomi add the twig infusion to medicines as a flavoring agent and the Ojibwa use the inner bark as a diuretic.[11]

Betula nigra (river birch) is used by the Cherokee as an antidiarrheal, by chewing the leaf or making an infusion with the leaf. The Cherokee and Chippewa take a bark decoction for stomach pain. The sap can be harvested in spring to make syrup.[12]

Betula papyrifera (paper birch) bark is used by the Chippewa for enemas and as a cathartic tea. The Menominee use the inner bark in a tea to treat dysentery and as a general tonic. The Ojibwa use the root bark in a tea for stomach cramps, and the Potawatomi use the twigs to flavor medicines.[13]

Betula populifolia (gray birch) bark decoction is taken internally as tea. The MicMac use the inner bark tea to treat infected wounds and also as an emetic. The Iroquois use the tea internally for bleeding piles.[14] The inner bark can be dried, ground, and added to flour as a famine food to make bread.[15]

Betula pumila (low birch) is used by the Ojibwa as a gynecologic aid; the cones are infused in a tea to ease menstruation and to strengthen a woman's body after childbirth. The smoke of the cones is inhaled to help clear catarrhal conditions in the lungs.[16]

To prepare a birch leaf tea use one tablespoon of fresh leaf in one-half cup boiled water and steep for twenty minutes. Take one-quarter cup, four times a day.[17]

To prepare a birch bark tea simmer one teaspoon of inner bark per cup of water for twenty minutes. Take up to two cups a day in one-quarter cup doses. Gather the bark from a twig using a sharp knife.[18]

CAUTION

When using the bark, please take the bark from a twig—never from the trunk of the tree. Girdling a tree can be fatal to the tree.

The best beverage tea is made from black birch and other birches, such as river birch, that have a distinct wintergreen smell when you crush the leaf or chew on a twig.

Spring Tonic

Each spring I like to make one batch of nonalcoholic beer using birch. The tonic warms the blood and increases circulation, a perfect antidote to the doldrums of a cold winter here in New England.

I am fortunate to have a small grove of sassafras trees by my house. Each year I sacrifice one small tree to make the tonic. (Sassafras trees grow in colonies, all connected by their roots. If you take one tree you are really just pruning a small part of the larger organism.)

I dig up a sassafras tree and cut off the root. (The leaves can be dried and powdered to make Fíle Gumbo, a Louisiana Cajun recipe featuring bell pepper, onion, celery, tomatoes, and a combination of fish and shellfish or chicken, sausage, and other meats. Powdered sassafras leaf is the traditional thickening agent for the gumbo, which is added only after cooking is done.) Using a sharp knife, I peel off the bark of the root. The root bark is where the sassafras flavor comes from.

Then I visit a river birch tree behind the house. I harvest a few feet of branches and cut them into one-inch sections. Then I slice up a large section of gingerroot (*Zingiber officinale*).

I place everything in a large, nonaluminum pot with a tight lid. I just barely cover the roots and twigs with spring water, and simmer these ingredients for about twenty minutes. I let the pot sit for about fifteen minutes longer and then add a sweetener, such as maple syrup, sucanat (dried sugar cane juice), honey, or organic sorghum, to make a syrup.

To make the birch beer I pour about two ounces of the syrup into an eight-ounce glass, and then fill the glass with a sparkling water such as Evian or Perrier. Voilá!

SPIRITUAL ASPECTS

In my spiritual work as a *ban-drui* (Druid priestess) I like to visit a large birch tree that grows behind the stone circle in the forest where my grove and I do our rituals. She blazes forth on moonlit nights like a column of white flame bursting out of the dark woods. It is obvious to me why birch is known as "the way shower."

The ancient Proto-Indo-European word for birch, *bherH-g-o*, is associated with the words for *it shines, glitter, flash, shimmer, brilliance, brightness, white,* and *bright* in several languages. The Gaelic word for birch, *beith*, is closely related to the Gaelic words *bith* (existence, enduring, constant) and *bithe* (womanly, feminine).[19]

Scandinavian couples would celebrate May Day by making love in a birch forest because birch forests were sacred to Frigga, goddess of fertility and love. The legendary Celtic lovers Diarmid and Grainne slept in birch-branch huts as they fled their pursuers. Birch trees and linden trees were commonly offered as sacrifices in Druidic groves.[20]

Birch is regarded in all cultures as a Goddess tree. Use her energy to put yourself in touch with the feminine aspect of the universe and within yourself.

Birch helps us to focus on what needs doing and gives us energy in the process. She tells us to honor our female side, our vulnerability, and our feminine life-giving, nurturing qualities as well as to honor those qualities in others.

Give all your honor and respect to the birches. They show us the straight path of wisdom, lead us safely through dark forests of the soul, and bring us home to the clear light within.

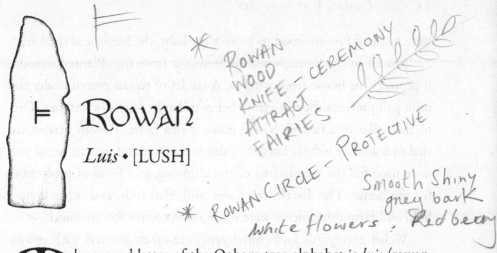

ᚂ Rowan

Luis • [LUSH]

Handwritten annotations: ROWAN WOOD KNIFE – CEREMONY; ATTRACT FAIRIES; ROWAN CIRCLE – PROTECTIVE; Smooth Shiny grey bark; white flowers; Red berry

The second letter of the Ogham tree alphabet is *luis* (rowan, also known as mountain ash). The *Word Ogham of Morainn mic Moín* designates rowan as *li sula,* "delight of eye." The *Word Ogham of Mic ind Oic* characterizes it as *cara ceathra,* "friend of cattle."[1] We also see *lúth cethrae* "sustenance of cattle" in *Briatharogam Con Culainn.*[2]

The word *luis* means "flame or radiance,"[3] which is a fitting description for this tree. When the mountain ash or rowan is covered with berries, it glows like a tower of red or orange (depending on the species). According to legend, the original rowan was brought from the Land of Fairy by the Tuatha de Danann, the tribe or peoples of the goddess Danu, who preceded the Celts in Ireland. One berry fell on the ground in Eire and thus the first rowan took root. Those who ate the berries were young and joyful ever after.[4]

Garlands of rowan berries were worn by ladies of the Scottish Highlands as a form of magical protection, and tied around the horns of cows and the necks of pigs to keep them healthy and safe.[5]

In Scotland, tiny crosses were made of rowan wood. With arms of equal length symbolic of the sun, they were bound with red thread and secretly sewn into clothing as a protection from sorcery. Rowan branches were placed in the cradle, laid over the lintel of the home, and hung in the barn to protect the cattle. Churn staffs were made of rowan wood to keep the butter safe from evil spells. Cradles, plow pins, pegs, and whips were made of Rowan wood to protect the baby, the horse, and the land.[6]

Rowan in the home is said to protect it from fire. Planted outside, it protects the house from witches. A circlet of rowan placed under the milk pail prevents the milk from being stolen by fairies or witches. Tied to the collar of a hound, it will make it run faster. Rowan berries are tied to a wild or unruly horse to calm it. In Scotland, rowan wood was once used for the crossbeams of the chimney, as a form of protection for the house. The distaff, the water mill, flail rods, and other household and farm implements were made of protective rowan wood.[7]

Welsh graveyards and churchyards are often planted with rowan trees. Rowan prevents the dead from rising and protects against evil spirits, thus Scottish coffins and biers were once made of rowan wood.[8]

Rowan is considered a powerful protection against being taken by the fairies. A rowan wood walking stick is used for this purpose. A green rowan stick allows the explorer to safely enter and exit a fairy fort (an ancient cairn or stone circle). It also affords protection when walking over a fairy hill (a cairn covered by grass). Wear rowan on a hat to avoid being "fairy led,"[9] an expression that means becoming unaccountably lost when traveling in familiar territory, usually on a country road or path. (The correct way to undo the fairies' charm is to take off one's clothing and put it back on inside out—that way one is no longer recognizable to the fairies.)

Rowan bark shavings were once used as fodder for cattle in Scandinavia,[10] which accounts for rowan's Ogham name "sustenance of cattle." The beauty of a rowan tree in spring, when it is covered in white flowers, and its beauty in the fall, when it is lush with berries, explains the name "delight of eye." Birds are very fond of rowan berries, adding to the delightful image.

Rowan was an important wood for the Beltaine festival, the celebration of the official start of summer and the light half of the year (please see details on how to observe this festival in the Celebrate the Celtic Fire Festivals chapter).

A rowan fire in the hearth brought luck on May Day morning. Sprigs of rowan were mixed with the cattle fodder and the cows were switched with Rowan to protect them from spirits who might be about. Rowan was tied to the tails of the cows, placed in windows, on doors, and in the fields. In Scotland, lambs and sheep were made to walk through a rowan hoop. In the Isle of Man, tiny rowan crosses were tied to cows' tails on Beltaine. The crosses had to be made without the use of a metal knife,[11] because fairies detest iron and helpful spirits might be repulsed by the use of iron implements.

In Scotland, sprigs of rowan were burned at the entrance to barns on the first day of every quarter.[12]

Rowan is called *fid na nDruad,* "the Druid's tree." The goddess Brigid, the great triple goddess of smithcraft, healing, and poetry and the patroness of the Druids and bards, has three fiery arrows made of rowan wood.[13] Druidic battle-magic spells were sometimes cast by lighting huge fires of rowan and uttering incantations to thwart the opposing army. Druids read the outcome of the battle in the flames and smoke.[14]

HERBAL USES

Rowan berries are highly pigmented and full of bioflavinoids and vitamins A and C, making them valuable boosters of the immune system. Their traditional use was as an antiscorbutic (scurvy preventive). *Sorbus americana* (American mountain ash) has orange berries, and *Sorbus aucuparia* (European mountain ash) has red berries. The herbal properties of both species are identical, and the berries should be picked only after the first frost when they develop a deep, bright color.

The juice of the fresh berries is laxative and can be used as a gargle for sore throats and mouth sores. Take one teaspoon of fresh juice in a little water as needed.[15] Rowan berry jam is made with apples and controls diarrhea.[16] (If fresh berries are not available, soak one teaspoon of dried berries per cup of water for ten hours.)

CAUTION

Children should not eat the raw berries, but may eat small amounts of the jam, about one tablespoon three times a day, to help with diarrhea.

To make a tea or gargle, simmer one teaspoon of berries per cup of water for twenty minutes in a nonaluminum pot with a tight lid. Adults can take up to one cup a day in quarter-cup doses.[17]

The Welsh once added the berries to ale recipes (the process has been lost) and in the Scottish Highlands, rowan berries and apples were simmered in honey to make a syrup for coughs, fever, and sore throats.[18]

Native American healers and medicine people used rowan as a medicine. The Cree scraped the inner bark of young branches to make a tea for pleurisy and inflammatory diseases. The Montagnais called the tree "bear berry" because bears like to eat the berries. They made a tea of the scraped inner bark to increase appetite and to purify the blood. They also made an infusion of the root to treat colic.[19]

CAUTION

Never take the bark from the trunk of a tree—you might kill it! Use only the inner bark of twigs.

The Ojibwa used the wood for objects that needed to be bent and flexible, such as canoe ribs, snowshoes, and lacrosse rackets.[20]

The Potawatomi steeped the leaves to make a cold remedy. Apparently the leaf tea is emetic and in this way mucus is driven out. The Potawatomi also used rowan leaves for pneumonia, diphtheria, and croup.[21]

CAUTION

Harvest the leaves only until summer solstice. After that they will contain too many alkaloids for human use.

The Tête-de-Boule made a decoction of the buds and inner bark for feebleness and depression, and to make a plaster that they applied to the kidneys of women who were in childbirth.[22]

SPIRITUAL ASPECTS

Evidence for the spiritual power of rowan appears as far back as the Bronze Age. In Maglehoj, North Zealand, Denmark, a mound was excavated in 1888 and the grave of a female healer was discovered. Within the mound was a stone coffin covered by a large slab of stone with smaller stones set on top of it to protect the tomb from dirt. Inside the coffin were cremated bones wrapped in woolen clothing with a double-headed fastener, a knife, and a fibula placed on top of the bundle of ashes.

Close by was a bronze box decorated with star patterns.[23] The box was filled with sorcerer's charms: horse's teeth, weasel bones, the claw-joint of a cat (possibly a lynx), bones from a young lamb or deer, a tiny section of a bird's windpipe, some snake vertebrae, two burned bone fragments, some charred aspen, two quartz pebbles, a lump of clay, two pyrites, a bronze sheet, a piece of bronze wire bent to make a hook—and a twig of rowan, the presence of which strongly hints at its magical protection and medicinal value to the sorceress.

Some years ago when I visited Ireland, I was gifted with a small carved rowan wood knife to use in the ritual circle. The fairies despise iron, so it makes sense to use a rowan knife. An iron blade will only repel the fairies. Using a rowan blade in ceremony demonstrates our sensitivity to the needs and desires of the spirits and strengthens our bonds with the spirit world.

As rowan protects the house and barn, it is also a protector for one's inner spirit. Rowan helps to strengthen your inner shields as it fortifies your strength, patience, and inner peace. Allow rowan to create a circle of protection around you, repelling evil and harm and allowing only good and uplifting forces to enter. Rowan is the ancient enchantress who holds all creation in her circle of light.

handwritten annotations:
BRAN CARRIED ALDER SPRIGS
PONDS, RIVERS, STREAMS,
GREY BROWN BARK SHALLOW FISSURED

ᚃ ALDER

Fearn • [FYEHRN]

Now we will examine the third letter of the Ogham tree alphabet, *fearn* (alder). The *Word Ogham of Morainn mic Moín* lists *airinach fian,* "shield of warrior bands." The *Word Ogham of Mic ind Oic* lists *comet lachta,* "guarding of milk."[1] And *Briatharogam Con Culainn* gives us *Dín cridi,* "Protection of the heart" (from).[2]

"Song of the Forest Trees," an Irish poem of woods-wisdom dating to the thirteenth century, lists which woods are best to burn in a fire.

> *Rowan, the wizard's tree, Briar, burn him that*
> *   is so keen and green,*
> *Oak, fiercest heat giver of all timber,*
> *Alder, very battle-witch of all woods,*
> *Holly, burn it green, burn it dry,*
> *Elder, him that furnishes horses to the armies*
> *   of the sidhe [fairy mound] burn,*
> *Birch, burn up most sure the stalks that bear*
> *   the constant pods,*
> *Aspen, burn it late or early.*[3]

When seeking alder, look to the edges of ponds, rivers, and streams because alder likes to have its feet wet. Alder is very resistant to rot. In ancient times its wood was used to make roadways and tracks. Alder was used in any construction that required protection from damp such as pilings for lake dwellings, water wheels, house foundations, canal locks, and wooden pipes. It was also used for milk pails, which perhaps was the reason for the Ogham name "guarding of milk."

Alder was also used to make charcoal for gunpowder, and as fuel in smiths' fires and in potters' ovens.[4] In a house that was plagued by fleas and other insects, alder leaves were gathered while damp and strewn on the floors. The insects stuck to the leaves and died.[5]

Alder, the "shield of warrior bands," was once used to make shields for warriors. Its wood turns from white to red after cutting, making it look like blood.[6]

HERBAL USES

The part of alder (*Alnus glutinosa*) (black alder) that is used herbally is the inner bark, which is gathered by scraping the bark off a twig or branch with a sharp knife.

CAUTION

Never take the bark off the trunk of the tree or you might kill the tree.

The inner bark is also simmered to make a wound wash, suitable for very deep external wounds, and a tea for internal injuries (perhaps another reason for the Ogham name "shield of warrior bands"). The bark must be dried before using it internally, because the fresh bark is emetic. Taken internally it stops bleeding. When the inner bark is decocted in vinegar it makes an external wash for eliminating lice and scabies. Alder bark tea can be used as a gargle for sore throats and as a dentifrice to clean the teeth and gums.[7]

To make this decoction, simmer one teaspoon of the inner bark or leaves per cup of water in a nonaluminum pot with a tight lid for twenty minutes. For internal use such as treating internal hemorrhage, take up to two cups a day in tablespoon doses.[8]

CAUTION

Gather the fresh leaves only until Summer Solstice. After that they will contain too many plant alkaloids.

Red alder (*Alnus rubra*) is used the same way as black alder, and the dosages are the same. Smooth alder or hazel alder (*Alnus serrulata*) is also used the same way and in the same dosages.

Native American medicine people and healers made use of alder for a variety of conditions. The MicMac used the inner bark to treat cramps and vomiting, for diphtheria, and for rheumatic complaints. Externally they used the bark and leaves to treat wounds. They used the inner bark and leaves internally as a tea for fevers, to stop internal bleeding, and for hemorrhage in the lungs.[9]

The Mohegan used the bark tea as a wash for sprains, bruises, headache, and back pain. The Montagnais made a tea of the twigs as a blood purifying medicine. The Penobscot made a decoction of the bark for cramps and vomiting.[10]

SPIRITUAL ASPECTS

Irish tradition holds that the first man was created from an alder, and the first woman from a rowan tree. Two Scottish tales associate alder with death. In one, a bridegroom who has died and has been buried returns to tell his bride that he was actually taken by the fairies. When his tomb is opened, there is a log of alder wood inside, but no corpse. In another story a woman is abducted by fairies and an alder log left in her stead. Alder, being a denizen of damp places, is associated with water spirits in Irish tradition, especially the white fairy horse.[11]

Alder had many sacred associations in ancient times. In Ebchester, near Hadrian's Wall in Scotland, a dedication to the god Vernostonus was found in which he is personified as an alder tree. Vernostonus is another name for Cocidius (the Red One), a local god of hunting and war, seen as a sacred warrior and tribal protector. The name Cocidius is possibly from the word "coch" or"red," a logical name for a god associated with warriors and with hunting."[12] A red dye is made from the bark of alder, furthering its association with warriors and blood.

Alder is also associated with the protector god Bran whose nephew, an Irish king, was named *Gwern,* the Welsh word for alder. In the "Battle of the Trees" by the poet Taliesin, Bran carried alder sprigs.

In ancient times it was the practice of warriors to keep the severed heads of their slain enemies as trophies. The Celts believed that once a warrior captured a head, he had the spirit of his enemy in his possession. He had captured his enemy's soul and his power. Bran's severed head was buried by his followers at the site of the present Tower of London, in Britain, to protect the land.[13] (King Arthur foolishly dug up the head, paving the way for the Saxon invasions.)

One of the Ogham names for alder is "protection of the heart." The spirit of alder is one of protection from the watery excesses of emotion. Call upon its spirit to help build a bridge in times of conflict, in order to avoid being storm-tossed on the oceans of passion. Use the protective sacred-warrior shield of alder to withstand tidal waves of fear, anger, and self-doubt. Let alder build a raft to float you safely over a sea of troubled feelings.

The oracular head of the god Bran sits on a shield.

Willow

Saille • [SAL-yuh]

Handwritten annotations:
Inflammation = Spring gathered Bark Tea.
BARK = GREY-BROWN DEEP FISSURED
HAIRY UNDERNEATH.
= ASPIRIN
Riversides

While we have no written evidence for Druid curricula in the Druid colleges of the Iron Age, we do know that Druids trained for up to twenty years to master their arts, and we do have written texts from the medieval poetry schools in Ireland.[1] From these, it appears that in the first year the student learned fifty oghams, in the second year another fifty, and in the third year fifty more.[2]

Given that no texts were being written in Ogham at the time, and that no literary composition of any length has ever been found that was written in Ogham characters, and because poets were masters of the harp, it is quite possible that all these Oghams were in fact musical notation.[3] It is well known that poetry and the harp were intimately related in classical Gaelic poetry[4] and that the wood of choice for ancient harps was willow.

Ancient Celtic culture had the same Indo-European caste system that is still seen today in Hindu areas. There was the sacred class, the *nemed* who were rulers and Druids. Below them in the social hierarchy were the warriors, then the farmers and producers, and finally the slaves, equivalent to the "untouchables" in India.

In ancient Ireland one could climb up or fall down the social ladder based on how much learning one attained. But there were limits—a grandparent who was a cow farmer had to contract by law for their grandchild to rise to nemed status based on learning and wealth. One could not jump from *boaire* (free farmer) to the nemed class in one generation.

Certain kinds of craftspeople and musicians had the possibility of attaining nemed status: "house-builders, builders of ships and boats, and of mills, wood-carvers, chariot makers, turners, leather-workers, fishermen, smiths and metal workers . . . among musicians, harpers only."[5] As Alwyn and Brinley Rees explain in *Celtic Heritage,* "according to the Brehon Laws only the harpist could aspire to the rank of noble, or *nemed*—and he only on condition that he 'accompanies nobility.'"[6]

A similar caste system existed in Wales, where in the pre-Christian era the highest social status went to the Druids, whose ranks included the poets. The *pencerdd,* the chief poet who had won his position in a competition, was equal in honor to the highest officers of the court. Under him in status was the *bardd teulu,* or house poet, one of the officers of the court. When the household bard took office, the king presented him with a harp, which was then his for life. Beneath the household bard were various types of minstrels.[7]

Of interest here is the fact that harps were traditionally made of willow wood. "Song of the Forest Trees," a thirteenth-century Irish poem, states, "The noble Willow burn not, a tree sacred to poems." The well-known so-called Brian Boru's harp, housed in Trinity College in Dublin (actually made in the fourteenth century) is made entirely of willow wood.[8]

Willow harps were associated with poetic secrets, the province of Druids. In one traditional tale, the Leinster king Labhraidh Loingseach had horse's ears, which he attempted to hide under his long hair. A young man was assigned to cut the king's hair and discovered the secret. The young man was sworn to secrecy on pain of death, which made him fall ill. To relieve his anxiety he told his secret to a willow tree. The tree was eventually cut down and made into a harp for the royal harpist. When the harpist sat to play for the king on his new harp, the only sound it would make was "Labhraidh Loingseach has horse's ears!"[9] Hidden in this story is the poet's secret: that truth will out, and that only truth can come from the mouth of a poet. The highest grade of poet (known as the *fili*) has "the tongue that cannot lie." When one of them speaks, his or her mouth utters prophecy.

And now we will examine the fourth letter of the Ogham tree alphabet, *saille* (willow). The *Word Ogham of Morainn mic Moín* lists *li' naimbi,* "hue of the lifeless" or "hue of the dead." The *Word Ogham of Mic ind Oic* lists *lúth bech,* "sustenance of bees." We also have *tosach mela,* "the beginning of honey," from *Briatharogam Con Culainn.*[10]

In "The Death of King Fergus," an Irish tale, Lubhdan, the king of the leprechauns, recites a cautionary poem when he sees a servant burning woodbine (Lubhdan lists all the trees that are unlucky to burn including the Willow) in the fire, a very unlucky act: "The noble willow burn not, a tree sacred to poems; within his bloom bees are a-sucking, all love the little cage."[11] This corresponds with the Word Ogham descriptions of willow as "sustenance of bees" and "the beginning of honey." But what do we make of the reference to the "little cage"?

We know that harps were made of willow wood and that willow is a tree "sacred to poems." The poet sits inside the cave of the willow to incubate a poem. The soft branches of willow resemble the strings of the harp, which is both the sustenance and the prison of the poet, who must wander the open roads to earn his or her keep.

The "hue of the lifeless" kenning for willow seems to relate to the pale moon of the night. Willow thrives beside streams, and it is very sensitive to the phases of the Moon. According to tradition, willow should never be cut in the waning moon or its wood will be brittle.[12]

In Britain there was a traditional game that was played on January 6 called Haxey Hood. The lead player was called King Boggan or Lord of the Hood, and he carried a wand made of thirteen willow sticks bundled together, symbolizing the thirteen moons of the year. The players wore red flannel coats and hats decorated with red flowers, symbolic of the sun and its rebirth. As they fought to gain possession of the willow wand, their actions and dress were meant to give energy to the newborn sun by sympathetic magic.[13]

Bride dolls, which were made of straw or rushes on Imbolc Eve in Scotland, sometimes held a willow wand, symbolic of Bride's power to affect the weather.[14] (Celebrated February 1–2, Imbolc is the festival of the lactation of the ewes, of first plowing, and of the goddess Brigid, who is known as Bride in Scotland.) In Herefordshire it is considered very lucky to bring a bit of willow into the home on May Day, to protect the home from sorcery. Willow catkins were once collected and spun in Scotland, to make cords to be placed under the milk pail, as protection from evil spirits.[15]

Willow wood is used in house building, especially for thatch (willow thatching is known as "Sally rods" in Ireland). It is also used in making wickerwork, and its lightness makes it an ideal material for making household tools and implements.[16] Willow is also used for wicker baskets, stockades, sieves for winnowing wheat, and building frames for a leather and canvas boat called a *currach*.[17]

HERBAL USES

Readers are already familiar with the herbal properties of willow, whether they are aware of it or not. The first synthetic drug of modern times was aspirin, which is synthesized from willow bark. All of the familiar properties of aspirin are also the properties of willow. Willow bark reduces fever and inflammation and helps with the pain of rheumatism, arthritis, and gout. It is protective of the heart (acts as a blood thinner) and can cause the same negative side effects as aspirin (such as internal bleeding) if abused or overused.

However, when ingesting a capsule of willow bark, many natural buffers and other components such as bioflavonoids are present. Willow is much easier on the body than synthetic aspirin.

There are about forty different species of willow in the United States alone. All have salicylic acid (the active ingredient in the bark that has beneficial qualities) but the best willow for human consumption is white willow (*Salix alba*). The bark can be simmered to deal with all of the above-mentioned ailments. The bark tea can also be taken as a gargle for sore throats and tonsillitis, and used as an external wash for wounds, sores, and burns.

The bark is collected in the spring.

CAUTION

Take bark only from a twig. Stripping bark off the trunk of the tree can kill it.

The medicinally active principles are in the inner bark (just under the dead outer bark) and the bark of the root.

Steep three teaspoons of the bark per cup of cold water for five hours. Bring to a boil and take up to one cup a day, in tablespoon doses. *Salix purpurea* (purple willow, purple osier) is used the same way and is probably more effective for fever than white willow.[18]

Salix nigra (black willow) is used the same way as white willow, however the bark and catkins are sexual sedatives (anaphrodisiac). *Salix caprea* (goat willow) can be used like white willow and the tea of the inner bark is also good for indigestion, catarrh, and whooping cough. It is disinfectant and has been used to disinfect bandages.[19]

Willow has been used for thousands of years as medicine. The Cherokee use white willow bark for fevers, for diarrhea, as a hair wash to encourage hair growth, and as a wound poultice. The tea is taken and the roots chewed for hoarseness and loss of voice.[20]

The Cheyenne use *Salix amygdaloides* (peachleaf willow) for diarrhea, as a poultice to stop bleeding, and as a sacred herb in the sun dance ceremony.[21] The Eskimo use *Salix arbusculoides* (littletree willow) as a bark poultice for sores and *Salix fuscescens* (Alaska bog willow) as an oral aid, by chewing the leaves to cure mouth sores. They also chew the leaves of *Salix arbusculoides* for mouth sores, and apply the leaves to sore eyes.

CAUTION

Tree leaves should be gathered only until Summer Solstice.
After that they will contain too many plant alkaloids.

The Cherokee use *Salix Babylonica* (weeping willow) for fevers, diarrhea, and as a poultice for wounds. Ball players chewed the roots to increase "wind" and for hoarseness and loss of voice.[22]

The Ojibwa use *Salix candida* (sage willow, silvery willow) for stomach problems, coughs, fainting, and trembling and *Salix discolor* (pussy willow) for stomach ailments. They use *Salix fragilis* (crack willow) bark as a styptic and as a poultice for sores.

The Houma use *Salix caroliniana* (coastal plain willow, Carolina willow) for fever. The MicMac use *Salix cordata* (heartleaf willow) for colds, to increase appetite, and as a poultice (from fresh bark) for bruises and skin eruptions. The Iroquois use *Salix discolor* (pussy willow) as an emetic. The Pima use *Salix gooddingii* (Goodding's willow) by simmering the leaves and bark for fevers.[23] Many other willow species are used similarly.

SPIRITUAL ASPECTS

Willow is above all a healer with a gentle touch. Native Americans call her "the whispering one" because of the way the breeze plays through her branches. In Celtic areas she is associated with the harp, the most ethereal of instruments, and with the gentle soul of the poet.

The blessings of willow were a part of ancient Celtic ceremonies. At Lughnasad (also called Lammas, this festival begins approximately August 1 and celebrates the first fruits of the harvest) milk pails were entwined with ribbons, flowers, and willow twigs and carried in procession. Willow was hung over the hearth to bless it and to ensure healthy cattle.

Willow is featured in the sacred iconography of the Gaulish Celts in

*The moon caught in the branches of a willow tree
that grows beside a silver stream.*

northern France. In 1711, in the choir of Notre Dame in Paris, a stone with a bearded god cutting a branch from a willow tree was found. On another face of the stone the same willow tree appears again, along with a bull. The bull has two marsh birds on its back and one between its horns. The name "Esus, Lord Master" is inscribed above the deity and "Tarvostrigaranus" (The Bull with the Three Cranes) over the bull.[24]

A similar stone was found at Tréves in 1895. On one side of the stone is the god Mercury, wearing a *torc* (a Celtic neck ring, symbolic of nobility) and accompanied by the goddess Rosmerta and a rooster. On another face of the stone a very similar Esus figure appears, cutting down a willow tree. A bull and three wading birds appear with the Esus figure. On a third face of the stone is a female figure. According to Anne Ross, "[the crane] is almost exclusively associated with transformed women, sometimes owned by a god." The crane is "a Goddess in the crane form in the service of, or as consort of, an otherworld god."[25] Both willows and cranes are beings that live between the worlds. Both have their feet in the water, the gateway to the ancestors, and their heads in the sky, world of the gods. Meanwhile their bodies exist as bridges between these worlds and the middle world of nature.

In Ireland there was a strong prohibition on eating cranes. The mysterious crane bag of the sea god Manannán, in which he stored his most precious possessions, was made of the skin of a woman who was changed into a crane out of jealous spite. The bag eventually became the possession of Finn mac Cumhaill, the leader of the Fianna warrior bands and one of the two greatest heroes of Ireland.

In another story, the hero Oisín sets out one day to visit his comrade in arms, Dearg, who is living in an otherworld mound. Along the way Oisín encounters a crane and asks it to tell him its story. The crane is a woman who was transformed into a crane and has been one for two hundred and ninety-five years.[26]

The crane is a water bird and willow is a water-loving tree, both have their feet in the water and their heads in the air. The transformed women live in the form of birds but can think and speak as human women—they too live between the worlds.

Music that is played on a Willow harp has the ability to move us and loosen our ties to mundane existence. We are transfixed by willow's otherworldly beauty. Willow heals our spiritual pain as she heals our bodily ills, with her gentle, healing touch.

Ash

Nion • [NEEN]

Ancient Ireland consisted of five provinces: Ulster in the north, Leinster in the east, Munster in the south, Connacht in the west, and Meath in the center. These correspond to the five sacred directions as understood by the Irish Celts. Each direction had certain inherent qualities.

The north was the direction of battle (*cath*) and its energy was associated with strife, pride, war, forced capture, and assault. The east was the direction of prosperity (*bláth*). Its energy was of the home, beekeeping, abundance, beautiful clothing, arts, hospitality, contests, nobility, and good manners. In the south was music (*séis*) and all manner of beautiful and poetic things—waterfalls, great gatherings, subtle wisdom, honor, learning of all kinds, teaching, the game of *fidchell* (a kind of chess), the art of poetry, modesty, and nobility.

In the west was learning (*fis*), science, history keeping, stories, eloquence, alliances, judgments, teachings, and abundance. The mystical Center was the direction of sacred rulership. In that direction were kingship, stewardship, dignity, fame, prosperity, charioteership, warriorship, mastery of arts, mead, ale, bounty, and mastery.[1]

The two sacred centers of rulership were located in the mystical central province: the royal seat of Tara, and the hill of Uisneach, home of the perpetual fire of the Archdruid. Tara and Uisneach were the "two kidneys" of Ireland, reflecting the constant pair, a ruler and his or her Druid.

41

No ruler could be effective unless a Druid was at his or her side. The Druids were the law keepers who kept the legal precedents in their heads, and without them a warrior king was unable to make competent judgments.

There were five legendary trees that seemed to reflect the same five-fold pattern of the sacred directions: the Ash of Tortu, the Bole of Ross (a yew), Eo Mugna (an oak), the Bough of Dathi (an ash), and the Ash of Uisneach.[2] Each of these trees was probably the *bíle* (sacred tree) of its district. Such trees were a strong source of local pride and the worst insult that could happen to a kingdom was for an enemy to cut down the sacred tree of the tribal area.[3] Three of the five trees were ash trees, hinting at the power of the ash's spirit.

The strength of ash is reflected in its practical uses. In ancient Europe, ash trees were used to make spear shafts, household crafts, and bows. The Proto-Indo-European word for ash, *os,* gave us the words for spear, lance, and javelin in several European languages.[4]

The folklore of this supremely useful tree is rich. In Greek tradition, it was said that Zeus created humans from ash trees. Yggdrasil was the cosmic ash upon which Odin hung for nine days until he discovered the runes.

The Icelandic word for ash, *aske,* means "blaze of great fire," ash being the very best firewood that can even be burned green. Ash was also an important fodder tree for Neolithic farmers.[5]

Ash was considered a solar tree, and its wood was used for the Germanic Yule log. Druids carved charms from its wood. Ashen divining rods were cut on Summer Solstice. A Druidic ash wand decorated with spirals was found on Anglesey, in Wales.[6]

Eating red ash buds at Midsummer was said to bring protection from sorcery. Witch's brooms, used for flying, were traditionally made of an ash pole with birch twigs and willow bindings. Ash "draws the flash" (attracts lightning) and so was used in rain magic.[7]

In Scotland it was believed that carrying the "keys" (ash seeds) brought protection from evil sorcery. Snakes were said to avoid ash trees and their fallen leaves; it was believed that an adder could be killed by a single blow from an ashen stick. A circlet of ash twigs was worn around the neck to heal snakebite, and ash sticks were carried in snake-infested woods. According to Pliny, drawing a circle with an ash wand around a snake would cause it to die.[8]

Ash trees were used in weather forecasting. If the oaks leafed first, dry weather would follow. If the ashes leafed first, wet weather was forecast. In Lincolnshire, England, it was said that the female ash, the sheder, could be used to overpower a male Witch and the male ash, the heder, could be used to overpower a female Witch.[9]

In Leicestershire a child with warts was carried to an ash tree in April or May. A pin would be stuck into the tree, then into the child's wart until pain was felt, and then into the tree again. The pin was left in the bark and this rhyme was recited: "Ashen tree, ashen tree, Pray buy this wart of me."

In the Highlands of Scotland, at the birth of a child a fresh branch of ash was placed in the fire. The sap that was forced out at the ends was collected in a spoon and fed to the infant to make it strong.

Children with hernias, weakness, or rickets were passed through a cleft in an ash sapling, before sunrise, while fasting. The slit in the tree was then bound and as the tree healed, so did the child. It was believed that if the tree was later cut down the child would be reinjured. To prevent this, the tree was pounded full of nails, to deter woodcutters. In Herefordshire, a lock of a child's hair was pinned to an ash to cure it of a bad cough.[10]

Turning once again to the Ogham alphabet, the *Word Ogham of Morainn mic Moín* uses the phrase *cosdad sida,* "checking of peace" while the *Word Ogham of Mic ind Oic* uses *bág ban,* "contest of women," to describe the ash tree. The description *bág maise,* "contest of beauty," comes from *Briatharogam Con Culainn.*[11] The *Auraicept na N-Eces (The Scholar's Primer)* states that "it is the maw of a weaver's beam as applied to wood: a sign of peace is that. A checking of peace with him is that from the ash of the weaver's beam."

The Ogham for N is translated by some as *nin* (fork) rather than *nion* (ash) based on ancient glosses.[12] But this should not trouble us. The fork is an upright Y that supports the weaver's beam.

The above Word Ogham meanings for ash can be more deeply understood with a little background on farm life at the time they were established. The Brehon Law text *Cáin Lánamna* states the rules for dividing a farm couple's assets in the event of a divorce. Based on the text, the normal tasks of a farm wife included plowing, reaping, caring for livestock in their pens, fattening pigs, grinding the grain, milking, cooking, and working with her husband in the fields. She was also responsible for carding, spinning, dyeing, and weaving.

The husband was often responsible for the beginning phases of farm work and the wife with the finished product. In a marriage where both spouses came into the union with equal wealth, the wife got only one-sixth of any wool that was still in fleece, one-third of combed wool, and one-half of any cloth. The husband had normally done more of the labor of caring for the sheep, but the wife had combed the wool, spun the thread, and wove the cloth.

With flax and woad the distribution was similar. The husband had done more of the work in the fields but the wife had processed the fibers for linen and the woad leaves for dyeing.[13] In the Laws women's particular possessions included tools for spinning, weaving and sewing, especially the distaff.[14]

Noble women were also occupied with cloth, weaving and sewing. They excelled at needlework and embroidery.[15] Whether of noble or base birth, all women competed to make the most elegant finery they could, for themselves and their families. Now the meanings of the Ogham become clear. It is the ash of the weaver's beam that makes the "contest of women" possible. As they ply the arts of weaving and embroidery they undergo a "contest of beauty," a hint that women competed to see who was most beautiful. A "checking of peace" resulted from the women's competition. The implication is that the contest was strenuous, even deadly serious, given ash's use to make warrior's bows, spear shafts, and very hot fires. Of course there is a double meaning to "checking of peace." In the hands of men, the ash becomes a deadly warrior's tool.

HERBAL USES

The tender tips and leaves of the European ash (*Fraxinus excelsior*) were used as a tea for gout, jaundice, and rheumatism. In winter the branch bark or the bark of the root was used for fever and as a vermifuge (to expel worms).

The leaves can be harvested in spring or dried for later use as a gentle laxative (the American white ash—*Fraxinus americana*—is used similarly).

To prepare ash leaves, steep one to two teaspoons of leaf per half-cup of water for about five minutes. Strain, and take up to one and one-half cups a day in tablespoon doses.

CAUTION

The leaves can be gathered only until Summer Solstice. After that they will contain too many plant alkaloids.

To prepare the bark, simmer one teaspoon per one-half cup water for about ten minutes and take up to a cup a day in tablespoon doses. Mint leaves or sweet marjoram can be added to improve the flavor of the tea.[16]

CAUTION

Only take the bark from a young twig, never from the trunk of the tree, or you might kill it.

The Cherokee used a decoction of white ash bark for liver and stomach complaints. The Delaware used the bark tea as a cathartic and an emetic. The Fox used the bark tea as an external wash for sores, itching, and vermin in the scalp. The Iroquois used the bark tea as a laxative and added the roots and barks to compounds that induced pregnancy. They also made a poultice of the roots for snakebite. The MicMac and Penobscot used the leaves to make a cleansing tea used after childbirth.[17]

Fraxinus nigra (black ash) was used in the form of bark tea by the Cherokee for liver and stomach complaints. The Fox used the bark tea as a laxative. The Iroquois took the bark tea for painful urination (strangury), and as a laxative, and used the roots and bark as a foot soak for rheumatism. An infusion of the roots was put in the ears for earache, and the roots and bark were taken together as tea to induce pregnancy.[18]

Fraxinus oregona (Oregon ash) was used by the Cowlitz who made a bark infusion for worms. The Yokia mashed the roots to make a poultice for wounds.[19]

SPIRITUAL ASPECTS

One survey of Irish holy wells found that out of 210 surveyed trees growing next to a holy well, 75 were ash trees (the most common tree was the hawthorn). Sometimes these trees were part of ancient well rituals in which the tree was circumambulated on holy days. Some of the ash trees had hollows carved into them, or natural hollows in their branches where rain water collected. This water was considered very holy and used for healing.[20]

Some sacred ashes had funerary associations. A funeral cortège that passed such a tree would stop for a few minutes so that participants could pray and throw a few stones on a cairn at the base of the tree.[21]

The Irish epic tale *Táin Bó Cuailnge* (*The Cattle Raid of Cooley*) says that every place the battle-leader Queen Maeve planted one of her ash horsewhips, a sacred ash grew. Any tree growing near a holy well is called a *bile Maedhbh* (sacred tree of Maeve) because Maeve was also the name of an Irish goddess of sovereignty, or land goddess.[22]

As mentioned above, three of the most famous legendary sacred trees of Eire were ashes. One, the Ash of Uisneach, *bile Uisnigh,* stood at the geographic center of Eire, on the hill of Uisneach. The Ash of Tortu, *bile Tortan,* stood at the center of a triangle formed by the sacred sites of Tara, Tlaghtga, and Tailltiu (Telltown), site of the ancient Tailtean Games that were held there from approximately 1500 BCE to approximately 1500 CE and were the model for the modern Scottish Highland Games. *Craob Daithi* grew in County Westmeath, about halfway between the others. Together, they made the sacred number three, symbolic of the three worlds of land, sea, and sky, implying completion and divinity.

The three trees stood until the reign of King Aed Sláin (murdered in 600 CE) when they were felled in the Christian era by poetic satire,[23] a method in which highly trained poets called *filid* placed a curse on a person, place, or thing by reciting magical formulaic verse.

The most beloved of the three was the bile Tortan, said to be so huge that all the men of Tortu could stand under its branches to take shelter from a storm. When it fell, the plain of Tortu lost two-thirds of its wealth due to the loss of magical and otherworldly protection. However, it is said that a new tree will one day rise from its roots, meaning that the mystical protection of the tree will once again bless the land,[24] and implying that the days of the great goddess of sovereignty will surely come again.

Hawthorn

Huath • [HOO-ath]

In ancient Ireland the highest class of poet was called a *fili* (poet) or *banfili* (female poet) while the lower class of poet or traveling minstrels were called bards. The poets had full professional standing and were responsible for upholding the honor and reputation of rulers via praise-poems. But a poet could just as easily destroy a reputation by satirizing a ruler.

Trained *filid* were able to raise blemishes on their victims' skin, merely by using words. In extreme cases they could even kill. In the year 1024, according to the *Annals of Ulster*, Cúan hua Lothcháin, the chief poet of Ireland, was dying, but he was still able to cause the bodies of his murderers to rot within an hour. The *Annals of Connacht* record that the Lord Lieutenant John Stanley died in 1414 from a poet's spell.[1]

Irish poets were said to be able to "rhyme to death" both humans and animals (especially rats) and the chief poet (*ollam*) was also expected to perfect less destructive magical skills. He had the job of protecting the king from sorcery and of divining the future.[2]

There were three magical techniques that the fili had to master in order to utter prophecy, answer questions, and to manifest that which he or she desired. These were *imbas forosnai*, "illumination between the hands" or "palm knowledge of enlightening"; *teinm laegda*, "extempore recitation, illumination of song"; and *dichetal do chennaib*, "recital from the ends of the fingers."[3]

When performing imbas forosnai, the poet chewed a bit of the raw flesh of a red pig, dog, or cat, laid it on a stone, sang an incantation over it, invoked the gods, and then went to sleep with his two palms against his cheeks. He was watched over so that his sleep was not disturbed, and he woke with the answer to his question.[4]

In teinm laegda, the poet put his thumb into his mouth and chanted, apparently going into trance to divine an answer. The hero Finn, who was Druid-trained, used this technique in several stories. In "Finn and the Man in the Tree," the *fian* (a band of warriors) are cooking a meal and Culdub emerges from a *sidhe* mound (elf or fairy mound) three times to steal their food as it is cooking. After the third theft, Finn chases the man and catches him just as he is reentering the sidhe mound. At the exact same moment, a woman is emerging from the mound with a vessel in her hand. She slams the door but Finn puts his finger between the door and the post, and then sticks his finger in his mouth. He begins to chant, his Imbas (a flash of poetic inspiration or enlightenment) comes on him, and he starts to recite.[5]

Later a mysterious man appears, hiding in a tree. Finn and the fian are unable to recognize the man until Finn puts his thumb into his mouth. When he takes out his thumb he begins to chant, and is then able to identify the man.[6]

Dichetal do chennaib involved the spontaneous uttering of a prophecy or a poem with no preliminary ritual other than some kind of mnemonic use of the fingertips. According to the *Senchus Mór* (*Great Old Law Book*), "when the poet sees a person or thing before him, he makes a verse at once with the ends of his fingers, or in his mind without studying, and he composes and repeats at the same time."[7] The highly trained poet could utter verse and prophesy spontaneously.

But the most awesome and frightening skill of the poet was the deadly art of satire. There were a number of different forms of satire that required a fine of the victim's honor-price. These included making fun of someone's appearance, broadcasting that someone had a blemish, coining a derogatory nickname, and formally composing a satire about a person, or repeating a satire composed by someone else. Mocking gestures, taunting someone, falsely accusing someone of stealing, and spreading an untrue, destructive tale about another person, whether that person was dead or alive, were grounds for legal action.[8]

A cutting satire could be legally nullified by issuing a praise-poem about the offended party. In one story, the poet Aithirne was angry at the river Modarn because it refused to give him a salmon for his supper. The poet satirized the river and the river rose up in anger. In fear of his life, the poet composed a praise-poem to calm it.[9]

Satire had its uses as a way to keep pressure on the nobles to obey the law. If a satire was justified, the king or lord had to pay whatever fine he owed because the satirist had publicly shamed the ruler, and he or she needed to make amends in order to save face. But if the satire was unjustified, the king or lord had to extract compensation from the satirist or lose his own honor-price because the ruler would lose face if he did not have the courage and determination to seek justice after being unfairly maligned by a public satire. The honor of a king could be restored simply by getting the satirist to recite a praise-poem on his behalf. Also according to the laws, a poet's praise-poem had to bear some resemblance to reality or else he or she was not entitled to payment for the composition.[10]

Illegal satirists were abhorred. Illegal satires included making fun of someone's appearance, inventing an insulting nickname that was shaming, falsely accusing someone of stealing, and repeating an insulting poetic satire about someone in a distant location. The satirist owed the victim of these actions the payment of their honor price.

A female illegal satirist was grouped with werewolves and vagrant women in the Laws. She was not entitled to sick maintenance in the event of illness because it was felt she would cause too much trouble in any house where she might be nursed. However, a woman could legally satirize the head of the kin of a person who had forfeited a pledge to her.[11]

There was a specific type of satire that was particularly deadly, which is of most relevance to us here. The *Uraicecht Na Ríar* (*The*

Poetic Grades of Early Irish Law) includes a description of the magical technique for composing a *glám dícenn* (a poet's black magic). The poet composed the satire in the shade of a hawthorn tree with no thorns and a dense, heavy top. The satire had to be repeated "three-times-nine" (twenty-seven) times, in the "circuit of the moon" (possibly over a one-month period). While chanting, the poet had to pierce a clay likeness of the person being satirized with thorns.[12]

Another description says that the "seven grades of poets" must go to a hilltop before sunrise. With their backs to a hawthorn tree, and with the wind from the north (the direction of battle, as we saw above) they should hold a thorn from the hawthorn tree in each hand as they chant the satire.[13]

And now to the Ogham alphabet. The *Word Ogham of Morainn mic Moín* describes Hawthorn as *comdál cúan,* "a pack of hounds," while the *Word Ogham of Mic ind Oic* uses *bánad gnúise,* "blanching of face," and *Briatharogam Con Culainn* gives us *annsam aidhche,* "most difficult by night."[14] All of these seem to relate to fear; *uath* means fearsome. Certainly this points to the fear of the satirist. A good satirist could raise a blemish, and anyone who was blemished was considered unfit to rule.

But if we examine the herbal uses of hawthorn we will see that it also relates to another kind of fear, that caused by pain in the heart.

HERBAL USES

Hawthorn is a valuable medicinal whose fall-picked berries and spring-gathered leaves and flowers make an all-purpose cardiac tonic that benefits virtually all heart conditions. According to the ancient Doctrine of Signatures, a medieval plant classification system that used the color, shape, and growing conditions of plants to classify their uses, a plant with thorns was likely useful for sharp pain somewhere in the human body.

Also according to that system, any plant with red fruit (or red stems, flowers, etc.) was likely useful for blood disorders and heart conditions.

Hawthorn is the perfect example of this. Other examples are raspberries (which build blood), beets, and elderberries.

Thus, hawthorn (whitethorn, May Tree, English hawthorn) is a classic herb for painful heart problems such as angina, as well as other heart conditions such as palpitations and arrhythmia.

Hawthorn (*Crataegus oxyacantha*) helps to regulate and normalize blood pressure. In my experience it is a good idea to monitor its action, because when taken for long periods of time it can cause a precipitous drop in blood pressure. It should not be taken in conjunction with other medications that lower blood pressure, or a rapid, steep drop in pressure can result.

Hawthorn benefits aged hearts and helps with inflammation of the heart (myocarditis). It benefits atherosclerosis and other heart conditions related to stress, insomnia, and nervous tension.

The ripe berries can be tinctured in the fall (gather them after the first frost when they are a deep red) and the young leaves and flowers can be tinctured in the spring. To make the tincture, place the plant matter in a clean glass jar and barely cover with 80 proof or higher alcohol (vodka, gin, whiskey, etc.). Cover tightly and allow to sit until the plant matter begins to wilt. Strain and add about 10 percent of water in relation to the amount of alcohol used plus a small amount of vegetable glycerin (about a teaspoon per quart). Take ten drops three times a day.

CAUTION

Be sure to use the tincture with medical supervision. Monitor blood pressure carefully.

To prepare a tea of the flowers, steep one teaspoon per half-cup of boiled water for fifteen minutes. Take up to one and one-half cups a day, in tablespoon doses. This tea is helpful for insomnia.

Simmer one teaspoon of the crushed berries per half cup of water, for twenty minutes. Take up to one and one-half cups a day in tablespoon doses.[15]

Native American medicine people used other species of *Crataegus* found in the Americas. The Kwakiutl used *Crataegus douglasii* (black hawthorn) in a chewed leaf poultice for swellings. The Thompson Indians used the same species' thorns to probe boils and ulcers, and made a tea of the bark, sap, wood, or root for stomach ailments.[16]

The Ojibwa used *Crataegus pedicellata* (scarlet hawthorn) root as an antidiarrheal. The Iroquois used *Crataegus punctata* (dotted hawthorn) shoots and bark to stop excessive menstruation and drank the tea to prevent cancerlike skin eruptions caused by witchcraft.[17]

The Cherokee used *Crataegus spathulata* bark tea to improve circulation and to prevent spasms. The Iroquois used *Crataegus submollis* as a witchcraft medicine, by using the decoction and a doll to make a person "break out like cancer,"[18] in a process reminiscent of the spells of the fili described above.

SPIRITUAL ASPECTS

Laying aside the darker aspects, there are many beautiful and positive traditions surrounding these trees. Tradition holds that where oak and ash and thorn are seen to grow together, one will be likely to see fairies. Another tradition is that a solitary hawthorn on a hill, especially if there is a spring or a well nearby, indicates a doorway to the Land of Fairy is close at hand. For this reason, hawthorn is sacred to the goddess Carnea, wife and mother of Janus, god of entrances and exits. People will deliberately avoid or seek out such a place, according to their predispositions.[19]

One of the duties of a Druid, in the days before television, radio, and newspapers, was to keep an eye on the local hawthorn tree. The day it first blossomed was reckoned as the official start of summer: the festival of Beltaine, or May Day. Hawthorn blossoms were used to decorate the house and May Pole, but it was considered very unlucky to bring them into the home, probably because of their attraction to the "fey folk." Hawthorn was woven into the crown of leaves worn by the

Green Man, a figure dressed in green leaves and ribbons who symbolized the return of summer's verdure. He was seen dancing through the
town in traditional May Day celebrations.[20]

Hawthorns are the most common sacred trees near holy wells, commonly known as clootie wells. A *cloot* is a cloth rag. People leave small
bits of cloth tied to the tree to personify their prayers and needs. As the
cloth disintegrates, so will their ailments and problems.

At marriage ceremonies on the Greek isle of Delos, singers and
dancers were crowned with oak, myrtle, and hawthorn, and hawthorn
blossoms, symbols of chastity, were included in the marriage wreath.
Athenian brides once wore hawthorn blossoms and used them to decorate altars sacred to Hymen, the goddess of marriage. In Ireland and
Celtic Britain, newly married couples danced around a hawthorn tree
to receive its blessing.

It is said that to cut down a thorn tree is so unlucky that the
offender is bound to lose his house, his children, or a limb.[21]

In Celtic tradition the wren is known as the "king of the birds."
To account for this there is a traditional tale. All the birds in the world
once gathered, declaring that whichever of them flew highest would be
declared their king. The eagle boasted that he would fly the highest,
confidently heading toward the sun. The eagle did not know that a
tiny wren had hidden in its feathers.

When the eagle could climb no higher, the wren popped out and flew
higher still, claiming the kingship. The eagle grabbed the wren in its claws,
and in a rage dashed it to the ground. For this reason, and to this day, the
wren has a stumpy tail and can fly no higher than a hawthorn tree.[22]

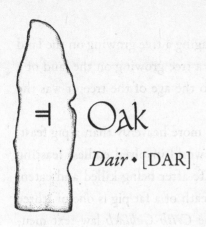

Oak

Dair • [DAR]

The postglacial Indo-European cultures came to fruition during the era when great oak forests covered most of their territory. Over half of all shelters and constructions in Europe were made from oak wood. Oak was an important source of heat, being a dense firewood, and was used to fashion bows, spears, oars, boats, and houses. The bark and leaf of the oak were boiled to make an astringent brew that could tan hides and nets as well as pull the edges of a wound together.

The *Bretha Comaithchesa* (ancient Irish law text on farming) lists seven "nobles of the wood" and outlines their economic value.[1] These are oak, hazel, holly, yew, ash, Scots pine, and wild apple.[2]

Oak is listed as a "noble of the wood" due to its acorns, its usefulness in tanning hides, and its value in woodwork. One commentator reported that a single oak tree gave enough acorns to fatten a pig for one year. Oak was called "the Tara of the wood" because it was the tallest tree in the forest.[3]

The fine for damaging an oak (or any other "noble" tree) was five *séta* (roughly two and a half cows). There were also fines for illegally stripping the bark from an oak for tanning purposes. If enough bark was taken to tan a pair of women's sandals, the fine was one cowhide. If enough bark was taken to tan a pair of men's sandals, the fine was one oxhide. The perpetrator also had to salve the tree's wounds with a mixture of clay, cow dung, and milk until there was new growth the width of two fingers. The fine for damaging a tree growing on the land of a noble called for a higher fine than a tree growing on the land of a peasant. No distinction was made as to the age of the tree; it was the species that counted.[4]

For the ancient Celts, nothing was more heavenly than a pig feast. In fact, their descriptions of the otherworld involved endless feasting on pigs that magically came back to life after being killed and eaten. A ninth-century triad states that the death of a fat pig is one of "three deaths which are better than life." The *Críth Gablach* law text mentions the boar that "removes dishonor at every season" and the *Audacht Morainn* (The Testament of Morann) describes a pig's fat side as "the freeing from shame of every face." In other words, pig meat was a fit meal for a high-ranking guest at any time of year.[5]

Pigs were commonly fed on *daurmess* or "oak-fruit," that is, acorns. Pigs and acorn mast were so linked in the Irish mind that an expression was born to describe a lost opportunity: "a pig which dies before the acorn crop."[6]

As to its meanings in the Tree Ogham, the *Word Ogham of Morainn mic Moín* describes oak as *ardam dossaibh,* "highest among bushes" and the *Word Ogham of Mic ind Oic* uses *grés sair,* "carpenter's work."[7] *Slechtam soíre* "most carved of craftsmanship" is from *Briatharogam Con Culainn.*[8]

These Ogham names suit the oak tree, the highest tree in the forest, and the carpenter's wood of choice. "Highest among bushes" may also have a double meaning, as the oak is strongly associated with the sacred (nemed) class of Druids, and with thunder, lightning, the gods, and high places (see Spiritual Aspects below).

HERBAL USES

Oak leaves and bark are astringent, meaning they will shrink and tone tissue as they heal. Oak makes a good enema for piles, helps with bloody urine, internal hemorrhage, fever, sore throat, and phlegm in the lungs. The tea can be used both internally and externally to help shrink varicose veins. It makes a fine wash for sores and skin irritations, and a hair rinse for dandruff and hair loss.[9]

A cloth can be soaked in the tea and wrapped around the neck to shrink goiters and glandular inflammations. A sitz bath will benefit prolapse of the rectum, fistulas, and tumors in the rectal area. A tea or poultice of the bark and leaf will benefit burns.[10]

The most palatable oak for internal use is the white oak (*Quercus alba*). A tea of white oak bark removes excess mucus and tones the stomach.

CAUTION

The bark must be collected from branches in early spring.
Do not take bark from the trunk of the tree, or you might
kill it. The leaves must be collected before Summer Solstice.
After that they will contain too many plant alkaloids.

To make the bark tea for internal use, simmer one tablespoon of bark (use white oak or English oak) per pint of water for ten minutes, in a nonaluminum pot with a tight lid. Drink up to three cups a day. To make an enema or douche, simmer one tablespoon of bark per quart of water for thirty minutes.[11]

For a wound wash use substantially greater amounts of bark; about a pound of bark and/or leaves per quart of water.

To make a leaf tea, steep two teaspoons of shredded white oak or English oak leaf per cup of freshly boiled water, for twenty minutes.

English oak (*Quercus robur*) can be used the same way as white oak. Other oaks, such as red oak (*Quercus rubra*) and black oak (*Quercus tinctoria*), are only used externally.[12]

Native American herbalists and healers of the Mahuna used *Quercus agrifolia* (coast live oak) externally as a pediatric aid to heal a newborn's navel. White oak was used by the Cherokee for diarrhea and dysentery, asthma, and loss of voice. They chewed the bark for mouth sores, and applied the bark tea as an antiseptic and as a wash for chill and fever.[13]

The Delaware used the tea of the bark for coughs and as a gargle for sore throats, and applied it externally to ulcers and bruises. The Houma crushed the root with whiskey and applied it to rheumatic parts.[14]

The Iroquois regarded white oak as a psychological aid for loneliness and for "when your woman goes off and won't come back." The Penobscot applied the bark tea to bleeding piles. The Ojibwa used the root and bark tea for diarrhea.[15]

The Iroquois used *Quercus bicolor* (swamp white oak) bark tea for cholera, consumption, and broken bones. They smoked the leaves and exhaled through the nose to get rid of excess phlegm. They also used it as a psychological aid—when "wife runs around, takes away lonesomeness."[16]

The Menominee used *Quercus ellipsoidalis* (northern pin oak) bark tea as an abortifacient. The Cherokee used *Quercus falcata* (Spanish oak) bark tea for dysentery, intermittent fever, asthma, and loss of voice. They used it externally as a wash for chills and fever, sores, and chapped skin. They chewed the bark for mouth sores.[17]

The Houma used *Quercus pagodaefolia* (cherrybark oak, red oak, shingle oak) bark tea for dysentery and made a decoction of the bark and root for sore throat, hoarseness, and use as a general tonic. The root and bark tea was applied to swollen joints.[18]

Many other oaks were used by Native American healers. For a comprehensive discussion of these, please see Daniel Moerman's excellent study, *Medicinal Plants of Native America*.

SPIRITUAL ASPECTS

The ancient Indo-Europeans could have been called "The People of the Oak." Because of their reverence for this tree and their dependence on it, many religious associations developed. Oak trees were sacred to the deities Taranis, Indra, Jupiter, Yahweh, Ukho, Rhea, Kybele, Thor, Artemis, Brigid, Balder, the Erinyes, and the Kikonian Maenads.

Perun, a Slavic god associated with oak trees, was worshipped on the summits of hills and mountains. Parjanyah, a Vedic oak god, was associated with rain clouds and storms. The Old Norse god Fjorgyn gave birth to Thor, associated with oaks, who helped his father by slaying his foes with a stone hammer. The Lithuanian god Perkunas was worshipped in sacred oak groves or in the guise of a single oak tree, usually growing in a high place.[19]

Among the Balts, oakwood fires were kindled in sacred oak groves to honor the high gods and the gods of thunder. The Teutons burned oak fires in honor of the thunder god. For them, harming an oak tree in any way was punishable by torture. In 1156, a bishop visiting Lubeck saw a grove in which there was an oak tree surrounded by a fence of stakes. The tree was dedicated to the god of the land.

The Greeks had groves of oracular oaks such as that in Dordona, where the will of Zeus could be heard in the rustling of the leaves. The ancient Greeks prayed to dryads, oak spirits, for rain. "Oak Brides" were burned alive on Mount Kithairon and dedicated to the oak god. The Akadian Greeks called themselves *eggenoi dryos*, "sons of oak." In Rome, the vestal virgins tended perpetual oak fires, and Jupiter was honored in the form of an old oak tree. The recurrent theme was the association of oaks with thunder, deity, lightning, high places, rain clouds, storm gods, paradise trees, and thunder gods. The oak tree was known to attract lightning, and for this reason was often planted near settlements and homes to ward off strikes.[20]

The Paleo-Indo-European root words for oak evolved into words for tree, trim, tar, beam, wooden peg, key to a sheepfold, godly tree, spoon, trough, bow, spear, rainbow, hard, strong, hale, firm, brave, true, tough, fixed, stout, belief, loyalty, trust, treaty, contract, agreement, sureness, confidence, chariot pole, fuel, log, post, woodsman, oak, acorn, Zeus grove, wood nymph/oak spirit, and Druid.[21]

The Proto-Indo-European word *dorw* (tree, oak) became the word for "door." The oak was said to be inhabited by a spirit who could open the door to the otherworld, either the Sky World through its branches or the chthonic world of the nature spirits through its root systems underground.

Dorw (and its variant *drew*, which became the Old English *treo*, "true") also embodied the meanings of truth, belief, and binding oaths/contracts. These qualities were undoubtedly associated with the Druids, the Celtic oak priests and priestesses, or "truth-knowers," who ate acorns to strengthen their powers of divination. Druids taught in oak groves, and early Christians such as Saint Kentigern, Saint Brigid, and Saint Columba took over the sites that were hallowed by Druidic oaks.[22]

Oak was the wood of choice for mortuary houses of the Hallstatt and La Tene Celtic cultures. Boughs of oak were recovered from a burial in an oak coffin found near Scarborough in 1834. Mistletoe was also found in the coffin, a plant that was gathered with great ceremony on the sixth day of the moon by white-robed Druids when it was found growing on oak trees, a rare occurrence.[23] The Welsh Mabinogion describes how the God Lleu took on an eagle form and perched on the branches of a magical oak that could neither be soaked by rain nor scorched by fire.

Many Celtic place names were associated with their local sacred groves. Drunemeton (from *dru*, and *nemeton*, sacred grove or enclosure) was the oak sanctuary of the Galatians of Asia Minor. Chartres Cathedral in France stands on the site of the most sacred oak grove of the Gaulish Celts. A typical Celtic *temenos* probably included the focal point of a sacred tree such as an oak, an associated well, and a simple shrine of wicker or stone. In English tradition, Herne the Hunter, a horned forest god, is said to walk under the oaks of Windsor Forest. At Wishford, in Wiltshire, England, on May 29, the local townspeople have the right to gather wood from the Forest of Grovely and to cut the largest branch of green wood they can carry away. They process through the town accompanied by a band, and stop at each house before entering the wood to cut their branches. This custom preserves the people's right to take wood from the forest by human power alone, no carts allowed.[24]

In former times, a representative of the town would dance in front of Salisbury Cathedral, but in the nineteenth century this was deemed irreverent. Now the ritual is limited to the laying of oak leaves on the altar.

In Oswestry, Shropshire, was the tree known as the Mile Oak. Death and disaster would result if any of its branches were cut. In Brampton, Cumberland, stood an oak around which newly married couples would dance. Until the end of the nineteenth century, the last load of wheat brought in from the harvest was decorated with oak branches.

Tradition states that acorns kept in the home or carried on your person will bring good luck. An ancient Welsh tradition held that good health could be kept by rubbing one's hand on a piece of oak on Midsummer Day while keeping silence. The dew under oak trees was held to be a magical beauty aid.[25]

Oak is above all a symbol of balance. Its roots go as deep as the tree grows high. Oaks are providers—they give of their excellent wood, and feed the people and the animals with their nuts. They attract the attention of the highest gods as evidenced by their tendency to attract lightning, yet they are not blasted by the stroke. They have their heads in the clouds and their roots firmly planted in the earth. For Druids, oaks symbolize the ideal way of life.

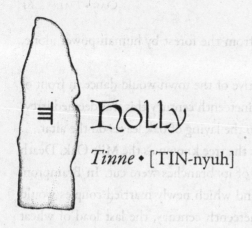

holly

Tinne • [TIN-nyuh]

The Gaelic word for holly is *cuileann*, yet the *t* sound has been given to the holly tree. Some translators attribute another meaning to this letter: *trian* or "a third," as in *trian roith* (a third part of a wheel) and *trian n-airm* (a third part of a weapon).[1] Others list *tinne iarn* (a bar of iron).[2] A related word, *tine*, means fire.

So what are the possible connections between holly, fire, iron, and a third of a wheel or a weapon? And why is holly important enough to be included in the Tree Ogham lists?

To begin with, holly (*Ilex aquifolium*) is classed as an *airig fedo* one of the "noble trees of the wood" in the *Bretha Comaithchesa*.[3] The text elaborates on why holly is so valuable: its use in making shafts for chariots, and its use in open-air cooking pits.[4]

Both holly and ivy (*Hedera helix*) were once valued as winter fodder. The upper branches of holly trees are relatively spine-free and thus suitable to feed to livestock.[5] Sickles were made that were especially used to cut holly and ivy for cattle feed. Apparently there was almost no haying in Ireland until the Normans invaded, because grass was available most of the year due to the mild weather, and the damp climate made hay storage difficult.

The second use of holly was in chariot making. The Irish chariot had two wheels and was pulled by two horses. The wheels had metal rims, and there was a pole that connected the main body of the chariot to the yoke. The shafts of the chariot were made of holly, either projecting from the back, or between the horses and the chariot.[6]

Finally, there was the use of holly in the *fulacht fian,* an outdoor cooking pit used to cook meat. Such pits were used in the Iron Age, the Bronze Age, and earlier. Meat was wrapped in grasses and placed in the pit, then the pit was filled with water. Rocks were heated in a fire nearby and then dropped into the water of the pit, thus boiling the meat.

A *fulacht* could also be used for bathing, to dye wool, to tan leather, and even to brew beer, according to modern archaeological experiments. Legal commentaries of the time describe holly as *crann fulachta fiannsa* "tree of the cooking pit."[7]

The *Crith Gablach* law text states that a farmer who is a *mruigfer* (landowner) should always have a sack of charcoal in his house for the purpose of making or repairing iron tools.[8] Holly wood was once used for charcoal to make axes and swords.[9]

Holly is a valuable tree for all kinds of fires. The "Song of the Forest Trees" states, "Holly, burn it green, holly burn it dry: of all trees whatsoever the best is holly."[10]

Now let us examine the Word Oghams connected to this tree. The *Word Ogham of Morainn mic Moín* describes Holly as *trian roith,* "the third part of a wheel." The *Word Ogham of Mic ind Oic* gives *smuir gúaile,* "marrow of charcoal" while *trian n-airm,* "one-third of a weapon," is the description from *Briatharogam Con Culainn.*[11]

From the above discussion, the derivation of these Word Oghams should be obvious. Holly is one of the best woods for making the charcoal that smelts the metal to make weapons and rims for chariot wheels. The metal part of a spear is roughly one-third of its length. *Tinne* is the bar of iron that is forged in the *tine* (fire) using charcoal made from holly.

HERBAL USES

The leaves of English (or European) holly (*Ilex aquifolium*) were once used as a tea substitute in Europe and for coughs, colds, and flu. It also benefits gout, stones, bladder conditions, chronic bronchitis, arthritis, and rheumatic complaints.

CAUTION

Holly berries are poisonous.[12]

Simmer two tablespoons of the leaf per cup of water for twenty minutes in a nonaluminum pot with a tight lid. Take up to one cup a day in one-quarter cup doses.

Native American herbalists and medicine people used American holly (*Ilex opaca*). The Alabama decocted the bark to make a wash for sore eyes. The Catawba drank the leaf tea for measles. The Cherokee scratched cramped muscles with the leaves and the Choctaw applied the leaf tea to eye problems. The Koasati rubbed the bark tea into itching body parts.[13]

The Iroquois used *Ilex verticillata* (winterberry holly, black alder) bark tea as an emetic (to vomit) and made a decoction of the roots for hay fever and allergies. The tea also made a wash for skin eruptions.[14]

To prepare the tea, simmer one teaspoon of the root bark (or berries) per cup of water for twenty minutes. Take up to two cups a day in one-quarter cup doses, cold. Or simmer two teaspoons of the bark per pint of water, and take one-quarter cup four times a day.[15]

The Alabama used yaupon holly (*Ilex vomitoria*) leaf tea to purge their bodies in preparation for ceremonies.[16] A mild tea of the leaves contains caffeine and makes a good beverage.[17]

There is a holly beverage called maté or yerba maté made from *Ilex paraguariensis,* a small tree that is native to Brazil, Paraguay, and Argentina. High in caffeine, it helps headaches, relieves fatigue, and increases mental and physical energy. It is a reputed blood cleanser, with less caffeine than black tea or coffee.[18]

SPIRITUAL ASPECTS

Holly is a chieftain tree of the Celts associated with Taranis, the Gaulish thunder god. Other Holly gods include Tina, the Etruscan thunder god; Taran, the Pictish thunder god; and the Scandinavian god Thor.

Holly was planted near homes to protect them from lightning, storm, fire, and hexes. Its wood was used in door sills to repel sorcery. With its blood-red berries and its spiny leaves, holly was understood to have a warrior's spirit. War clubs and chariot wheels were made from its wood.[19]

In England a ritual combat was enacted each year involving the "oak king" who ruled in summer and the "holly king" who ruled in winter. At Midsummer and again at Midwinter these "divine kings" would battle for the hand of the "queen" (the land goddess). The oak king always won in summer, initiating the season of green and light, and the holly king in winter, initiating the cold, dark season.

In ancient Rome, gifts were decorated with sprigs of holly at the Saturnalia, a midwinter festival that took place on December 25. The use of evergreens as decoration has traditionally been associated with good luck—holly and other evergreens in and around the home are a signal to the nature spirits that they are welcome to find shelter and comfort within. A round evergreen wreath on the door is a solar symbol and a sign of faith that life, like the sun, is cyclical, and that a dark phase such as the apparent "death" of the trees and herbs at winter is merely temporary.

In English tradition it was unlucky to bring holly into the home before Christmas and unlucky to take it down before Twelfth Night. A sprig was kept in the home to perpetuate luck in the coming year. By Imbolc (Candlemas) on February 2, all greens had to be out of the house.

The ancients regarded holly with its red berries as a powerful protector. A branch was placed in the cowshed to keep the cattle from harm. The common dark green English holly was regarded as a male tree and the variegated variety a female tree. In marriage ceremonies, holly represented the male principle and ivy the female principle. Both herbs were twined into wreaths and used to decorate carts, tables, and the house.

In the forest of Bere, Hampshire, herbal potions to treat whooping cough were drunk from a bowl made of variegated holly.[20]

Prickly holly is a warrior tree that will forcefully defend the body from cold, as it repels harm to the spirit.

A holly tree adorned with blood-red berries rises from the flames of a fiery forge.

Hazel

Coll ✦ [KOL]

As I mentioned in the Willow chapter, Celtic society was divided into four classes: the nemed (sacred class of Druids and kings), the warriors, the farmers and producers, and the slaves. Kings and queens were born into the warrior class and had to be ritually elevated to nemed status. Druids were nemed by hereditary right.

We have a surviving remnant of the *teagasc ríogh* (elevation ritual of a king) called the *Audacht Morainn* (The Testament of Morann), which was first written down in the seventh century but before that would have been part of the oral tradition. It was recited by a Druid to a new king on the occasion of his king-making ritual. This was done in Ireland until the time of the Norman invasions. There is evidence that Alexander III of Scotland underwent a similar ceremony in the thirteenth century, when a bishop girded the king with a military belt and explained to him in Latin and then in Gaelic the sacred duties of a king.[1]

In the *Audacht Morainn* the new ruler is advised to be humble because his rule is young. He is given counsel on how to have a prosperous and peaceful kingdom, and how to care for his tribes. He is told that his rule must be just, or the land and the people will suffer. The condition of the kingdom—good weather, bountiful harvests of grain, healthy forests, strong herds, great quantities of milk, plentiful fish, beautiful children—all depend upon the truth and justice of the king. The kingship is revealed to be a ritual function as much as a military one.

The *Audacht Morainn* states: "It is through the justice of the ruler that abundances of great tree-fruit of the great wood are tasted."[2] By inference, an unjust ruler would cause the failure of crops of nuts and fruit, and many other disasters. Of course, having been raised as a warrior, the king would not have memorized the laws and precedents. For this reason, every ruler had to have a Druid at his or her side in order to preserve justice. Thus the ruler and his Druid were like "two kidneys." (The mythical tales of Arthur and Merlin are a throwback to this sacred relationship between a ruler and his Druid.)

Hazel was an important tree-fruit in ancient Ireland. The Irish countryside was once covered with hazel (*Corylus avellana*), an important source of carbohydrates and protein. The nuts could be stored for up to a year, making them a critical winter food source, and they were widely traded.[3]

The hazel was classified as airig fedo, one of the "nobles of the wood" in the *Bretha Comaithchesa*. It was a valuable tree due to its nuts, and the strong and pliable rods that could be taken from it to be used for fences and house walls (wattling). One cartload of rods a year was part of the rent a client owed to his lord, which probably included both hazel and willow "Sally rods." Both of these woods were used for thatching and basket making.[4]

I mentioned above that pig meat was the food of choice for noble feasts. In "The Tale of Bricriu's Feast," the three bravest warriors in Ulster, CúChulainn, Conall, and Loegaire, compete to see who is worthy of the "champion's portion," the choicest cut of meat. The story mentions that a boar was reared especially for this feast. In the spring he was fed porridge and milk and gruel, in the summer curds and milk, in the autumn nuts and wheat, and in the winter stewed meats.[5]

Of interest here is an ancient lament for a pig, *"truagh truagh an mhuc,"* that describes the pig as *siúr na gcnó gcuill*—"sister of the hazelnuts."[6]

Finally, the hazel has a role in the legal system in ancient Ireland.

The smallest liquid measure mentioned in the laws is "the half-shell of a hazelnut." This measurement was used in determining compensation due to victims of crime, depending upon the amount of blood they had shed. Half of a hazelnut was said to hold five drops of blood (the next larger measure was a halved hen egg).[7]

The Word Oghams connected to this tree are as follows. In the *Word Ogham of Morainn mic Moín,* hazel is *caíniu fedaib, ithcar cnocar,* and *caincar fid*—"beautiful tree, edible nut, fairest tree." In the *Word Ogham of Mic ind Oic: carae blóesc,* "friend of cracking"; and *milsem fedo,* "sweetest tree" from *Briatharogam Con Culainn.*[8] The meanings should be obvious from the above discussion.

HERBAL USES

Homeopaths use the buds of hazel (*Corylus avellana*) in a low potency (2X) as a "drainage remedy" to restore elasticity to lung tissues. This tincture is used for emphysema, pulmonary fibrosis, and some liver conditions. The dose is fifty drops, once a day, taken in water.[9]

The herbalist Nicholas Culpeper recommended powdering the nuts and mixing them to a paste with mead or honey water for coughs. Adding pepper to this "electuary" helps to expel mucus from the sinus passages.[10] Among the Celts, hazelnuts were chopped and added to oatmeal as a strengthening food for invalids.

Hazelnuts are said to benefit kidney infections when eaten. The Huron used the bark of *Corylus rostrata* (beaked hazelnut) in poultices for ulcers and tumors. The Iroquois mixed hazelnut oil and bear grease to make a salve that repelled mosquitoes. The Chippewa made a decoction of hazel root from *Corylus americana* (American hazelnut), white oak root, chokecherry bark, and the heartwood of ironwood for bleeding from the lungs. They made drum sticks from hazel wood.[11]

The Meskwaki made brushes from fine hazel twigs to clean out their houses, and hazel twig baskets for carrying. The Ojibwa boiled the bark and used it to poultice wounds. The Mohawk made a tea of young hazel stalks and field horsetail root to relieve teething pains in babies. The Tête-de-Boule made a tea of the branch tips for heart problems.[12]

SPIRITUAL ASPECTS

Hazels figure strongly in Celtic magical tradition. There are stories concerning a sacred well of knowledge surrounded by the "nine hazels of wisdom." The well is said to be under the ocean, in the otherworld, or at the source of several rivers in Ireland. The seven streams of wisdom (the perfection of all the senses) flow from this well, and back to it again. Sometimes it is referred to as Connla's Well, the source of the Shannon River; or it is called the Well of Segais, which is the source of the Shannon or the Boyne.[13]

The nine hazels that hang over the well represent wisdom, inspiration, and poetry. The trees put forth leaves, flowers, and nuts simultaneously, which fall into the water to be eaten by the salmon of wisdom who swim in the well. For every nut a salmon eats, it develops a spot (possibly a reference to a lost series of initiations or poetic grades) and any person who eats one of these magical salmon will become wise. The waters of the well develop bubbles of inspiration from the dropping of the nuts that flow out to be drunk by all people of arts (*áes dána*).[14]

The hero Finn mac Cumhaill gained his prophetic powers and wisdom by eating a salmon of wisdom that had fed on the hazelnuts that dropped into the Well of Segais. This happened when Finn was a young apprentice. His teacher, the seer Finnégeas (Finn the Seer), had captured the salmon and intended to eat it himself in order to gain its knowledge. He set his young apprentice Finn to watch the cooking salmon. As it cooked, some of the hot juices popped onto Finn mac Cumhaill's thumb, which he immediately put in his mouth to salve the pain. (This begins to look a lot like the Druidic art of teinm laegda described above.) Finn instantly gained the knowledge of every art.[15]

Salmon of Wisdom

Based on the older seer's name, both Finn and the seer may be the same person in the story, before and after tasting the salmon of knowledge. Or perhaps before and after a significant Druidic initiation. And the flesh of salmon is red, which may be a hint that the initiation involved mushrooms, specifically *Amanita muscaria*, which is red with white spots.

In rivers there is a mysterious reverse current, which salmon utilize in their ascent of waterfalls and rapids. The salmon wisdom who venture out into the great sea of life unerringly return to the Source, an inspiring feat for any seeker of wisdom. This is related to a problem.[16] Druidic art of going within to find the answers oral tradition.

The tenth-century encyclopedia of *nmón,* "the hazel The *Cormac* (Cormac's Glossary), refers to composition break entific composition," from which hazel symbolizes the hard work of attaining knowledge—breaking the hard shell to get at the sweet meat inside.[17]

Ancient Druids and early Irish bishops carried hazel wands. Aengus Og, the Celtic young god of love, carried one as well. So revered was hazel among the ancient Celts that a tiny twig was enough to protect the home from lightning strikes or a ship from being lost at sea. A hazel collar worn by a horse was said to protect it from ill-intentioned fairy folk. At Beltaine (May Day) in ancient Ireland, cattle were driven between two ritual fires as an act of purification. Hazel rods singed their backs as they passed between the pyres.[18]

Hazelnuts were a common postglacial food for the Indo-Europeans. Hazel wood was used to make spears for small game such as hare. Hazel shoots were used as canes, barrel hoops, fishing poles, spits for roasting, and as wands and scepters of authority.

Hazel is a tree of choice for water witches, or dowsers. A forked hazel twig can be seen to tremble when a current of water is crossed. A hazel divining rod cut on St. John's Eve was used until the sixteenth century to detect thieves.[19] The spirit of hazel is one that helps us to divine the mysterious unseen Source of all things.

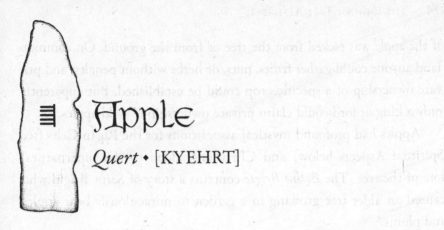

Apple

Quert • [KYEHRT]

s I mentioned above, the Gaelic word for apple is *aball* (Scots Gaelic *ubhal*). There is much confusion as to why the name *quert* was associated with this tree. Howard Meroney concludes that quert is actually a corruption of *ceirt* (a rag).[1] Given that other Ogham word lists were consistent (i.e., lists of birds, pigs, rivers, etc.) it is a mystery why a "rag" should suddenly intrude here. The word *cert* has the meanings of "fitting, proper, right." Perhaps the *imbas* (poetic inspiration) of another scholar will unravel the knot.

The wild apple (*Malus sylvestris*) was the original apple in Ireland. It is classed as a "noble of the wood" due to its fruit and its bark. The bark is certainly medicinal (see below in Herbal Uses) and can be used to dye cloth yellow.[2]

The wild apple has sour fruits. By the ninth century, the *Bethu Brigte*, the ninth-century biography of St. Brigid, makes reference to crops of "sweet apples" and in an eighth-century law text there is a reference to "wild" apples, implying domesticated varieties. The fine for destroying an apple tree was twenty *séta* (ten cows) if the tree belonged to the highest class of person (nemed), and only five *séta* (two and a half cows) if the tree was a commoner's. The perpetrator also had to replace the tree with one of the same variety, implying that there were different kinds of apples to be had.[3]

Apples were an important source of vitamins and carbohydrates in winter. One legal passage states that the fine for stealing just one apple from a tree was two ounces of silver, a huge sum. A different fine was if the apple was picked from the tree or from the ground. On common land anyone could gather fruits, nuts, or herbs without penalty, and private ownership of a specific crop could be established. But apparently only a king or lord could claim private ownership of wild apples.[4]

Apples had profound mystical associations for the Pagan Celts (see Spiritual Aspects below) and Christians added to the supernatural lore of the tree. The *Bethu Brigte* contains a story of Saint Brigid who caused an alder tree growing in a garden to miraculously bear apples and plums.[5]

Here are the Word Oghams connected to *quert: clithar mbaiscaill* ("shelter of lunatics," from the *Word Ogham of Morainn mic Moín*), *bríg anduine* ("substance of an insignificant person," from the *Word-Ogham of Mic ind Oic*) and *díghu fethail .i. cumdaigh* "worst of ornaments or worst of coverings," from *Briatharogam Con Culainn*.

Ceirt or rag does seem to relate to these three Word Oghams, but *ceirt* was never spelled with a *q*, and so the original name of this letter remains a mystery.[6] That said, according to Seán O'Boyle, the *Word Ogham of Morainn mic Moín* lists *clithar mbaiscaill*, which O'Boyle translates (quoting Calder) as "Shelter of a Hind," which makes eminent sense.[7] Deer are very fond of apples and will shelter near the trees in order to get at the fruits.

HERBAL USES

Apples can be peeled and then eaten raw to stop diarrhea. (Adding some powdered cinnamon to the raw, peeled apples will make an even more effective antidiarrheal.) Apples eaten whole or baked with the skin on will have a laxative effect.

Baked apples can be applied as a poultice to sore throats and to the chest and throat for fever. Apply a baked apple poultice to inflammations.

After a course of antibiotics it is important to replenish intestinal flora. Leave a dish of applesauce or a glass of unpasteurized, raw apple cider at room temperature overnight and eat or drink the beneficial bacteria the next day.

Eating raw apples benefits the gums, cleans the liver, eases tension and headaches, and helps insomnia. The best variety for general consumption is the sour green apple, which has less of a hypoglycemic effect on the pancreas.

Use the dried peels to help ease rheumatic conditions. Steep two teaspoons of dried peel per cup of freshly boiled water for twenty minutes. Take up to three cups a day.

Apple peel can ease heartburn, and can be simmered in boiled milk to help diarrhea.

The bark of the root has been used to treat intermittent fevers and the tree bark contains quercin, an astringent also found in oak trees. Simmer two teaspoons of bark or root bark per cup of water for twenty minutes. Take in quarter-cup doses, three or four times a day.

CAUTION

Do not take bark from the trunk of the tree or you can kill it. Please take the bark from a branch only. Apple seeds can be poisonous to young children if eaten in significant numbers and chewed (about twenty-five seeds could be fatal due to their strychnine content).[8]

Native American herbalists and medicine people made extensive use of crab apple. The Cherokee used *Malus coronaria* (sweet crab apple) bark as a tea for gallstones and piles, and as a wash for sore mouth. The Iroquois applied a cold infusion of the bark to sore eyes, used an infusion of the twig bark for labor and used the roots in remedies for consumption.[9]

The Bella Coola used *Pyrus diversifolia,* or *Malus fusca* (Oregon crab apple) bark or root tea as an eyewash. The Gitksan used a tea of the inner bark for consumption and rheumatic complaints and as a "fattening" agent. They also used the bark tea as a laxative and diuretic, and scraped juice from the peeled trunk to use as an eye medicine.[10]

The Makah used the bark tea for dysentery and diarrhea. They also soaked and then chewed the leaves for lung complaints. The Samish used the bark tea as a wash for cuts.[11] The Cherokee used *Malus pumila* (sweet apple) bark tea for piles and gallstones, included it in formulas to increase wind in ball players, and added it to drinks for hoarseness and loss of voice. The Iroquois applied a poultice of the bark and fruit peels to black eyes and bruises, put drops of the bark tea into the ears for earaches, and used a tea of the bark and leaf as drops for blindness.[12]

(For more on the medicinal uses of apples and of apple cider please see my book *Tree Medicine, Tree Magic*.)

SPIRITUAL ASPECTS

"The Song of the Forest Trees" states, "Burn not the precious apple tree of spreading and low-sweeping bough: a tree ever decked in bloom of white, against whose fair head all men put forth the hand."[13]

As we have seen above, apple trees were regarded as precious in ancient times. In my experience, apples have sweet and welcoming spirits. I know an old apple orchard that is hidden in the midst of a wilderness area, in the hills of western Massachusetts. Some of the trees are so ancient that their trunks bend to touch the ground and are filled with holes and fissures.

If you sit quietly in that orchard, and hold out a handful of seed, chickadees and nuthatches will eat right out of your hand. There is a small herd of deer that frequents the orchard. They usually travel with a flock of fat wild turkeys. It is funny to watch the baby deer jump like puppies and try to get the huge turkeys to play. It is a very magical spot.

All apples seem to like humans. There is no sadder sight than an unkempt apple tree that has not been pruned in years. Apples seem to go out of their way to get our attention. The crab apples in particular put on tremendously showy displays in an effort to be seen and appreciated.

The common wild apple was a component of the mixed hardwood forests of the postglacial Indo-European homeland. The domesticated apple was probably developed in the southern Caucasus as part of the Neolithic farming revolution and soon spread to Switzerland, Britain, and Ireland. Apples were an important and popular food source being sweet, high in calories, and easy to dry. According to the historian Tacitus, milk, deer, and apples were the main diet of the Germanic tribes.[14]

Apples had magical and religious significance for Celtic, Greek, Slavic, and Germanic peoples. They are so embedded in our cultural imaginations that the biblical story of Adam and Eve is said to revolve around an apple even though no apples are mentioned in the Bible!

Scandinavian tradition relates that Loki stole the apples that the goddess Ithunn had bestowed upon the gods to keep them immortal. When the gods began to age, Loki had to return them.

In English folk tradition warts can be cured by rubbing them with two halves of an apple, which are then buried. As the apple decays, so will the warts. Cutting down an apple tree was considered sacrilegious. In Herefordshire it was said that hops would never grow in a felled apple orchard.[15]

A piece of common land could be claimed in Britain by fencing it and planting an apple tree. And as long as the yearly crop was taken, the landowner maintained his claim. In Yorkshire it was said that one apple must be left on each tree after harvest as a gift for the fairies. If a bloom appeared on a tree that had already borne fruit, it was an omen that someone would die.

Wassailing the orchard is an old custom of Twelfth Night. Farming families ate hot cakes and drank cider and then proceeded to the orchard where a cider-soaked cake was placed in the fork of an apple tree. More cider was poured on the cake as a libation and then noisemakers were employed, such as pots and pans, to drive away evil spirits. Cider was then sprinkled on orchard and field to encourage the vegetation fairies.[16]

Apple wood is a traditional choice for magic wands, and the scent is considered a potent love charm. Associated with immortality and the Summerland, Arthur's island of Avalon (*Abhalloch*) was said to be covered with apples.[17]

In the eighth-century tale "The Voyage of Bran, Son of Febal," Bran goes outside the gates of his fort and hears beautiful music, which lulls him to sleep. When he wakes he sees a silver branch with white blossoms and apples on it, which he carries back to his hall. All who have gathered in the hall are amazed to see a strange woman appear suddenly in their midst, even though the gates were closed. She sings a hauntingly beautiful song about an island in the otherworld and then disappears, taking the apple branch with her.[18]

The god of the sea, Mannanán Mac Lir, lives on an otherworld island to the east of Ireland called Magh Meall (The Pleasant Plain), Tír Tairngire (The Land of Promise), or Emhain Abhlach (The Place of Apples). Emhain Abhlach is an island of golden apples that is the same place as Arthur's Avalon.

One day Mannanán appeared to Cormac Mac Airt carrying a branch with nine golden apples upon it. When shaken, the branch produced beautiful music, and anyone who heard the sound was instantly cured of their troubles. Mannanán later took Cormac to the Land of Promise and gifted him with the Cup of Truth.[19]

When the Celts arrived in Ireland from Spain, their Druids did battle with the Druids of the Tuatha De Danann, the resident peoples of Erin. The latter were eventually driven underground and into the sídhe (fairy) mounds. Each of these fairy hills was an entrance to the otherworld, where apple trees were always in fruit and pigs were roasted, only to come magically back to life again and again.[20]

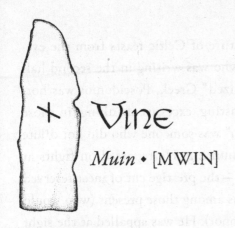

Vine

Muin • [MWIN]

Muin is not the word for grape or vine. It may be a corruption of *mídiuit* (unsimple), or it may be related to the Welsh *mwn* or the Gaelic *muin* (the back) or the Latin *munus* (which carries the meanings of gift, present, spectacle, function, tribute, and service).[1] I will examine the Word Oghams associated with this letter in the Herbal Uses section to unravel the kennings, but first let us acquaint ourselves with the role of wine in Celtic life.

We know that wine was a prestige drink for the ancient Celts, suitable for sacred feasts and to honor the dead. Large numbers of wine containers (amphorae) have been found in Gaulish graves, along with other prestige items such as helmets and bronze vessels. Based on the very large percentage of wine containers in relation to other pottery vessels in certain places, it can be concluded that wine played an important part in ceremonial or political events at these sites.[2]

Wine became a feature of Celtic life around 600 BCE as can be discerned from Greek, Etruscan, and Roman wine-drinking vessels that were imported into Celtic areas. Wooden barrels and skin bags were used to transport the valuable drink. Based on grave deposits in Britain, Austria, Switzerland, France, Germany, and other Celtic areas, evidence exists for wine as a ritual and prestige item all through the Pagan Iron Age.[3] Christians continued to regard wine as a sacred and prestigious drink after that, as evidenced by the use of wine as a sacramental drink in the mass.

We know that wine was a feature of Celtic feasts from the eye-witness accounts of Poseidonios, who was writing in the second half of the first century BCE. A "civilized" Greek, Poseidonios was horrified by Celtic culture and its boasting, excessive drinking (in those days one definition of a "barbarian" was someone who did not dilute their wine with water), and headhunting. He reported on fights at feasts for the "champion's portion"—the prestige cut of meat reserved for the warrior of the highest status among those present (who would fight and sometimes kill for the honor). He was appalled at the sight of heads nailed to the doors of houses, to which the homeowners pointed with special pride when the decapitated enemy was particularly eminent.[4]

Poseidonios also reported on Celtic hospitality and manners at feasts. He said it was considered impolite to question newly arrived guests, and that the Celts were "leonine" in their appetites but had clean table manners. Armed warriors were present at feasts where wine was usually drunk straight, not blended with water. Hospitality and politics were intimately connected, and generous feasts along with gifts of silver and gold enabled warriors to win leadership positions.[5]

There is evidence that grapes were grown in Britain from Roman times, but there is no such evidence for Ireland in old Irish sources. Only the apple and plum were cultivated (cherries and other fruits arrived after the Norman invasions).[6] In general, all food consumed was produced by the household in which it was grown, but the old Irish law text *Muirbretha* (Laws of the Sea) refers to "wine-jars," vessels used for measuring wine among Gaulish and Frankish traders, implying that wine was being imported.[7]

The *fled* or feast was as important in Irish Celtic culture as it was to the Gaulish Celts. Any client with a lord over him was expected to provide food rent, and also feast his overlord in accordance with the lord's station. The feast *cóe* was called "winter-hospitality" because the lord and attendants were feasted in late winter. In spring the lord might be entertained at a *crimfes* or garlic feast, and at Samhain (Halloween) the lord might be entertained at a pig feast.[8]

The laws of hospitality also extended to visitors and passers-by. Failure to feed such a person could result in a fine of the offended person's honor-price. But poor farmers were exempt from this obligation, and there was no duty to feed a criminal.[9]

There were other precise rules concerning food, for example, which foods were due to workers. A master builder got meat and bread and his assistant vegetables or salt, and bread. A turner who made vessels from yew wood got three-quarters the ration of a master builder.[10]

A client was supposed to attend a feast in honor of his lord when the lord died. The lord in turn used the food rent he received (live animals, meat, milk products, grain, malt, bread, vegetables)[11] to feed his household and also to gain prestige via feasts. Kings were expected to give lavish feasts for their own households and for their subjects. Great feasts were held at the inauguration of a new king and on important holy days such as Samhain.[12]

One text, *Suidigud Tige Midchúarda* (The Seating of the House of the Mead Circuit), describes the correct seating arrangements for a feast, according to the rank or profession of the guest and also what cut of meat was to be served to each. The highest-ranking guest got the *loarg* (haunch) or the *lónchrúachait* (tenderloin steak). Those below them got the shank or center-cut loin steak. The lowest ranking guests got the belly or shoulder fat.[13]

Drink at such noble feasts held a deep ritual significance to the ancients. Mead (*mid*) was the most common drink, with a higher status than the usual beer (*cuim*). Wine (*fín*) is also mentioned as a drink fit for such celebrations.[14] The distribution of an alcoholic drink such as wine or mead held an important political significance, because the highest-ranking person got served first followed by others of descending rank. In this way the distribution of an alcoholic drink could raise or lower a person in status before the tribe. Oaths were spoken over the cup as it was passed, and marriages were sanctified simply by passing a cup from one half of a couple to the other.

HERBAL USES

Grapes (*Vitis vinifera*) are an excellent food for those with a fever. The leaves were once boiled with barley meal and applied to inflamed wounds as a poultice. Dried raisins are beneficial for those with a cough and are slightly laxative.[15]

The ash from burned vines was once used as a dentifrice to make teeth white by rubbing on the teeth each morning. Red grape juice is rich in iron and antioxidants and is known to help clean the blood. Conditions such as weak circulation, low blood pressure, anemia, a congested liver, and skin eruptions will all benefit from grape juice. Grape fasts have been used to treat cancer and other chronic conditions.[16]

CAUTION

Please see a medical professional before undertaking a prolonged grape fast.

Grapes are not suitable for gouty conditions. The sap can be applied to weak eyes. Ripe grapes are diuretic. Grapes help to restore the system in cases of anemia or exhaustion. Persons with "torpid" livers can take three to six pounds of grapes per day (and nothing else except water). Those who need cleansing of the liver (as evidenced by skin blemishes) should eat the grapes when not quite fully ripe. Those who are losing weight rapidly, and are exhausted and chilly, should eat fully ripe grapes, which will have a higher sugar content.[17]

Native American herbalists used several species of grapes. Summer grape (*Vitis aestivalis*) was used by the Cherokee as an antidiarrheal. They infused the leaf for liver complaints and to poultice sore breasts after childbirth. The Choctaw used the grapes as a "refrigerant" (to bring down body temperature).[18]

The fox grape (*Vitis vulpina*) was also used by the Cherokee as an antidiarrheal, and the leaf tea was used for liver complaints. The wilted leaves were used to poultice sore breasts, and the bark tea was used for urinary complaints. The Mohegan applied the leaf poultice to the head for headaches and fevers.[19] The Delaware applied the sap to the hair.[20]

The Cherokee used the frost grape (*Vitis cordifolia*) leaf infusion for liver problems and diarrhea. They also used the leaves to poultice sore breasts after childbirth. The Chippewa used the root tea for rheumatism and diabetes. The Iroquois gave an infusion of the plant to children with urinary or stomach ailments. The Menominee squeezed grape juice into the eyes to remove foreign bodies.[21]

SPIRITUAL ASPECTS

The *Word Ogham of Morainn mic Moín* describes vine as *tresim fedma* or "strongest of effort." The *Word Ogham of Mac ind Oic* uses *aruusc n-arrligh* or "condition of slaughter."[22] Meroney offers *conair gotha .i. tre muin* or "path of voice," that is, through the neck.[23] And the *Auraicept na N-Eces* (Calder translation) states, ". . . back of man or ox, for it is they that are the strongest in existence as regards effort."[24]

The themes of wine, effort, slaughter, back of the neck, sacred drink, and feasting point to a basic Indo-European mystical understanding: the idea of the sacrifice that regenerates the world. Birth and death, creation and destruction happen in a continuous cycle. Sacrificial animals (or in the Christian mythos, the dying God) bequeath their body and substance to the world so that the world may continue to be created anew.[25]

In Persian tradition, fifty-seven species of grain and twelve species of healing plants were created from the first ox that was offered as a sacrifice. These healing substances and foods emerged because the blood of the ox was spilled. Different plants sprang from the different body parts; sesame from the marrow, the vine from blood, and so forth. Food and medicines emerged from the act of sacrifice. The act of eating was also seen as a sacred function that was part of the continuum; wine that was blood (of the sacrificed animal) became blood again (by nourishing the one who drank the wine) and the sacrifice was reversed.[26]

All Indo-European cultures have similar beliefs. In the *Senchus Mór* it is said that the Druids "claimed that they made the sky and earth and sea . . . the Sun and Moon and so forth." The Indian *Aitareya Brahmana* (instructions to Brahmin priests on the handling of sacrificial animals) instructs the sacrificer to send the animal's eye to the sun, its breath to the wind, its life force to the atmosphere, its ear to the directions, and its flesh to the earth.[27]

Work is also a form of sacrifice: the man and the ox work with the most sustained effort to give of their life force so that all lives may continue to exist. Whether through a cut in the neck that spills blood or through strongest effort, the sacrificial victim's body becomes the basis for the continuing survival of all creation.

A Green Man sprouting vines from his mouth
and drinking from a golden chalice.

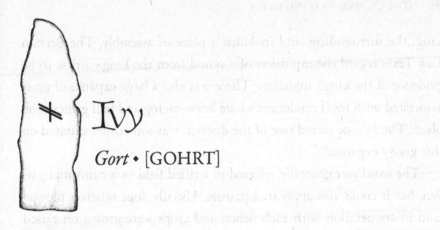

Ivy

Gort ◆ [GOHRT]

The herb ivy (*Hedera helix*) has been associated with the letter *g*, however, *gort* actually means "tilled field" or "garden." To unravel the kennings we must examine both the nature of fields and gardens in ancient Ireland and the uses of ivy.

As I mentioned above, ivy was used (along with holly) as winter fodder for cows.[1] There was a special sickle called a *cromán tige bantrebthaige* (hook of a woman householder's house). This *corrán* (sickle) was used specifically to cut holly or ivy. It was an essential tool for women of poorer farming families, so that they could feed their herds in winter.[2]

Ivy was a useful plant for fodder and for medicine (see below in Herbal Uses) and was classed in the Brehon Law Texts with the *losa fedo* (bushes of the woods)[3] along with bracken, bog-myrtle, gorse, bramble, heather, broom, and wild rose.[4]

Work in a garden was the province of the farming and producing class in ancient Ireland. For a person of higher rank to work a garden was considered shameful and "one of the three failures of a minor lord" according to the poets.[5]

The area that was cultivated for vegetables, grain, and fruit trees was called the *airlise,* which was supposed to extend the length of a spear-cast on every side of a farmstead. The fields around a farm were rectangular and radiated outward from it like the "petals of a flower."[6]

The ownership of land was divided evenly among heirs but the oldest also got the farmhouse and the surrounding area. In the case of a king, the surrounding land included a place of assembly. The Brehon Law Texts regard the expulsion of a synod from the king's airlise to be evidence of the king's injustice.[7] There was also a large expanse of grass associated with royal residences where horse-racing and ball games took place. The *bíle,* or sacred tree of the district, was sometimes situated on this grassy expanse.[8]

The word *gort* generally referred to a tilled field or a cultivated garden, but it could also apply to a pasture. Usually, four relatives plowed land in cooperation with each other, and crops were grown on raised beds in rectangular fields, with a drainage trench between each bed.[9]

Land ownership and status were intimately connected. It was assumed that a farmer who accumulated livestock would sell off the extra animals to purchase land. The Law Texts enumerated professions that were likely to be profitable enough so that their practice would result in land ownership. These included poetry, learning, wood or stone craftsmanship, smith craft, metal work, and law. When these professionals bought land, they also got the serfs who came with the land.[10]

Some professionals could attain status without land, but that was very rare. Merchants could do so, but they are barely mentioned in the laws. A hermit who was a *díthir Dé* or "landless one of God" had enough status that evidence he provided could overturn a contract, and his oath was binding.[11]

Being landless was usually a bad position, though. A landless person could not make a contract unless it was authorized by someone of property. To be landless implied that one was a shiftless wanderer. In the Brehon Law Texts such a person was called a "fox of a cooking pit" or a "marsh dweller." Landless persons survived by gleaning, scavenging, and by charity, and were assumed to be disreputable outcasts from their kin. However, one who had been away studying or one who had been abducted when young could claim and use land if he could prove his case.[12]

Members of a *fian* (an independent group of wandering warriors) were landless, but it was assumed that these wild warriors would eventually settle down. As the *Técosca Cormaic* wisdom text says, "Everyone is a warrior till farming."[13]

With the above facts in mind, the implications of the Word Oghams for *gort* are made clear. The *Word Ogham of Morainn mic Moín* describes *milsiu férai; glaisem gelta,* "sweetest grass; greenest pasture." The *Word Ogham of Mic ind Oic* offers *ined erc,* "suitable place for cows"; and *sásad ile,* "satisfaction of all, sating of a multitude" is from *Briatharogam Con Culainn.*[14]

These Word Oghams describe fields, pastures, and a field fit for the assembly. Ivy is a type of grass that is suitable for the herds when grasses fail. Every person, from the lowest to the highest, has access to provision for their kine.

HERBAL USES

Hedera helix (English ivy) twig and leaf can be simmered into salves for sunburn. The leaf infusion makes a douche for vaginal infections. Ivy can be used externally to poultice injured nerves, sinews, ulcers, glandular swellings, boils, and abscesses. (For detailed instructions on salve making and poultices please see my book *A Druid's Herbal for the Sacred Earth Year.*)[15]

Ivy was an herb used in the *spongia somnifera* (soporific sponge) of the Middle Ages. A fresh sea sponge was soaked in a mixture of opium, henbane, mulberry juice, lettuce seed, hemlock, mandrake, and ivy and then sun-dried. When it was needed for pain relief, it was reconstituted with water, and the patient inhaled the vapors, or the liquid was dripped into his or her mouth.

CAUTION

Do not try this at home. Some of these herbs are deadly and could easily prove fatal.[16]

English ivy is used as an external wash for sores, cuts, burns, dandruff, and skin irritations. The cold extract can be taken for phlegm in the system.

The herb causes contact dermatitis in some people. Small amounts of the tea are said to dilate blood vessels, while large amounts may cause the blood vessels to contract. Ivy can break down blood corpuscles by releasing their hemoglobin. The berries are poisonous, and the leaves should be used internally only with professional supervision.[17]

CAUTION

While the plant has been used internally for fevers, gout, rheumatism, whooping cough, and bronchitis, extreme care must be taken not to overdose with it, because diarrhea, vomiting, and even coma have been reported. It is probably best to use it as an external wash for burns and cuts and as a poultice for painful rheumatic joints. The leaves are antibacterial and paraciticidal, making them useful for infections and parasites on the skin. The twigs can be gently simmered in oil to make a sunburn remedy.

To prepare a cold tea, steep one teaspoon of crushed leaf per cup of cold water for eight hours. Take one-quarter cup four times a day, not with meals. (Make a stronger tea for use as an external wash.) Before steeping the leaves, soak them in a quart of cold water with a few tablespoons of vinegar or sea salt added for about twenty minutes to remove parasites and germs, and rinse well.

SPIRITUAL ASPECTS

There is an old Welsh expression that "the day the bees stop humming the world will end." Ivy blooms in the fall and provides the last bit of sweetness for the bees. For Druids the bee symbolizes the intelligence that navigates by the sun (divine guidance) to visit fields of flowers (the world) to gather sweetness (wisdom) and bring it back for the benefit of the tribe.

To be a Druid is to perform an active role on behalf of the people; it is a tribal function. The Old Irish *druí* (or ban-druí for a female Druid) was a priest or priestess, a prophet, an astrologer, and a teacher of the children of the nobility.[18] Druids did not isolate themselves in order to perfect their inner spiritual development. They served the whole and, like bees, went far and wide to gather knowledge on behalf of their kingdoms.[19]

Druids supervised the lighting of sacred fires on hilltops on the holy days of the Celts. At Midsummer herbs were ritually smoked over these fires, to be hung in houses and barns as protective amulets. These magically protective herbs included figwort, ivy, mugwort, yarrow, vervain, elder, fennel, chamomile, melilot, St. John's wort, plantain, hawthorn, lavender, and male fern.[20]

Ivy was equated with female energy and holly with male energy. Both herbs featured in Yule celebrations and in wedding wreaths for the bride and groom. Ancient poets were crowned with ivy to give them honor. An early Christian church council tried to ban the use of ivy in decorations because of its Pagan associations.[21]

Ivy clings to a sheer rock wall, a wolf's face forming in its leaves.

Reed

Ngetal • [NGYEH-dul]

ere is another case where the word assigned to the tree is not the name of the tree—*ngetal* does not actually mean "reed." (There is no word in Irish that begins with "ng.") Ngetal may be a corruption of *gétal*, "wounding, or act of wounding" (related to the Welsh *gwanu*, "to pierce or stab") or *cétal*, meaning "charm."[1] The Word Oghams associated with the letter are related to the practice of medicine, so we can assume that a physician's charm is meant here.[2] The case is very strong for a connection between reed and a physician's chant or incantation, as we will see below.

According to the Laws, a *liaig* or *midach* (Old Irish for "physician") had an honor-price of seven séta (or seventeen-and-one-half cows), regardless of their level of expertise. Three things were required of them: "a complete cure, leaving no blemish, a painless examination." The profession was usually hereditary, with training handed down within families.[3]

According to the *Táin Bó Cúailnge* wounds were healed by the application of bone marrow or by herbal poultices. Specific diets were prescribed for invalids and surgery was done. By law, a liaig was allowed to cause bleeding during the course of treatment, but if a sinew or joint was cut the liaig had to pay a fine and assume all costs for the care of the patient.[4]

There were female physicians who, along with several other types of women, had independent legal capacity. If they had no husband, their honor-price was based upon their value to the tribe and their possessions. Such women included "the woman who turns back the streams of war" (likely a *ban-druí*), the "hostage ruler," a *ban-sáer* (female wright), the *banliaig túaithe* (the woman-physician of the *túath* or territory), *airmitnech túaithe* (the woman revered by the túath), and *maínech ferta* (the woman who performs miracles, a female hermit).[5]

Besides using herbs and surgery, the liaig also chanted magical charms. In the *Táin* there is a description of how two wounded warriors arrived with their physicians who used medicinal herbs and spoke a healing incantation over the wounds.[6] Here is one example of a healing charm, recorded in an Anglo-Saxon book of leech-craft: *"I wound the worm, I strike the worm, I kill the worm."*[7] ("Worm" was a generic term for disease.)

The *Carmina Gadelica*, a collection of hymns and incantations collected in the Western Isles of Scotland around 1900 CE, preserves some old incantations for us. We cannot assume that the Druids used these charms, but they may have used something similar.

> *Bone to bone,*
> *Vein to vein,*
> *Balm to balm,*
> *To the left foot.*
> *Sap to sap,*
> *Skin to skin,*
> *Tissue to tissue,*
> *to the left foot.*
> *Blood to blood,*
> *Flesh to flesh,*
> *Sinew to sinew,*
> *to the left foot.*
> *Marrow to marrow,*
> *Pith to pith,*

Fat to fat,
To the left foot.
Membrane to membrane,
Fibre to fibre,
Moisture to moisture,
to the left foot . . .[8]

FROM CHARM FOR SPRAIN (NUMBER 432)

In the story of the Battle of Maige Tuired (Moytura), there is a description of a magical bath that was prepared by the god of medicine, Diancecht, and his children, Octriuil, Miach, and Airmid. The physicians sang magical incantations over a spring, and when mortally wounded warriors were placed in it, the warriors emerged completely healed.[9]

Now as to the subject of reeds, we know that they were used for thatching roofs and that there was a profession built around gathering reeds. Reeds were classed in the Laws as *losa fedo,* "bushes of the wood" based on their economic importance.[10] Of particular interest to us here is the use of reeds to administer medicine. The physician would use the reed as a straw to blow powdered herbs onto the back of the throat of a sick person, and reed has many other medical uses as well (see Herbal Uses below).

The *Word Ogham of Morainn mic Moín* describes reed as *lúth legha,* "a physician's strength, or a physician's cry." The *Word Ogham of Mic ind Oic* calls it *rtiud midach,* "robe of a physician." *Tosach n-échto,* "beginning of murder" is from the *Briatharogam Con Culainn.*[11]

Each of these meanings points neatly to the role of chanting and incantations in the healer's art and to reed as the tool of the physician, as seen in the medicinal uses of this valuable herb. The practice of making arrows from the stems probably explains the Word Ogham "beginning of murder."

HERBAL USES

The common reed (*Arundo phragmites, Phragmites communis L.,* and *Phragmites vulgaris*) grows in ponds and bogs and is ubiquitous in a damp climate such as Ireland's. Every part of the plant is useful. The roots can be eaten raw or cooked like a potato, and can be gathered in spring before the leaves form, to be dried and ground to make porridge.[12]

The stems are high in protein, fat, and carbohydrates, and very sweet—the plant is about 5 percent sugar. The stems and stalks can be boiled in water and the liquid boiled off to get the sugar. There is a sweet gum that exudes from the stems that can be eaten like candy.

The young shoots of the leaves can be eaten raw or cooked and can be dried, powdered, and added to flour. The seeds can also be eaten raw or cooked, and can be dried, ground, and added to flour.[13]

CAUTION

Before eating the raw leaves or roots please soak them in a quart of water with a few tablespoons of vinegar or salt for about twenty minutes. This will cause any parasites or germs to come loose. Rinse carefully and then prepare as food.

The stems and leaves are very tough and durable. Roofs thatched with reed can last a hundred years. The stems and leaves are also used for lattices and fencing, to weave mats, and to make arrows, carrying nets, baskets, brooms, and corks. The plant fibers can be used to make string or rope, and the flowers yield a light green dye.

The leaves and stems are mixed with mud to make plaster, and the stems have been used to make quills for writing on parchment.[14]

Medicinally, the plant is a virtual pharmacy from the bog. The leaves have been used to treat bronchitis and cholera. The ash of the leaves is styptic (stops bleeding) and can be applied to infected sores. The flowers are simmered to make a tea for cholera and for food poisoning. The stem helps to counteract poisoning, is antiemetic (stops vomiting), antipyretic (checks or prevents fever), and refrigerant (lowers body temperature).[15]

The root is febrefuge (lowers fevers), antitussive (stops coughs), depurative (cleans toxins from the blood and the liver), diuretic (increases urination), lithontropic (removes stones from the kidneys and bladder), sedative (calming), a sialagogue (increases saliva and thus aids in the digestion of foods), and stomachic (helps the stomach). It has been used historically for diarrhea, fever, vomiting, cough with a thick, dark mucus, lung abscesses, urinary tract infections, and for food poisoning (especially from seafood). The roots are harvested in the fall and juiced or dried for later use.[16]

Native American healers and medicine people made use of this plant. The Apache used it as an antidiarrheal, decocting the root for stomach ailments and diarrhea. The Paiute used the sugary sap for pneumonia, to loosen phlegm and calm pain in the lungs.[17]

It is easy to see how a liaig might have depended on this plant as part of a now lost Druid medical pharmacopoeia.

SPIRITUAL ASPECTS

The Celtic goddess most associated with the reed is the great goddess Brigid. Known by many names across the Celtic speaking world (Bride, Brigit, Brighid, Brigantia, Brigidu, Bricta, Brixia, Bricia, Brigindu), the root of her name, *brig,* means "high" or "exalted" and is found in many languages from Ireland and continental Europe. Brigid was the goddess of sovereignty for many tribes, and was the most popular and venerated pan-Celtic goddess. Brigid's stories and traditions were later grafted onto those of Saint Brigid or Saint Bride in Christian times.

Brigid's mother was Boann, cow goddess of the moon and of the Boyne River in Ireland, and her father was the *Daghda.* Brigid was a triple goddess, one of three sisters, each named Brigid. Her spheres of influence were poetry, smithcraft, and healing. She was patroness of the Druids and bards, and was especially associated with healing wells and springs.[18]

The later Saint Brigid of Kildare was born of a Druid father and a Christian slave mother and was sold briefly to a Druidic poet from whom she probably received training. She eventually converted to Christianity and became the first Irish nun, forming the first Christian religious community for women in Ireland. Her sacred Fire Temple was located at Kildare (Kil Dara—Church of the Oak) and a perpetual fire was maintained there by nuns—a mirror of the perpetual fire of the archdruid at Uisneach. It was a place where people could come with questions or to seek healing. The nuns would scry into the flames to divine answers.

Saint Brigid's Fire Temple continued to be maintained after her death in 525 CE and was tended faithfully by nuns until extinguished by the pope in 1220 CE. It was later rekindled for four hundred years, until the Protestant reformation shut it down once again. Thankfully, the flame has been relit in recent times, and nuns are carrying on the tradition of tending the flame once more. There are also numerous Pagan and Druidic groups that tend the flame worldwide, honoring Brigid in her ancient guise as goddess of healing, smithcraft, and poetic inspiration.[19]

Each year at Imbolc or Oimelc (February 2) at the fire festival that honors Brigid and the lactation of the ewes, equal-armed crosses are made from reeds in Brigid's honor. These crosses predate Christianity and are a version of the ancient swastika, or sun symbol, fitting for a fire goddess. Once made, the crosses are hung on the front door or in the byre, to bless the people and the animals.

Another custom is to leave *brat* or a mantle outdoors all night on Imbolc Eve. It is said that Brigid will pass by and bless it. The mantle can then be used for healing work all year. One can also leave a cloth outside on Imbolc Eve for Brigid to bless. The cloth is brought in the next morning and torn into strips, which can be tied to a person's limb or to an animal, when they are sick.

BLACKTHORN

Straif • [STRAF]

Some have equated *straif*, the Ogham word for blackthorn, with a corruption of *sraiph* (sulphur) and associated it with the alchemists' art based upon the Ogham Tract of the *Auracept na N-Eces*, which states: "For among dyes *straif* is stronger for the coloring of bodies, since it acts on white silver so that it becomes bluish in making pure silver thereof; it is boiled through urine into white gold so that it makes red gold of it."[1] Though this could just as easily be referring to the dyer's art. According to Vincent de Beauvais in *Speculum Naturale*, "Pure white mercury, fixed by the virtue of white noncorrosive sulphur, engenders in mines a matter which fusion changes into silver and united to pure red clear sulphur it forms gold." Also, the Word Oghams "increasing of secrets" and "seeking of clouds" seem to point to alchemy.[2]

I believe the explanation may be different. From ancient times, women in Scotland and Ireland used the bark of the blackthorn (*Prunus spinosa*) to make a red dye. The addition of stale urine as a mordant brightened the color. The chemical name for the active property of stale urine that makes it so valuable in the dyeing process is aluminum sulfate.[3] Hence the connection with sulphur (sraibh). (The actual Gaelic word for the blackthorn tree is *draighean*.)

Other parts of the tree were used as dyeing agents: a green dye was obtained from the leaves, and dark gray and green from the fruit (which may explain the reference to silver above). The bark boiled in alkali yielded yellow (which may explain the reference to gold above).[4] I prefer these plant references to the alchemy explanation, since alchemy wasn't even a part of ancient Irish thinking!

Blackthorn (*Prunus spinosa*) is native to Ireland and is a type of wild plum. The berries, called sloes, are edible and taste best just after the first frosts of autumn. Blackthorn was the "barbed wire" of the ancient world. It made a thick and sturdy hedge that could survive in marine environments and was strong enough to hold cattle. Its wood is very hard and was used to make *shillelaghs* (a large clublike weapon). In "The Destruction of Da Derga's Hostel," warriors were said to carry blackthorn clubs made with a band of iron around each one. The thorns were used as awls in leather-working.

The importance of blackthorn as a dyeing agent is mentioned above. The color of clothing was serious business in caste-conscious early Ireland. The lowest class of people were only allowed to wear clothing that was grayish brown (*lachtnae*), yellow (*buide*), black (*dub*), or white (*find*). The nobility could wear red (*derg*), gray (*glas*), or brown (*donn*). Princes and rulers wore blue (*gorm*) or purple (*corcra*).[5] Also, one's rank determined how many colors one could wear together: the highest ranking nobility could wear as many as six colors at once. The color of one's outfit was a kind of calling card; everyone knew instantly who they were dealing with.

Purple could be obtained from shellfish, but vegetable dyes were the norm. Bracken (*Pteridium aquilinum*) yielded a yellow-green, lady's bedstraw (*Galium verum*) produced gray, and juniper (*Juniperus communis*) made brown. The lichen *Parmelia saxatilis* yielded a brownish red. The famous herb woad (*Isatis tinctoria*) was an import from the Aegean that gave a permanent blue color to wool and also to bodies, according to Pliny.[6] Woad may also have been used in tattooing. The *Cauldron of Poesy* (an eighth-century text) contains a gloss that refers to the poet Amargen, who had a blue tattoo on his shank.[7]

Another important dye plant was madder (*roid*), which was introduced from Asia. The roots of madder produced a brilliant red. The stronger red the color, the more the cloth was worth. Madder also provided a facial cosmetic.[8] Leona Arthen, a spinner and dyer of Scottish heritage now living in New England, was able to produce bright red wool, and then purple (after soaking the fiber in vinegar), from the lichen *Umbilicaria pustilata*.

Su Grierson, author of *The Colour Cauldron*, experimented with blackthorn flowers and was able to obtain a deep orange-yellow (gold) by boiling an alum-mordanted wool for several hours. The bark from a bush was chopped up and soaked for a week, then boiled for a day to yield brownish orange with an alum mordant.[9]

Blackthorn is classed with the *fodla fedo*, "lower divisions of the wood." It was valuable as a field boundary that "a small pig should not be able to penetrate because of its closeness, and an ox should not be able to penetrate because of its firmness and height" according to the Brehon Law Texts. Such a fence was made of four-foot stakes, spaced about eight inches apart. Three bands of rods were woven in and out of the stakes, and the whole thing was topped with blackthorn, woven in and around the crest of the fence.[10]

Blackthorn was also used to help establish the quality and price of a piece of land. The very best land was flat and suitable for growing corn, flax, woad, madder, and fruit. It could maintain cows for their milk and nourish bees for their honey. It had soil that did not require manure, and it was free of clinging and prickling weeds such as bramble (*dris*), blackthorn (*draighean*), burdock (*gleslige*), or thistles (*omthann*). To test the quality of land a horse was set loose upon it, and if anything stuck to the horse's hair the land was not of the best quality.[11]

The *Word Ogham of Morainn mic Moín* lists *tressam rúamnat, aire srábae,* and *aire adhon draigin,* which translate as "strongest reddening dye," "chief of streams, dam of a river," and "hedge of blackthorn." The *Word Ogham of Mic ind Oic* gives for blackthorn *mórad rún,* "increase of secrets" while *saigid nél,* "seeking of clouds, arrow of the clouds," is the definition from *Briatharogam Con Culainn.*[12]

Blackthorn may be used to build dams and fences. The secrets of the dyer's art yield the reddest color from this tree. The clouds are the steam that rises from the dyer's vat, or the cloud of unknowing that surrounds the dyer's art. And there may be another meaning here; blackthorn is the fearsome weapon that causes bright red blood to spill.

HERBAL USES

Blackthorn flowers appear before the leaves emerge. Its branches are said to be a home for the fairies, pointing to the magical strength of this tree in the eyes of the ancients.[13] There were prohibitions on burning the wood, another indication of the value placed on it. As the "Song of the Forest Trees" states: "The surly blackthorn is a wanderer, and a wood that the artificer burns not; throughout his body, though it be scanty, birds in their flocks warble."[14]

The fruits of the blackthorn, called sloes, are quite sour and astringent until just after the first frosts. Then they can be eaten raw or cooked, and are used to make jams (the jam is slightly laxative), jellies, and to flavor liqueurs. The dried fruits can be added to herbal teas as a flavoring agent. The flowers can be crystallized in sugar.

The flowers, bark, and fruits are medicinal. The flower tea is useful for diarrhea, especially in children, and helps bladder and kidney complaints and stomach cramps.[15] The flower tea also stimulates appetite, clears skin problems by cleaning the blood and liver of toxins, and clears edema and stone formations.

The juice of the fresh berries can be applied to mouth sores and sore throats. The root bark is simmered to make a tea for fevers.[16] In the Highlands of Scotland the flower tea was used as a laxative in spring, and in the fall the berries were used for fevers (probably as a cooling drink).[17]

To prepare the flower tea, steep two teaspoons of the flowers per one-half cup hot water. Take one half cup twice a day, made fresh each time.[18] For root bark, inner bark, and berries, simmer two teaspoons per cup of water for twenty minutes in a nonaluminum pot with a tight lid. Take one-quarter cup four times a day, not with meals.

Prunus spinosa does not occur in North America. Native American herbalists and medicine people used *Prunus americana* or American wild plum. The Cherokee used the inner bark to make cough syrup and made an inner bark tea to benefit the kidneys and bladder. The Cheyenne applied the crushed fruits to mouth diseases. The Chippewa used the roots in a worming tea and applied the inner bark in poultices for cuts and wounds. They also made a disinfectant wash from the bark.[19]

The Fox made an astringent application from the root bark, which they applied to mouth sores. The Mohegan took a tea of the twigs for asthma. The Omaha poulticed the boiled root bark and applied it to abrasions. The Ojibwa used the small rootlets as a tea for diarrhea.[20]

CAUTION

The leaves and seeds of Prunus species contain cyanide, which in small amounts has been shown to improve digestion and respiration, but in large amounts can cause respiratory failure and may even prove fatal.[21]

Native American herbalists also used *Prunus americana* as a dyeing agent. The Chippewa made a mixture of two handfuls of bloodroot (*Sanguinaria*), one handful of the inner bark of wild plum, one handful of the bark of red osier (*Cornus stolonifera*), and one handful of the inner bark of alder (*Alnus*), which they boiled in one quart of water to produce a brilliant scarlet color on porcupine quills.[22]

SPIRITUAL ASPECTS

From the discussions above it should be obvious that blackthorn has both positive and negative connotations. It carries the meaning of a strong protective fence, shield, or barrier that can insulate from harm. It also carries the meaning of a dreaded weapon that causes others to bleed.

I was told in a personal conversation with a witch in Ireland that the shillelagh was sometimes deliberately made with thorns sticking out of it. The idea was that the thorns of the *draighean* would puncture the skin and cause more infection than a simple blow from a cudgel. In the old days such puncture wounds would likely lead to death. At the same time, it was said that by carrying a blackthorn stick one would be *protected* from evil spirits.

The ambiguous nature of the blackthorn is illustrated in a traditional Irish tale. A man's grain was stolen, and when he fell asleep under a blackthorn a voice told him that the fairies had taken it. The voice also told him what he had to do to get it back. He got the grain back, but the fairies had their revenge: any of his livestock that ate it died.[23]

Because of its association with the fairies, blackthorn, like hawthorn, was considered very unlucky to bring into the home. In England there is a type of bad weather that coincides with the blooming of the blackthorn known as "the blackthorn winter." Yet in some areas of Britain, blackthorn was added to mistletoe in Christmas decorations to bring good luck.[24]

The particular fairies that inhabit and protect the blackthorn are called Lunantishees. These are of a fairy tribe who punish anyone who cuts a blackthorn stick on May 11 (Old Beltaine Eve) or November 11 (Old Samhain Eve).[25]

The seven sons of Queen Maeve (Meadhbh) once kept a hostile army at bay by erecting a fence made of blackthorn and briar. Her sons remained behind the fence until Queen Maeve herself came to relieve them.[26]

ELDER

Ruis • [RUSH]

The word *ruis* (redness) is very well suited to this tree. Elder has red berries and red stems and is a beneficial medicine to build the blood. Elder is associated with a strong mother spirit, probably because of the medicines that can be made from it, to benefit even the youngest children. The Gaelic word for elder is *trom,* so the appellation *ruis* is really a kind of poetic description of the tree and its properties rather than the name of it. (There is no word *ruis* in the dictionary, rather the words *rus* and *ruise.* The words must have been mixed up over time.[1])

Elder is said to be especially protective of children. There are two law texts that deal with the rights of children in ancient Ireland: *Cáin Iarraith* (on fosterage) and *Maccslechta* (on inheritance). From these we can develop a picture of what children's lives may have been like. (Neither text survives complete; only portions remain.[2])

By the age of fourteen a female child was considered marriageable. Between fourteen and twenty a young man lived in a temporary house on his father's land. He had the honor-price of a yearling heifer (*dairt*) until age seventeen and the honor-price of a two-year-old heifer (*colpthach*) from age seventeen to twenty.[3]

Normally, a father or foster father was liable for his son's transgressions, but seven fathers were exempt: a king, a bishop, a poet, a hermit, an insane or senile father, a father who was an alien (in that case the mother's kin were liable), or the father of a child of a tenant (*fuidir*) whose offense was paid for by his lord.[4] From the age of twelve to seventeen, if a child stole something, the only requirement was that it be restored, or that something of equivalent value be given. There were no further punishments.[5]

Children were treasured in ancient Ireland and much compassion was shown to them in the Laws. Until the age of seven a child had the same honor-price as a cleric, no matter what class they were born into. After that, their honor-price was half of their father's. A sick child under seven was entitled to the same medical care as a cleric, and if still nursing, had to be accompanied by its mother. Sometimes a fine was substituted for the usual sick-maintenance if a child was injured, because children of the nobility, or a poet, or a favorite child, a "pet of a household," were probably cared for at home.[6] Elder would have been a very important remedy for childhood fevers of children of every class because the flowers are safe for even the smallest babies.

Both parents were responsible for the upkeep of a child, unless the child was the result of rape, in which case the father's kin had to pay all expenses. The father was solely responsible for upkeep if he impregnated someone else's wife, or a servant, or a slave, or if he tricked a woman into sex. He was also responsible for a child's upkeep if a woman's father had forbidden his union with the mother.

Sick or disabled mothers were exempt from childcare, as were insane, blind, deaf, maimed, leprous, or diseased mothers. Female outcasts and satirists were also exempt (they weren't deemed worthy to raise a child). If the mother died, the father had sole responsibility for the child's maintenance.

The father had no responsibility if he was an alien, a slave, a satirist, or an outcast. If a woman was impregnated by a dependent son and his father had forbidden the union, she was responsible for the upkeep of the child. In Christian times, a woman who was impregnated by a priest was solely responsible for the child if he refused to marry her and chose to remain in the priesthood (and did penance). A prostitute was solely responsible for her offspring.[7]

Fosterage was very common as a way to bind communities and kin groups by the mutual exchange of children. Children were sometimes closer to their foster parents than to their biological ones; the most intimate terms of endearment, such as *muimme* (mummy) and *datán* (daddy), were reserved for the foster mother and foster father. Sometimes the fosterage was free and sometimes a fee was paid. The price for fostering a girl was higher than the price for fostering a boy; no clear reasons for this are given in the texts, but it may be because boys repaid more of their keep via their labor.[8]

A foster child was maintained according to his or her station. The son of a king was given a horse to ride, fine cloth for clothing, and a proper education. He was taught *fidchell* (a type of chess), horsemanship, swimming, and use of weapons. A noble girl was taught to sew, cut cloth, and embroider. The son of a farmer was taught to care for animals, dry grain, comb wool, build and mend fences, weed the garden, and chop wood. A farmer's daughter was taught the use of the quern (a grinding tool for grain), to sieve grain and to knead dough.[9]

Sometimes a foster child got specialized training. For example, the child of a poet would get poetic instruction, and the son of a craftsman would get training in new skills that he could later bring back to his biological father. Druids taught Druidic arts, such as divination, to their fosterlings. There are references in the Laws to female poets, wrights, and physicians, so evidently some fostered girls were given specialized training, especially if their father had no sons.[10]

A foster child was expected to stay until his or her fosterage was complete, unless there was child abuse, in which case the contract was voided and any fees went back to the father. Both the father's and mother's kin had the right to intervene in cases of abuse. Fosterage was usually complete by age fourteen.[11]

Parents could sell their child into slavery. A man who impregnated someone else's slave woman had to pay all costs for the child. If a free woman became pregnant by a slave she alone was responsible for the child. Children of slaves, no matter what their parentage, were prohibited from entering the nobility. In Christian times, if a man made a slave woman pregnant he was required to set her free.[12]

Children were fed according to their station in life. A child who was sick and being cared for was due certain foods from age seven to ten: egg yolk, butter, porridge, and curds. All children had to be fed porridge. The child of a farmer or producer was given oat porridge with buttermilk or water. A small serving of curds was also allowed. A child of the nobility got porridge made with milk and barley-meal, and a blob of butter on top. A prince or princess got porridge made with milk and wheat-meal, and a blob of honey on top.[13]

There were magical traditions surrounding childhood. A child had to be watched carefully to see if it might be a young hero waiting to reveal him- or herself. There were stories of young children who emerged from the womb making prophetic statements, passing judgments, or uttering poetry. Such children undertook incredible tasks while still infants—slaying monsters, or appearing at court and dazzling the bards with their knowledge.

In the tales such children had been set adrift and rescued from the water; in effect, being twice born. (For example, the child poet and bard Taliesin emerged from a leather bag caught in a weir on a Beltaine, speaking poetry. But he had been caught in the bag for *forty years,* implying that this was actually a reference to some kind of poetic initiation.) Baptism was a reenactment of this magic—until a child was baptized by water it was very susceptible to being taken by the fairies, who might leave an ugly or sick changeling in its stead.[14]

Stories were told of magical births and conceptions. In one story we are told that there was a prophecy concerning the death of Cumhal mac Airt predicting that he would die in the first battle he fought after being married. This made him avoid marriage for a long time until he secretly married a princess. His wife had been kept hidden because there was a prophecy that her son would cause her father, the king, to lose his realm.

When Cumhal was about to go into battle, he asked his mother to see to it that if he had a son, the child would be carefully concealed. A child was born, and on hearing of this, the king ordered that he be drowned in a lake. But the child emerged from the lake with a salmon in his fist. Cumhal's mother took the child and secretly raised him in a hollow tree.

At age fifteen the child appeared suddenly at the king's fort and defeated all the other boys in a game of hurling (a game very similar to hockey that is played with a stick and ball). The king asked, "Who is that *finn cumhal* ["white cap," so named because he was a tow head]?"And that was how Finn mac Cumhaill got his name. The king pursued Finn in a rage, but he was only able to kill Finn's grandmother.[15]

The *Word Ogham of Morainn mic Moín* describes elder thus: *tindem ruccae,* "most intense blushing; most painful of shames." The *Word Ogham of Mic ind Oic* offers *rúamnae dreach,* "reddening of face." And the description *bruth fergae,* "glow of anger," is from *Briatharogam Con Culainn.*[16]

The Word Oghams seem to allude to conditions of redness, the red glow of anger in the face, and the red blush of embarrassment, as poetic metaphors for the red-branched elder tree.

HERBAL USES

There is a lovely drink that can be made from the flowers of black elder (*Sambucus nigra*). You have to have the variety of elder that smells like sweet perfume (which I have found only in Britain) or the recipe won't work. Take fresh, very fragrant, elder blossoms and steep them for just a few minutes in freshly boiled water. Add lemon juice and sweetener and allow the brew (flowers and all) to sit in the refrigerator in a tightly sealed glass container for a day or two. The result is a drink called Liquid Light that I have been assured is a favorite of the fairies.

In the Highlands of Scotland, birch bark was simmered in water and then the flowers of black elder (*Sambucus nigra,* also called

European elder) were steeped in the brew to make a spring tonic. (See the birch chapter for advice on how to select a birch species for beverage teas.) Elderflower water was also used as a skin wash. Young elder leaves were used in healing salves and ointments.

CAUTION

The leaves MUST be young or they will have too much natural plant pesticide in them.

Elderberry tea was given for coughs, colds, flu, asthma, and bronchitis.[17]

American elder (*Sambucus canadensis*) root is used for headaches, mucus congestion, and to promote labor. A tea of the young leaf and flowers makes a good wash for wounds, inflammations, and blemishes. An inner bark decoction can also be used as a skin wash.

A warm tea of the flowers causes sweating, is helpful in fevers and headaches due to colds, and can help rheumatic pain. The tea, used cold, is a diuretic (increases urination). The tea of the leaf buds is purgative (laxative). The juice of the berries is mildly purgative. The dried berries make a tea that will benefit diarrhea and cholera. The berries can be cooked into pies, used in muffin recipes and sweet breads, and made into wine and liqueurs.

CAUTION

All parts of the fresh plant except the ripe berries can cause poisoning, especially in children who chew on the bark. The berries are completely safe when cooked.

To make a tea, use one teaspoon of plant matter per cup of water. Steep young leaves and flowers, or simmer the inner bark or berries, for twenty minutes in a nonaluminum pot with a tight lid.[18]

The bark of the twigs or the root of black elder (*Sambucus nigra*) are purgative and diuretic.

CAUTION

The inner bark and bark of the root must be used fresh.

Used wisely, the tea can benefit kidney and urinary problems, edema, colds, rheumatism, and constipation by increasing urination.

The flower tea promotes sweating in fevers and colds and in rheumatism. The berries should be cooked slightly before use (the juice of the fresh berries causes diarrhea and vomiting) and can be made into jam, which will be gently laxative. The jam is suitable for children.

CAUTION

Large doses can irritate the bowels.

Steep two tablespoons of the flowers per cup of boiled water for twenty minutes and drink up to three cups a day, hot. Or decoct (simmer) one teaspoon inner bark or root bark per one-half cup of water for twenty minutes, in a nonaluminum pot with a tight lid. Take no more than one quarter cup, four times a day.[19]

Sambucus racemosa is the red elder. Its roots are purgative and diuretic. The berries can be used for jam or jelly but the seeds must be strained out as they are poisonous. Simmer one teaspoon of the root in one cup of water for a few minutes. Take one-quarter cup four times a day.[20]

CAUTION

Elder seeds must be strained out from any herbal preparations because they are poisonous.

Sambucus ebulus is the dwarf elder. The root can be used in burn salves and is diuretic and laxative when taken as a tea. Steep one teaspoon of the root per cup of boiled water until cold. Take up to two cups a day in mouthful doses.[21]

Native American herbalists and medicine people used *Sambucus canadensis* berry tea for rheumatism. The Cherokee infused the flowers to promote sweating in fevers, and made a wash from the young leaves for wounds and sores. They used the young leaves in poultices for burns and in healing salves.

The Chickasaw made a tea of the branches, which they applied to headaches. The Chippewa used the root tea as an emetic and the Choctaw used a tea of the seed and roots for liver ailments. The Creek used the pounded roots as a poultice and applied them to sore breasts. The Delaware made a poultice of the leaves and scraped bark for wounds and swellings. They also gave the flower tea to children with colic.

The Fox used the root bark tea for lung conditions with phlegm. The Iroquois used a tea of the pith for heart diseases and gave the twig bark tea to children as a laxative. The MicMac used the berries, bark, and flowers as a purgative. The Mohegan specified that when gathering the bark, if you scrape in an upward motion with your knife the tea will be emetic and if you scrape downwards the tea will be physic (a cathartic purge).[22]

The Cherokee also used *Sambucus nigra* berries in tea for rheumatism and infused the flowers to sweat out fevers. They used the leaves in wound washes and salves.[23]

SPIRITUAL ASPECTS

Elder trees are intimately associated with the fairies. On the Isle of Man an elder would be planted by the door just for them. Cutting one down is a profound insult to the fey folk, who will desert a house where that has happened.

Elder is also associated with Elda Mor (Hylde-Moer), the Elder Mother, a powerful female spirit who lives in the tree. Other names for the Elder Mother are Frau Holle or Frau Ellhorn. Elda Mor is a good goddess to petition whenever there is sickness, especially in children.[24]

A face marked with the juice of red berries
and ringed by a wreath of elder branches

The Elder Mother is sometimes regarded as a goddess of death and the underworld. Irish witches' brooms are made from elder twigs. Slavic gypsies wear a wreath of elder at Halloween so that they can see the spirits soaring by.

Lithuanians leave offerings for Puschkeit, lord of the underworld, under an elder tree at twilight. The Jews of old Prague planted elder trees in their cemeteries. In the Tyrolean Alps, elder wood crosses were planted on graves. Elder trees planted near a grave are said to protect the dead.

Elder branches are easily hollowed, making them ideal for bellows and pipes. Tradition holds that the sweetest music comes from panpipes made from elders growing far from human habitation. If an entire tree is cut down, however, any furniture made from it will likely be haunted by the Elder Spirit and it is bound to buckle, split, or warp.

In Shropshire, England, it was said that burning elder in the fireplace would lead to a death in the family, and it was a very bad idea to use its wood for a cradle, as the tree's spirit would attack the child. This was no doubt a way of discouraging the cutting of these valuable medicinal trees.

The fresh branches are hung in the cowshed and the house to repel flies. Mature elder leaves are used in natural insecticides. In 1772 Christopher Gullett reported that cabbages, turnips, and fruit trees could be healed of blight by whipping them with leafy elder branches. (You can make a sun tea of mature elder leaves and old cigar butts that will kill aphids and other garden pests when you spray it on your plants. Just fill a jar with the leaves and butts, cover with water, and allow to steep in the hot sun for a few days. Add some castile soap and a little oil to make the pesticide stick, and apply it with a spray bottle).

Witches are said to be able to transform themselves into elder trees, which is not surprising given the extraordinary healing virtues of this tree.[25]

In Scotland, the elder was second only to rowan as a magically protective tree. Crosses made of elder wood were hung in stables. Drivers of hearses carried elder whips to repel evil. It was said that if one stood under an elder on a fairy hill at Samhain, one could see the fairies. When walking in the Highlands it was the custom to put a little of the elder into one's buttonhole, to repel unfriendly spirits.[26]

Silver Fir

Ailm • [AL-um or AL-uv]

The Scot's pine (*Pinus sylvestris*) is listed among the *airig fedo* (nobles of the wood) in the Laws due to its resin, which was used to caulk boats and to preserve wood. It was also used in building construction and for the masts of ships.[1] Silver fir (*Abies alba, Abies pectinata*) has the same uses and deserves to be classed among the noble trees of the forest.

Silver firs are majestically tall trees that grow on mountainous heights, at three thousand feet above sea level or higher. The wood of the silver fir is light yet durable, and has been used traditionally as a building material and to make furniture and barrels. Resin is tapped from sixty- to eighty-year-old trees in the spring and is used to caulk ships.[2]

In ancient times, boats had mundane as well as spiritual functions. Farmers who lived near the sea could fish from wickerwork coracles (*clíab*) or from a boat (*náu*).[3] The great mystical *navigatio* (sailing adventures) of Saint Brendan and others before him were undertaken in hide boats. The shell of the boat was wood and the wood was covered with oak-tanned leather hides, stitched together and soaked in butter. Small leather boats were made with one hide, a larger boat was made with as many as three.[4]

The bards told stories of *echtrai* (adventures) and of *immrama* (mystical voyages). In the apple tree chapter I mentioned the story of Bran and the magical branch from the apple tree of Emain Ablach, the land of apples.[5] After meeting the fairy woman with the apple branch,

Bran went to sea with his foster brothers, each leading a company of nine men. After two days and nights on the ocean they met the sea god Manannán mac Lir. Manannán told Bran that the sea was really a land with many flowers (The Plain of Delight), where salmon were the leaping calves and lambs and the waves were horses. He said that there was a forest of fruit trees just under Bran's boat.

Bran continued on his voyage and came to several other islands and though many years passed, Bran and his followers thought only a year had gone by.

Eventually Bran and the others returned to Ireland, where there was a group of people assembled to greet them. Bran announced who he was and no one recognized his name, but they had heard of "The Voyage of Bran" as an ancient tale. Bran jumped to shore, wrote the verses of his journey in Ogham, and collapsed in a heap of ashes as if he had been dead for centuries.[6]

In "The Voyage of Maeldúin" we are told that Maeldúin built a boat of three skins on the advice of a Druid, in order to find his father's slayer. The Druid told him which day to begin making the boat, which day to set sail, and how many men to take with him.

The first island Maeldúin and his men came to was filled with the noise of carousing warriors, one of whom was boasting about how he killed Maeldúin's father. Maeldúin prepared to land, but a sudden strong breeze carried his boat back out to sea. The company surrendered their fate to the gods and were eventually guided to thirty-three magical islands, after which they returned to their native country.[7]

One interpretation of "The Voyage of Bran" is that it is a record of an actual sea voyage across the Atlantic. The fierce beast they encountered that looked like a horse with claws could have been a sea leopard. Giant horses could have been walruses, and the river that burned like fire could have been a lava flow from a place in Iceland. The transparent sea of glass under which they saw herds could have been a sheet of ice under which were shoals of fish or other wildlife. A silver column and a fortress with a glass bridge that they described may well have been icebergs. Islands of birds and solitary monks seem to be literal descriptions, and the island of trees with intoxicating and slumber-inducing berries might describe Vinland, the name the Vikings used for North America.

There is another possibility here. The voyage could be the description of an otherworld journey, on which the hero sees the islands to which the dead must go, in the West.

For ailm, the *Word Ogham of Morainn mic Moín* gives us *ardam íachta,* "loudest groan." The *Word Ogham of Mic ind Oic* offers *tosach fregra,* "beginning of an answer." And we have *tosach garmae,* "beginning of expressions," from *Briatharogam Con Culainn.*[8]

The *Auraicept na N-Eces* characterizes ailm as "loudest of groanings, that is wondering . . . for it is ailm or 'a' a man says while groaning in disease, or wondering, that is marveling, at whatever circumstances."[9]

Silver fir is the tallest tree, growing on the highest heights. It symbolizes the far-seeing of the visionary, whether he or she is a hero voyaging into unknown lands, or a mystic gazing at the wonders of the otherworld with unflinching courage. Ailm symbolizes vision, both inner and outer, that enables us to see into the mysteries of the unknown.

HERBAL USES

Silver fir (*Abies alba, Abies pectinata*) is a medicinal tree found in mountainous areas. The inner bark can be cooked, dried, and ground to a powder, and used to thicken soups or added to flour.

The buds are antibiotic, antiseptic, and balsamic, meaning that they will prevent infection and soothe tissue. The inner bark is antiseptic and astringent and can be gathered all year. The leaves are expectorant and sedate bronchial spasms. Gather the leaves in spring and dry them for later use.

The resin is antiseptic, balsamic, diuretic, eupeptic (aids digestion), and expectorant. It can be gathered from holes in the trunk of the tree or by boiling knots from the wood. The resin is also an excellent vulnerary (used for wounds).

The young needles and resin can be used together in teas to soothe coughs and colds, or inhaled for bronchitis. They are also used in douches and teas to benefit cystitis and colic. Externally the resin is added to baths and used in rubbing oils for rheumatic pain and neuralgia.[10]

To make a decoction, simmer two teaspoons of plant matter per cup of water in a nonaluminum pot with a tight-fitting lid for about twenty minutes. Take one-quarter cup four times a day, not with meals.

Native American herbalists and medicine people used *Abies balsamea* (balsam fir). The Chippewa burned the resin on a hot rock and inhaled the vapors for headache. They used the root tea in the sweat lodge to treat rheumatism and headache, by pouring it over hot rocks.

The Iroquois used the tea in the sweatlodge after childbirth and made a decoction of various tree parts for coughs, colds, and rheumatism. They applied the decoction externally to cuts, sprains, and sores.

The Menominee used the inner bark to flavor medicines and used the balsam from the trunk for lung conditions and sores.

The MicMac used the buds in laxative teas and the buds, cones, and inner bark for diarrhea, and applied the gum to burns.

The Ojibwa used the needle tea in the sweat lodge and inhaled the leaf smoke for colds. They also used the needle tea as a wash for sores and applied the balsam to sore eyes. The Potawatomi swallowed the gum fresh to treat a cold.[11]

The Paiute, Shoshone, Tewa, and Washoe used *Abies concolor* (white fir) in similar ways. The Cherokee used *Abies fraseri* for wounds, ulcers, and kidney and bladder conditions, as a laxative, and for venereal diseases.

The Bella Coola used *Abies grandis* root bark or stem tea for stomach problems and tuberculosis. They warmed the gum and ate it for sore throat. The Chehalis used the needle tea for colds and the Gitksan used the bark to poultice boils and ulcers. The Kwakiutl held the root in the mouth to heal mouth sores and took the bark tea as a general tonic. The Thompson Indians used a strong tea of different parts of the tree to cure gonorrhea, and gave it to girls who were bewitched (the branches were a witchcraft medicine).[12]

The Blackfeet burned *Abies lasiocarpa* as a ceremonial incense and applied the poultice for fevers and lung conditions. The Cheyenne burned the needles to cure people who were afraid of thunder and to revive a dying person's spirit. They also used the smoke to chase away illness and bad energies. The Crow burned the needles in ceremony.[13]

SPIRITUAL ASPECTS

Firs, like all conifers, have long been understood as symbols of immortality; their evergreen branches defy the seeming death of winter. Their cones are "tree-eggs" that grow in a sunwise spiral, showing their connection to the solar year and making them an ideal magical "sender" when placed on the tip of a magic wand.

In Greek tradition, Attis, the young god of spring, was reborn each year as a conifer, his blood transformed into violets at his feet. At the spring rites of Kybele, a pine tree was carried to the Phrygian sanctuary

The pine is a tree of ecstasy and elation.

decorated with violets. Egyptian priests of Osiris hollowed out a pine tree and placed within it a carved statue of their god, whom Isis had restored to life.[14]

Christian missionaries put strong prohibitions on the worship of trees and tree spirits, making a point of chopping down sacred trees and groves wherever they could. In the second Council of Arles (452 CE) this canon was issued: "If within the territory of a bishop infidels light torches or venerate trees, fountains, or stones, and he neglects to abolish this usage, he must know that he himself is guilty of sacrilege."

Charlemagne issued the following edict: "With respect to trees, stones, and fountains, where certain foolish people light torches or practice other superstitions, we earnestly ordain that that most evil custom detestable to God, wherever it be found, should be removed and destroyed."[15]

The church was never able to completely eradicate tree, stone, and water worship. Wells once dedicated to the old gods were resanctified in the name of saints, and images of Mary were placed in grottoes once sacred to the Earth Goddess. We have seen how Saint Brigid established her nunnery in a place made sacred by oaks.

There was once a pine tree considered sacred by the people of Tours, which Saint Martin wanted to destroy. The people agreed—on the condition that Saint Martin allow the trunk to fall on his head as it fell. The tree was not cut down.

In Carmarthen, Wales, an ancient oak called Merlin's Oak was preserved by casting it in cement because an old prophecy had declared that if it fell, Carmarthen would fall with it. In recent times an oak sapling was planted right next to the old and dying trunk, to keep the tree spirit from deserting the town.[16]

To this day, evergreen wreaths, symbolic of the sun, grace doors at Yuletide, and Christmas trees bring a spirit of sacred serenity into the home. Orthodox Jewish burials still require that the coffin be made of pine, the ancient tree of immortality.

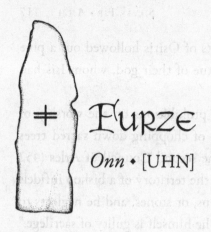

Furze

Onn • [UHN]

Onn is translated as "wheel." The Gaelic word for furze (gorse, whin) is *aitenn*. But this should not trouble us overmuch. The word "wheel" was probably associated with this letter because the letter *o* is round, in a kind of pun relating to the shape of the letter and the *onnaid,* or wheels, of a chariot.[1] As we examine the Word Oghams, the association of onn, or wheel, with furze will become more obvious.

Aitenn (furze, gorse, whin) is classed with the losa fedo or "bushes of the wood" in the ancient Law texts.[2] The presence of furze (or heather) on land was an indication of its poor value. Any land where these flourished was called *antrenn* or "very rough." Such land was probably mountain pasture, common land, or wasteland suitable only for sheep.[3]

Furze blooms all year and stays in leaf all year, though it can be damaged by a hard frost. The bees love it, and it can be grown as a shelter for young trees because it fixes nitrogen in the soil, which helps trees to take hold. Eventually, as the trees mature they shade out the furze, which needs full sun, and it dies back. Furze makes an excellent windbreak and can be used as a hedge to pen livestock. It thrives in marine environments.[4]

Furze can be burned as fuel or used as kindling. The ashes that result from burning it can be used in soap making and to fertilize pastures. In some areas, furze is burned to the ground every three years, and the resultant new shoots make excellent fodder for cattle and horses. The mature branches can also be milled and fed to cattle, horses, and sheep. The species that grows in Ireland, *Ulex strictus*, is the softest variety and best suited for animal feed.[5]

The wood of furze was once used to make *camáin*, or hurleys, and walking sticks. In the fall it was cut for bedding and fodder for cattle and horses.[6]

The *Word Ogham of Morainn mic Moín* describes furze as *congnaid, congnamaid ech*, or "wounder; helper of horses." The *Word Ogham of Mic ind Oic* gives the meaning *fétham soíre*, "smoothest of craftsmanship."[7] *Lúth fiann*, "desire of the *fianna* (warrior-poets)," is the poetic description from *Briatharogam Con Culainn*.[8]

It is not difficult to understand why prickly furze is the "wounder of horses." We have already seen that land where it grows is unsuitable for them, and is proper only for sheep. We have also seen that it is a "helper of horses" when burned, because they can eat the new shoots and the carefully milled branches. There is yet another meaning here—the letter *o* (Furze—*Onn*) is the wheel that helps a horse to pull the cart.

Furze is a craftsman's friend, making hurleys and walking sticks. And finally, the warriors of the Fian can hide behind a thick, protective hedge of furze. The plant has a warrior's spirit, as we will see below.

HERBAL USES

Gorse or furze flowers can be pickled in vinegar and eaten like capers. The flower tea has been used for jaundice and scarlet fever in children. A tea can be made from the tips of the shoots. The seed tea has been used for diarrhea and stones.[9] Furze tea was once used as a mouthwash for "whiskey breath."[10]

The seeds are slightly astringent and contain tannins. The seeds and the herb contain plant alkaloids and can be used to make insecticide, especially against fleas.[11]

Furze is a great dye herb. The bark and twigs yield a brown dye when used with alum and iron as mordants. With iron as a mordant it can be used to dye cloth or wool green. In Ireland the bark, flowers, and shoots were used to make a yellow dye, using alum and cream of tartar as mordants, and gold by using chrome as a mordant.

I can find no evidence that Native Americans used this plant.

SPIRITUAL ASPECTS

The ancient Celts divided the year into two halves. Samhain (Halloween) began the dark half of the year and Beltaine (May Day) the light half of the year. Beltaine marked the date when the cows were driven out to their summer pasture and Samhain marked the date when the herds were brought back to the winter safety of the farm. Both were "spirit nights," liminal portals between summer and winter, when the ancestors and the fairies were said to be abroad and the walls between the worlds were thinnest. (The official date for Beltaine was when the hawthorn blossomed.)

The color yellow was particularly associated with Beltaine. It was considered lucky to bring furze blossoms into the home at Beltaine, to hide them in the thatch, or to hang them in the barn for luck. A protective sprig of furze could be twined around the butter churn or the milk pail to thwart fairy mischief. It was lucky to insert furze blossoms into a bridal bouquet.[12]

In Celtic areas it was a May Bush rather than a May Pole that was used in the celebrations. Furze blossoms were used to dye eggs yellow, and they were hung on a bush to honor the sun (soak the eggs in white vinegar before dyeing them—it will make the shells more porous). Yellow flowers such as marsh marigold and yellow ribbons completed the May Bush decorations. Everyone danced around the May Bush, with a large bonfire nearby and liberal portions of whiskey for all.

A yellow-haired maiden of the Land of Youth stands
in her stronghold of furze, adorned with its golden flowers.

Furze can be used in the Beltaine bonfire. In ancient times cattle were driven between two fires at Beltaine as they were led out to their summer pasture in an act of ritual purification. The fires had to be so close that a white cow passing between them would have her hair singed brown.

Ꞁꞁeather

Úr • [OOR]

eather (*Calluna vulgaris, Erica cinerea, Erica vulgaris*) is classed with the *losa fedo,* which are the fourth class termed "bushes of the wood" in the ancient law texts on farming. The fourth class of plants included things that grew on scrub land and in waste places such as heather, gorse, broom, bracken, wild rose, bog myrtle, and bramble (sometimes useful plants such as rushes for floor covering and ivy for cattle fodder were also included in this category) Heathery mountainsides were considered very rough land, suitable only for sheep.[1] But heathery mountains make a wonderful habitat for deer and other wildlife, and attract moths, butterflies, and bees.[2]

The use of heather in Scotland goes back to the Neolithic and Mesolithic periods. On the Hebridean island of Rum, evidence of brewing from two to five thousand years ago was discovered. Meadowsweet (*Filipendula ulmaria*) and heather (*Calluna vulgaris*) were used in the brewing, and royal fern (*Osmunda regalis*) was used to halt the fermentation process, according to the pollen record.[3]

To Make Heather Ale

According to the historian and cleric Boethius, the sixth century Picts were brewing heather ale without the use of barley. Here is a modern recipe to make the ale:

Collect the flowering heather in August or September and fill a large pot with the purple blossoms. Cover with water and boil for one hour. Strain off the liquid and add ginger, hops, and golden syrup (a type of golden yellow molasses). Bring to a boil again and strain; add yeast when cool. Allow to "work," or ferment for a few days and then gently pour off the liquid.[4]

To Make Heather Wine

Boil 1¼ pounds of the blooming tips in one gallon of water for one hour. Strain off the liquid and add more water to restore one gallon. Add two sliced lemons, three sliced oranges, and three to four pounds of sugar. Heat to 70°F, add one teaspoon yeast and one teaspoon yeast nutrient. Ferment for two weeks, strain. Strain again and bottle when it stops "working."[5]

(Of course, the ancient Picts and other prehistoric peoples would have used honey as their sweetener when making these drinks.)

Heather branches were once used for thatching and to make baskets, ropes, and brooms. (Heather rope is very resistant to rotting in seawater and a great tool for sailors.) The branches were dried and used for fuel, and the roots were used to make musical pipes.[6]

Mattresses filled with heather were said to be very soft and springy and would regain their shape each morning after the sleeper got up. They were very fragrant and produced a scent that was a sleep aid. Tough heather branches were used as a type of scouring agent for pots and pans, and the roots were used to make handles for *dirks* (knives).

Heather was an important dye plant. It produced ocher with the use of alum and chrome as a mordant, yellow with alum, gold with chrome, and green when mixed with indigo and alum. The darkest green was obtained from heather growing in shady areas.[7]

As I mentioned above, heather is a favorite of the bees. Bees were so important to the ancient Irish that an entire law text was devoted to bees called the *Bechbretha* (Laws of Beekeeping). It is unknown if bees were native to Ireland or imported, but there are native words that point to a very ancient, pre-Christian history for the art of beekeeping: *bech* (bee), *mil* (honey), and *mid* (mead).[8]

In earliest times holes were made in trees to attract bees, and beehives were made from hollowed-out logs. The word *crann,* meaning "tree," also meant "beehive" in the seventh century. Later, from the eleventh century on, the word for hive was *cleis* or *clíab,* meaning "basket." Straw hives came in around the seventeenth century.[9]

The law texts on bees are based on the principle that a bee visiting another person's property is actually trespassing and taking strength from the landowner's flowers. A beekeeper was exempt from a fine for trespassing for three years. At the fourth year, any swarm had to be given to the closest neighbor upon whose property the bees had heavily grazed.

Later swarms were given to other neighbors, who had to keep an eye out for the likely swarming. If the neighbor failed to witness the swarm he had to wait another year for his bees. However, if a swarm stopped only temporarily on someone's property, the beekeeper was entitled to take them back and the neighbor received one-third of the beekeeper's honey for a year. But if the bees had taken up permanent housekeeping on a neighbor's land and were living in a tree that would be damaged by the process of removing the bees, the neighbor got to keep the bees, and the original beekeeper got one-third of the honey for three years.

Anyone who found a stray swarm in the forest could keep the bees, provided he donated one-ninth of the honey to his clan leader or the church. The whole system seems to have been devised to ensure that bees and honey kept circulating throughout the community, a very healthy thing for the farmers and their crops.[10]

Honey was used in bread baking, as a food, and as a medicine. Mead, a special drink suitable for feasts was made by fermenting honey. (The everyday drink was beer—*beóir*.) The banquet hall at Tara was called *tech midchúarta,* "the house of the mead circuit." *Brocóit,* or *bragget,* a type of beer, was also made with honey. Beeswax was used for candles, seals, writing tablets, and as an adhesive.[11]

An old Irish saying advises: "Gold under furze, silver under rushes, famine under heather." And in Yorkshire they say, "Where there is bracken there is gold, where there is gorse there is silver, where there is heather there is poverty."[12] Heather grows in damp areas and is associated with boggy land that is unsuitable for farming. Any home that relied heavily on heather for fuel, medicine, mattresses, and the like was apt to be a poor home in a damp area.

The Gaelic word for heather is *fróech,* which has no obvious relationship to the word *úr* (humus) associated with this Ogham letter. But in the Word Oghams we see the rationale for heather's Ogham name. The *Word Ogham of Morainn mic Moín* gives the description *uaraib adbaib,* "in cold dwellings." The *Word Ogham of Mic ind Oic* calls it *sílad cland,* "propagation of plants," while *forbbaid ambí,* "shroud of the lifeless," appears in *Briatharogam Con Culainn.*[13]

Humus or soil is that medium in which plants are propagated. It is also the substance that covers the dead. There is no colder dwelling than the grave, and those who depend upon heather for food, shelter, and medicine live in cold, damp areas.

HERBAL USES

Common heather, ling, or Scotch heather (*Calluna vulgaris, Erica vulgaris*) is gathered in late August and September when the plant is in full bloom, and carefully dried in the shade for later use. The flowering tops are astringent and antiseptic, meaning they can be used to make a wound wash.

Heather tea taken internally cleans the liver and the blood of toxins, is slightly sedative, and can be used for fevers. The tea of the flowering tops is also used for coughs, colds, and cystitis, and for other bladder and kidney conditions. The tea is antiseptic and mildly diuretic and helpful for gout, rheumatism, and arthritis.[14]

The herb is used to poultice arthritis and rheumatism—both are conditions made worse by the damp climate in which heather thrives.[15]

Heather is a vasoconstrictor that also strengthens the heart.

CAUTION

Heather can slightly raise blood pressure.

To make a sleep aid, steep one teaspoon of the tops in one-half cup of boiled water for twenty minutes, add honey to taste. For other conditions, simmer four teaspoons of the herb per cup of water for five minutes. Take up to one-half cup a day in small doses.[16]

I can find no evidence that Native American healers used this plant. It was introduced to the Americas by European settlers when colonization was already widespread.

SPIRITUAL ASPECTS

Heather is strongly associated with bees, a very sacred animal to the Forest Druids. As I have mentioned elsewhere, "The day the bees stop humming the world will end." There is much truth to this ancient Welsh saying. Honeybees are now a threatened species worldwide due to pesticide poisoning, and we depend on them to pollinate our food crops.

Bees symbolize the work of the Druid, which is a tribal function. The Druid serves his or her order, tribe, and all lives. The Druid is not a solitary mystic, she is a teacher, a healer, a philosopher, and a naturalist. Like the bee that is guided by the sun, the Druid navigates by the light of her own higher self. She forages among the blossoms to bring nectar back to the tribe. She perfects her wisdom and then shares it for the benefit of all.[17]

Lovers lie in a bed of sheltering heather
under the rising sun.

Heather (especially white heather) is a plant that brings good fortune. It can be tucked into the wedding bouquet and in ancient times was tucked into the caps of warriors to bring success in battle. Several Scottish clans chose heather as their totem plant for this reason.

Heather is used in rain-making magic. One method is to dip heather and fern into water and sprinkle it around.[18] Another method is to burn a bunch of heather. A sprig of heather can be placed under the pillow to alleviate insomnia.[19]

Aspen

Edad • [ETH-ath]

dad is not the word for aspen (*Populus tremuloides*). The Gaelic word for aspen is *crithach*. The letter *e* has been associated with this tree because of the *e* sound made by those who grieve. Aspen is primarily associated with death and with a measuring rod called a *flesc idaith* (wand of aspen) or *fé*, which was once used to measure graves and corpses.[1]

There is a rich tradition of death and burial customs throughout the Celtic world, which changed from period to period and place to place. There was the Iron Age "pit tradition" from central England, where bodies of both sexes were interred in grain storage pits. The bodies were in a fetal position, usually lying on the right side with the head to the north, either singly or in a group. Sometimes the bodies were dismembered, hinting at ritual sacrifice. In the same area, other bodies were cremated or exposed and then deposited in rivers or outlying areas.[2]

At about the first century BCE the Durotriges of the Dorset area of southern Britain buried their dead in earthen graves or stone cists (square stone boxes) within cemeteries. The bodies of both sexes were usually placed on the right side with the head oriented between northeast and southeast. There were locally produced offerings such as ceramics and meats placed in the graves, and occasionally, jewelry.[3]

In the first century CE in southeastern Britain corpses were cremated and the ashes were buried in ceramic, wood, or metal containers of Gaulish-inspired design. Some of the graves had brooches, drinking vessels, and feasting paraphernalia associated with them. Most of the burials of this type were of males.[4]

In the Yorkshire area around 400 BCE, corpses were placed in long barrows in a style similar to that of the Gaulish Parisi tribe. The bodies were tightly crouched, usually on their left side, head to the north, and accompanied by grave goods. Warriors had swords buried with them, and chieftains had chariots and carts. Commoners had personal jewelry, pottery, and pig meat as grave deposits. The lowest-ranking burials had no deposits at all. Males and females appeared in equal numbers.[5]

In the early Iron Age in the Western Hallstatt bodies were laid flat with their heads to the west in cemeteries. In the late Hallstatt culture in southwestern Germany and eastern France, the elite were buried in wooden chambers, with deposits of imported Greek and Etruscan bronze and silverware, wagons, horse trappings, feasting implements, gold jewelry, glass, amber, coral and lignite decorations, jewelry, and silks.[6] Those of lesser rank were buried with weapons or jewelry, and some were buried in barrows that were constructed in groups from as few as four to as many as one hundred in a single area.[7]

Gaulish burials featured cremation, and in northern France in 300 BCE there is evidence of complex funeral rites. In Gournay there was a ritual enclosure (45 × 38 meters) set within a fort of the Bellovaci tribe. There were ditches around the enclosure and walls to ensure privacy. The implication is that the small space was not designed for public rituals. About two thousand sacrificed weapons and animals were found in the ditches around the temenos and many human remains, which seem to have been dismembered during funeral ceremonies.[8]

In the Romano-Celtic period cremation was common and an east-west orientation for burials became the norm. Grave goods were far fewer, limited to jewelry, hobnailed boots, and sometimes a coffin. Some of the dead were decapitated, with the head placed between the knees or feet. Roughly the same numbers of males and females were represented.[9]

Cairns in Ireland were raised mounds of stones over a burial, marking a special spot with otherworldly associations. According to tradition, any collection of five stones, or five things, marked a cairn. There were five provinces in Eire, making the whole island a sacred cairn. There were five great roads in Eire, five famous hostels, five paths of the law, and five prohibitions on the provincial kings. Finn mac Cumhaill was one of five "masters of every art," and was killed by the five sons of Uirgriu. Cúchulainn had five wheels on his shield, and when he lay on his sick bed he had one companion at his head, one at his feet, and on each side, with himself in the middle, making a sacred cairn.[10]

Sometimes stone burial cairns became so old that they were covered with grass. After that they might be termed a "fairy hill." According to Irish tradition the fairies are the spirits of dead ancestors, and if you have many deceased friends you will have many fairies looking after you. But if you have many deceased enemies, the fairies will try to do you harm.[11]

Walking on a fairy hill is always a tricky matter because one is never quite sure what type of fairy lies below. The fairies are divided into classes that reflect the caste consciousness of the ancient Celts. There are the red-capped leprechauns who live near springs of pure water, and the *lunantishees* who are the spirits of the blackthorn bush—and who cause misfortune to anyone foolish enough to cut a sloe branch on Old Beltaine (May 11) or Old Samhain (November 11).

The *daoine maithe* are the "gentry."[12] According to eyewitness reports the "gentry" are a superior class of fairy, aristocratic warriors, tall and strikingly beautiful, who can shape-shift at will and see through the Earth with their sight. Their voices are sweet and silvery in tone. They are ever young and play fantastically beautiful music. They are capable of striking humans with paralysis, or may choose to "take" intellectually gifted young people.[13]

According to Irish tradition there are Isles of the Blessed offshore in the western Atlantic. There is also an invisible island between Inishmurray and the mainland that can only be seen every seven years. These are the islands of the dead.[14]

It is only polite to have a small altar somewhere in the house or garden, where you leave food offerings, flowers, and bits of cloth for the benefit of the fairies. In Scottish tradition it is important to do this on the "Quarter Days" (solstices and equinoxes) because that is when the fairies move house. Good dishes for the fairies are oatmeal with cream and honey, mashed potatoes and butter, berries, and peppermint candies. (Do not leave chocolate, as that can harm animals who might wander by.) Of course, food is put out for the fairies and dead ancestors at rituals and important family feasts and on holy nights such as Samhain and Beltaine. A portion of the feast can be left out on a plate for the local fairies and spirits who will partake of the essence of the food.

Offerings should be placed in a new home before moving into it. If the food is not consumed by morning it is best not to move in. There is a tradition of turning a piece of sod and leaving it upside down overnight, if one is planning an addition to the western side of a house. The western side is sacred to the fairies, and they require notice. It is also tradition that a family altar be placed somewhere in the western side of the house. Pictures of dead ancestors and other memorabilia are displayed there.

Every garden needs to have a "goodman's croft," or a special place set aside for the fairies, where no human dares to tread.

One way to know if someone is about to cross over to the otherworld land of fairy is if you see a "death candle." It appears as a patch of very bright light that illuminates a room, even in the dead of night. It is a blue or green luminous mass that rolls and dances as if it were held by an invisible hand.[15]

When I was visiting the Loch Tay region of Scotland, my traveling companion, who is a native of Fife, told me that he had once seen these kinds of fairy lights moving along the top of Schie Hallion, a local mountain said to be the home of the fairy queen.

In the *Word Ogham of Morainn mic Moín* aspen is called *áerchaid fid* (destroying wood). In *Word Ogham of Mic ind Oíc* it is named *commaín carat* (exchange of friends), and in *Briatharogam Con Chulainn* it is termed *bráthair bethi* (brother of birch) Other glosses give *ed uath* (horrid space, horrid measure) *(f)é a tuth* (fie on its odor), *(f)é at uath*

(woe, they are terrible), and *adéitche* (hateful).[16] The aspen is destroying because its wood is used for the measuring rod to measure a corpse.
Its fluttering leaves whisper on the breeze like a conversation between
friends and it is "brother of birch" because both trees grow in similar
locations and soils, and both trees are of similar size.

HERBAL USES

Quaking aspen (poplar) (*Populus tremuloides*) bark and buds are used as
medicine. The resinous winter buds are collected and used in salves, as
medicinal tea, and as an external wash. The tea of the buds is helpful for
colds and sore throats and can be used as a gargle. Externally it is used as
a wound wash and is helpful for burns and inflammations.

The inner bark can be collected from twigs and used to make a tea
for fever and to aid digestion.[17]

CAUTION

Do not take bark from the trunk of a tree or you might kill
the tree.

To make the tea, use two teaspoons of plant material per cup
of water. Simmer in a tightly covered nonaluminum pot for about
twenty minutes. Take one-quarter cup four times a day. Make a
slightly stronger batch for external use only.

Balm of Gilead (*Populus candicans*) buds can be used in the same
ways described above for the buds of *Populus tremuloides* and the tea
helps relieve minor aches and pains.

Tacamahac (*Populus balsamifera*) buds are even better than balm of
Gilead for the above uses.[18]

Native American healers and medicine people made liberal use of
poplars. The Iroquois used *Populus alba* (white poplar) bark as a tea
for colds and as a body wash for antilove spells. The Ojibwa used the

bark tea as a general wash for rheumatism and other illnesses. They also made a tea of the bark and roots for blood illnesses.[19]

The Montana used *Populus angustifolia* (narrowleaf cottonwood) inner bark as an antiscorbutic and in *kinnikinnik* (an herbal smoking mix).[20]

The Chippewa used *Populus balsamifera* (balsam poplar) root tea for back pain and made a salve of the buds for wounds, frostbite, and sores. They applied the buds in poultices and decoctions to sprains and strained muscles. The Iroquois added the bark to worming medicines and to laxative formulas. The MicMac used the buds and other parts as a salve for sores and venereal chancres.

The Ojibwa cooked the buds in grease and applied them to the nostrils for bronchitis and colds. The Potawatomi used the buds in salves for eczema and sores.[21]

The Bella Coola used *Populus trichocarpa* (black cottonwood) branches and leaves in the sweatlodge for rheumatic pains. They made a decoction of the roots for body pains and a poultice of the buds for pain in the lungs and hips. The Northern Carrier chewed the green roots and applied them as a poultice to stop bleeding. They used the inner bark tea as an eyewash.

The Paiute simmered the sap for stomach problems. The Southern Carriers made a tea of the buds for lung problems and coughs. They also used the resin of the buds to repel stinging insects such as mosquitoes and flies. The Shoshone applied the root tea as a headache remedy and used it internally as a general tonic. They used the bark tea for venereal diseases.[22]

The Delaware used *Populus deltoides* (cottonwood) as a women's tonic. The Montana used the inner bark for kinnikinnik and applied the bark tea as a wash for sprains. The Kawaiisu used *Populus fremontii* (Fremont cottonwood) inner bark tea to wash broken bones and for injuries. The Yuki used the bark or leaf tea for sore throat, colds, and sores.[23]

The Cherokee used *Populus gileadensis* (balm of Gilead) bud juice on sores and tinctured the buds for colic and bowel complaints, rheumatism, and venereal problems. The Iroquois made a wash of the tree parts for mouth sores, and the Menominee applied a salve made with the buds to the nose to cure a head cold and used it as a wound salve.[24]

The Iroquois used *Populus grandidentata* (large-toothed Aspen) by applying the bark to itchy skin, and the Ojibwa used the tea of the roots to stop bleeding. The Cherokee used *Populus nigra* (English poplar) buds on sores and tinctured the buds for rheumatism, long standing venereal diseases, colic, and bowel complaints.[25]

The Bella Coola used *Populus tremuloides* (quaking aspen) root bark decoction for gonorrhea. The Chippewa made a poultice by chewing the bark or root and applying it to wounds. The Fox made a cold remedy by applying the decoction of the buds to the nasal passages of adults and children. The Gitksan took the bark tea as a purgative. The Iroquois used a tea of the bark for worms (in adults and children, cats, dogs, and horses) and for measles. They applied the bark poultice for pleurisy and used teas of the roots and bark both internally and externally for venereal diseases. The Montana used the inner bark for kinnikinnik and as an antiscorbutic. The Okanagan made a wash for rheumatic parts from the stems as well as a tea for dyspepsia.

The Penobscot took the bark tea for fevers and colds. The Salishan used the root and stem decoction for syphilis. The Sikani made a poultice of the powdered bark for wounds. The Thompson Indians rubbed the tea on adolescents' bodies as a ritual purification.[26]

The Klallam used *Populus trichocarpa* (black cottonwood) bud infusion as an eyewash and the Quinault applied the gum as an antiseptic for wounds. The Squaxin used the leaf tea as an antiseptic wound wash and the bark tea as a sore throat gargle.[27]

SPIRITUAL ASPECTS

The ancient Indo-Iranian word for poplar is related to the words for oar, pole, boat, scapula, shovel, and a certain sacred instrument used for cutting or furrowing the soil prior to a sacrifice (possibly a sword-shaped ritual instrument). In later European belief it was said that a magic stake of aspen driven into the ground near a grave was enough to stop the corpse from leaving it.[28]

At Aston-on-Clun in England there is a traditional tree-dressing ceremony on May 29. A black poplar at the crossroads in the village center is decorated each year to commemorate the marriage of a local heiress, Mary Carter, to John Marston, the Lord of the Manor, in 1786. It is most likely that this ceremony is a continuation of an ancient tree-blessing rite established long before the marriage.

The Greeks associated poplars with grief and death. The Heliades were the sisters of Phaethon who died when he crashed to Earth after driving the chariot of the sun. The sisters in their grief turned into poplar trees, and their tears turned into amber as they fell into a nearby stream. Hercules was said to wear a crown of poplar when he went into Hades to kill the triple-headed dog Cerberus.

The Greeks used poplar wood to make shields. It is said that Persephone, the young goddess of spring, had a sacred grove of poplars in the west, the direction of the sunset. There was a poplar grove dedicated to the goddess of death on Kalypso's Island of the Blessed.[29]

In Irish tradition when aspen appears in a story it presages death. When Oscar, son of Oisín, is dying, his trembling is compared to a falling aspen tree. The Cailleach (the death aspect of the Land Goddess) is sometimes described as having on her head "gnarled brushwood, like the clawed old wood of the aspen root."[30]

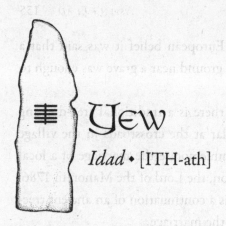

Yew

Idad • [ITH-ath]

As I have previously mentioned, there were five especially sacred trees in Ireland. One of them, the Bole of Ross, was a yew according to the *Dindsenchas* (traditional stories and lore regarding landscape features).[1]

Among the ancients, tree names were given to men: Mac Cuill (Son of Hazel), Mac Cuilin (Son of Holly), and Mac Ibar (Son of Yew). Women were also given names derived from trees, such as Caer Ibormeith (Yew Berry). It was an honor to be compared to a tree, as in the Scots Gaelic tribute, *Craobh a b'áirde de 'n abhall thu*—"You are the tallest tree in the orchard."[2]

Yews featured in traditional tales such as the story of the lovers Aillinn and Baile. After they died, an apple and a yew grew from their graves. The poets of Ulster cut down the yew that had grown from Baile's grave and used it to make a tablet upon which they inscribed "the visions, the espousals, the loves, and the courtships of Ulster." Then they did the same thing with Aillinn's apple tree, upon which they inscribed the "courtships, loves, and espousals" of Leinster. One day the two tablets sprang together and could not be pried apart again.[3]

We have seen how the magical apple branch that bears fruits and flowers simultaneously is associated with the otherworld. Here we have an intimation that yew has similar associations. Yew is a traditional tree to plant in graveyards, due to its associations with death and immortality.

The Druids held the yew in high regard as a sacred tree. The island of Iona in the Inner Hebrides of Scotland was once a Druid sanctuary, and the name of that island may be derived from the word for yew. There is a fairy haunt in Inverness called *tom-na-h-Iubhraich* (tom-na-hurich—"knoll of the yew wood"). Juniper or mountain yew bushes were burned by Highlanders to purify the house and barn on New Year's morning.[4]

I was told by a Forest Druid in Ireland that the ancient Druids would carry a section of yew or juniper wood from which they would shave thin slivers of wood with a knife, which they would burn to purify a place or an area (in the same way that Native Americans burn sage or cedar to purify a space and purge negative energies in preparation for ritual).

In the "Song of the Forest Trees" we read, "Patriarch of long-lasting woods is the yew, sacred to feasts as is well-known: of him now build dark-red vats of goodly size."[5] The yew is classed with the *airig fedo* (nobles of the wood) in the law texts due to its value in making "noble artifacts" such as bows and spears.[6] Yew wood was the wood of choice for domestic vessels, and there were skilled craftsmen who specialized in working with this wood.[7]

Yew wood is a very hard wood, and it was used to judge the quality of iron objects such as axes. The Laws specify that an ax must be made by three separate heatings: red heat, white heat, and the heat of tempering. The resulting iron should be strong enough that it cannot be dented by oak or yew.[8]

Yew is a tree that naturally grows deep in shady forests, far from human habitation. Plants that grow at a distance from human settlements and which are normally hard to find (when in their natural habitat) are plants that need to be respected. These plants are powerful medicines for very special conditions and uses. (Every part of the yew tree is a violent poison, except for the red flesh of the berry, which can be safely eaten provided the poisonous seed is swallowed whole or spat out.)

In the law texts on farming there is a list of plants including yew that can make livestock (and humans) seriously ill or even cause death,[9] and there was a mistaken belief that yew was fatal to bees. Bee mortality was more likely a result of damp cold weather and starvation.[10]

Yew trees live many thousands of years (see Spiritual Aspects below) and can be grown as ornamentals in a garden for a thousand years or more.

The *Word Ogham of Morainn mic Móin* names yew *sinem fedhaib*, "oldest of letters" or "older than letters."[11] In the *Word Ogham of Mic ind Oic* yew is *caínem sen; aildem aís* or "fairest of the ancients; most beautiful in age." Yew is *lúth iobair*, "sustenance of a leper" from *Briatharogam Con Culainn.*[12]

Yew is the longest-lived tree of all in the islands and continent of Europe, and lepers and outcasts probably ate the berries as food. But there is another secret here. Yew is a powerful healer, and those with deadly diseases may have spent time with this tree and its spirit to repair their ravaged bodies and resurrect their health.

HERBAL USES

As I mentioned above the yew tree is poisonous, except for the flesh of the berries. But yew is also a powerful healing agent when used by knowledgeable practitioners. In 1962, Monroe Wall of the National Cancer Institute began the first experiments with *Taxus brevifolia*, the western or Pacific yew, that had been found growing in the Willamette National Forest in Oregon. He discovered that taxol, a substance extracted from the tree, had a powerful effect on cancer cells.

CAUTION

Extreme caution must be used with this tree, and no one should use it as a domestic remedy without expert medical advice and supervision.

Clinical trials began at Johns Hopkins Hospital in Baltimore, Maryland, in 1988. Forty women with ovarian cancer who were not responding to standard chemotherapy were given either taxol from the yew or a placebo, and followed for two years. A 10 percent response to taxol would have been astounding, but 30 percent of the women who received taxol went into complete remission.[13]

That was the good news. The bad news was that the tree was very hard to find. The Pacific yew is found widely scattered beneath the shady understory of Douglas fir and red cedar forests, which are home to the spotted owl, an endangered species. Cedar and fir are logged for lumber, and yew has customarily been considered just a weed to be burned. Further, it takes about one hundred years for a yew tree to mature, and it takes the inner bark of four to six yew trees to make enough taxol to treat just one person.[14]

Eventually scientists understood that they could harvest taxol from yew shrubs and bushes, a renewable resource.

The medicinal property of the yew lies in the shoots and the bark. Decoctions of *Taxus brevifolia* (Pacific yew, western yew) branches have been used for lung conditions. The needle infusion can be used as a wash to induce perspiration and to poultice wounds. A tea of a very minute portion of the inner bark can be used for bloody urine. Gather the needles in spring or early fall and the bark from fall to spring.[15]

CAUTION

Every part of the tree is poisonous except for the red flesh
that surrounds the seed. Use only with expert supervision.
Do not chew the seeds. Do not experiment with this tree.
It can kill you.

Taxus baccata (English yew, European yew) can be used in similar ways. The leaf tea has been used internally for asthma, bronchitis, hiccups, indigestion, rheumatic pains, and epilepsy. Homeopaths make a very dilute potency that is used for cystitis, skin eruptions, headache, heart and kidney ailments, and rheumatism.[16]

Native American herbalists and medicine people used *Taxus brevifolia* (Pacific yew) in their pharmacopoeia. The Bella Coola made a decoction of the leaves and branches for lung troubles, and the Chehalis used an infusion of the leaves as wash to induce sweating. The Cowlitz poulticed the ground leaves and applied them to wounds. The Karok used a tea of the twig bark for upset stomach. The Klallam made a leaf decoction for internal injuries and pain, and the Quinault chewed the leaves to make a poultice for wounds.[17]

The Chippewa used *Taxus canadensis* (American yew) twig tea in the sweat lodge for rheumatism and took it as an herbal tea for rheumatism. The Potawatomi used the leaf tea as a diuretic and added the leaves to compounds for gonorrhea. The Iroquois used *Taxus baccata* (ground hemlock) as an abortifacient and to promote menstruation. They used the leaves and bark for coughs, colds, tuberculosis, and for numbness in the fingers and legs. The Menominee used the branch tea in the sweat lodge for rheumatism, numbness, and paralysis.[18]

SPIRITUAL ASPECTS

Yew trees, with their attractive red berries, are thought of today as ornamentals for the garden, but in their natural state they are stately trees that can grow to fifty feet in height. When the "mother tree" reaches a certain age, she dies back and sends out shoots in a large ring around herself. Thus an undisturbed yew has the potential to live almost forever. This fact of its growth cycle has made yew a powerful symbol of death and resurrection, of rebirth, and of eternal life.

Some of the oldest trees in the world are yews. The oldest tree in Europe is the Fortingall yew of Scotland, near Loch Tay. It is three thousand years old and presently lives surrounded by a cast-iron fence in a churchyard. It is fifty-six and a half feet in circumference, the center having died back. The churchyard is noted for its eighth-century baptismal font, once used by Adamnan, biographer of Saint Columba. Nearby in the town of Fortingall are the "Druid stones," three sets of three large stones in a field overlooked by Schie Hallion, a large mountain said to be the home of the fairy queen.

Yew forests were once common in France and Germany. The wood of the English yew was used for bows by Celtic and Teutonic warriors, a practice that eventually led to the demise of the great yew forests of Western Europe. In Teutonic areas the yew had important symbolic significance: judge's staffs were made of its wood, and the tree was planted in graveyards as a form of protection from malevolent spirits. Its needles were used in rituals to communicate with the dead.

Among the Hittites the *eyan* (yew) was said to protect from evil demons and from disease. Yew trees were planted in front of the homes of those who were tax-exempt, such as priests, while royalty were compared to yews as being blessed with everlasting reigns. In ancient Britain, yews were planted in graveyards and their branches placed on graves.

Relic boxes and magical tools were once made from yew wood. A sprig of yew was used by dowsers to find lost objects. The sprig was held out in front of the seeker and was seen to jump when the object was located.

Yew was one of the "nine sacred woods" used in the ritual fires of the Celts. The fires were started by friction using oak branches rubbed or rotated against one another using a drill, and then the nine sacred woods were added, having been ritually gathered in the forest. According to the *Carmina Gadelica* these nine woods are: the willow of the streams, the hazel of the rocks, the alder of the marshes, the birch of the waterfalls, the rowan of the shade, the yew of resilience, the elm of the brae, and the oak of the sun. The ninth wood might have been holly, ash, or pine according to other sources.

The Greeks sacrificed a black bull wreathed in yew to Hecate,

A great yew tree stands in a dark grove, the gaping
hollow of its trunk opening like a gateway.

goddess of crossroads and of death. Pictish warriors dipped their arrows into a poison made from yew.

A type of fairy is said to inhabit yew groves. They are said to be able to conjure a fairy darkness into which they or unwary mortals can instantly disappear.

I was told by a Forest Druid that the ancient Druids would bathe the dead in a bath of yew to "bring them back to life." Were they resurrecting their patients or simply sending them on to their immortal homes? Or did they understand a type of cancer treatment involving baths of yew?[19]

Part Two

The Druidic Arts

Druid Magic

The practice of Druid magic is called *druidecht* (druidism). *Druidecht* is also the word for magic, thus Druids and magic are synonymous. The word for sorcery is *corrguinech,* which is the practice of casting a spell while standing on one foot, with one arm extended, and one eye closed.[1] This is known as the Heron's Stance or the Crane Posture.

I have heard differing explanations for the Crane Posture or Heron's Stance. It may be a yogic posture of concentration that enables the adept to focus. It may be an allusion to the crane, a bird that exists between the worlds, with its feet in the water and its head in the air (as we saw in the willow chapter). By shapeshifting into a crane the Druid is better able to move into a liminal space between the worlds in order to bend reality.

Another interpretation is that the Druid is assuming the shape of a mushroom by standing on one leg, a veiled allusion to the use of hallucinogenic substances that open psychic awareness. By closing one eye and depriving him or herself of the use of two limbs, the Druid is only half in this world. One half of his sight and limbs are being used, the other half are hidden, or in the otherworld, giving him better access to the Spirits.

After adopting the Heron Stance the Druid utters a satire, incantation, or curse, aimed at a particular target. The magician may also adopt the stance when casting other kinds of spells. CúChulainn adopted the stance while cutting an oak sapling, which he bent into a ring, onto which he inscribed Oghams ordering Queen Maeve's army not to move until one of them had performed the same rite and issued a response on a wooden ring, to be placed on the same pillar stone where CúChulainn had issued his challenge.[2]

Other accounts relate that Druids crawled on all fours while uttering their incantations, or bent over with their backsides facing their targets.[3] They may have been shapeshifting into other creatures by adopting these postures. Either posture would certainly add insult to injury!

Druids were responsible for using their divinatory powers to help pick the next ruler of a tribe. In the *tarbh feis* (bull feast) a white bull was ritually slaughtered and the Druid who was charged with divining who should be the next ruler ate of its flesh and drank of its broth. Four Druids stood over him chanting a Spell of Truth as he slept (or went into trance) wrapped in the hide of the newly slaughtered bull. The hide was placed over a bed of rowan branches, and when the sleeper awoke he had his answer.

The Scottish version was the *taghairm,* in which the Druid lay wrapped in a newly sacrificed bull's hide (called a "cloak of knowledge") behind a waterfall or near the tide line (both liminal places between the worlds). The sound of the water and the bull's spirit helped the Druid seer to divine an answer. The Druid who performed this type of divination was called a *taibhsear,* or "spirit-seer."[4]

Druid magic also helped the nobility by providing protection in battle. The *celtar* was a magic "mantle of concealment" that Druids could make in order to enable someone to become invisible. CúChulainn used one once when going into battle. Druids could also raise a Druid mist called a *ceó druidechta* that bestowed invisibility. The method has been described as a poetic incantation or a fog spell that hid objects. It was said that every "shee" or fairy mound had one around it, to protect it from mortal eyes.

According to legend, Saint Patrick and his followers were able to recite a Christian hymn that was a *fe-fiada* (an invisibility charm) that made them look like a herd of deer to would-be attackers. Apparently a magic mantle, fog, spell, incantation, or hymn could produce a cloak of invisibility.[5]

I have had occasion to appreciate the usefulness of such spells. As a Druid priestess I have participated in numerous all-night vigils. On one memorable vigil I had climbed a hill dressed in a dark blue cape, carrying a large basket of sacred herbs and other ritual items, and my staff. I was all alone. The moon was full that night, and a gang of drunken teenage boys appeared. When they saw me they started screaming "Witch! Witch!" and "We are going to get you!" in very ugly tones.

Luckily, the grass on the hill was uncut and fairly tall. I simply pulled my dark hood over my head and dropped to the ground, becoming invisible in an instant. The boys staggered around for a time, bellowing at each other. They came within a few feet of me but I remained completely hidden, by the grace of my dark cape. Eventually they gave up and careened off, back down the hill. I have thought of my dark blue cape affectionately as my "cloak of invisibility" ever since.

Druids practiced many other arts: battle magic, bird augury, wind augury, cloud divination, magical healing, scrying into flames or water, and the like. *Fidlann* was divination by lot casting. *Fid* means "wood," so it probably means divination by Ogham sticks.[6] Druids also maintained strong relationships with their gods and goddesses by giving them gifts and praise. When the Druids needed help, they knew they could appeal to their gods for magical assistance.[7]

Magical Tools of the Druids

While we do not know for sure which tools were used by Druids, we can make very educated guesses by looking at the stories and the archaeological evidence. The sickle was a ubiquitous tool of the Druid, also used by Indo-European clergy such as Hindu Brahmins, for thousands of years. Ash wands have been found in Celtic burials, along with sprays of mistletoe and oak.

According to tradition, when the Tuatha Dé Danann (People of the Goddess Danu or Danann) came to Eire they brought with them their magical talismans: the Stone of Fál, which shrieked when stood upon by the true king; the Spear of Lug, which made its bearer invincible; the Sword of Nuadu, from which no one escaped alive once it had been unsheathed; and the Cauldron of the Daghda, from which unlimited food issued.[1] Here we have four magical tools hallowed by tradition: the stone, the sword, the spear, and the cauldron. Many variants of these appear in traditional tales.

In the Mabinogion of Wales, Bran gives Matholwch a magical cauldron called the Cauldron of Rebirth, which originally came from a lake in Ireland (anything that issues from a lake or pond or the sea can be assumed to come from the underworld of the fairy). Dead warriors could be placed in the cauldron overnight, and they would emerge fully healed but mute.[2]

An early Welsh poem describes the cauldron of the head of *annwfn* (the otherworld), which is kindled by the breath of nine maidens (nine is a very magical number that, like five, symbolizes the whole) and which will not boil food for a coward.[3] In "The Second Battle of Maige Tuired," an Irish tale, the same story is told of a magic well from which dead warriors are restored to life.[4] The cauldron of the sorceress Cerridwen boiled for a year and a day and produced three drops of magical inspiration and rebirth.[5]

Other objects that appear in the stories are often objects of quests: the Sword of Light, the Vessel of Plenty (probably the origin of the Grail mysteries), and the Waters of Life.[6] In the stories we are told that the Sea God Manannán Mac Lir brought Cormac to the Land of Promise, and gave him a drink from the Cup of Truth that would enable him to distinguish truth from falsehood.[7] In a different story, when Conn is lost in a mist with his Druids and poets he comes to a house near a golden tree where the God Lugh and the Goddess of Sovereignty are sitting. He sees a crystal chair, a silver vat, a vessel of gold, and a golden cup beside the goddess. The goddess serves Conn meat and red ale in the golden cup as Lugh recites the name of every royal prince from Conn into the future. A Druid records the names on yew staves and the vision disappears. But the vat, the golden vessel, and the yew staves remain.[8]

The Bell Branch is a magical tool to which we have numerous references. In one story, Cormac was on the rampart of Tara when a warrior appeared bearing a silver branch with three golden apples hanging upon it. The warrior had come from a land where there was no age, decay, gloom, sadness, envy, jealousy, hatred, or arrogance. The music of that branch was so magical that the wounded, the sick, and women in labor fell asleep as soon as they heard its music.[9]

As I mentioned in the apple chapter, Bran, son of Febal, was walking near his royal fort when he heard music that lulled him to sleep. Upon waking, he discovered a branch of silver beside him with white blossoms upon it. He carried the branch into his hall where a woman magically appeared, singing a song of islands in the sea, where treachery, sorrow, sickness, and death were unknown. When she left the hall, the silver branch from Emain Abhlach (the Island of Apples) disappeared with her.[10]

We know that branches were carried by poets as an emblem of their status and grade. The *Uraicecht Na Ríar* (Poetic Grades in Early Irish Law) states, "It is thus then that the boy went, with a silver branch above him, for it is that which was above the *ánruth's*. A golden branch, moreover, above the *ollam's*. A bronze branch above the other poets."[11] (An *ollam* has mastered all of the poetic art, the *ánruth* has mastered half of the poetic art, and the other *fílid,* or poets, are below them.)

Forest Druids use a tool called a Bell Branch with three or nine bells upon it. It is shaken while circling a sacred space, in order to repel negative energies. The sound of the bells is delightful to friendly fairies, and this attracts them into the ritual space.

Another tool of the Druid is the harp. In the tales we are told that the Druid harpist was master of the three kinds of music: "laughing music," which was the sound of young men at play; "sleeping music" that would lull listeners to sleep; and "crying music" that was the sound of a woman in childbirth. A Druid harpist would insert a gemstone into the wood of his or her harp, placed in such a way that it faced the audience. The Druid would focus his or her magical intention through the stone, sending it out to listeners.

The Magical Arts of the Forest Druids

A PRACTICAL GUIDE

One of the duties of a Forest Druid is to know the indigenous plant and animal species of her area, and to be aware of the condition of the land, the air, the water, the stones, the trees, the plants, and the animals of her immediate environment. The Forest Druid works to stop the forces of destruction that threaten endangered local species. Every Forest Druid forms a relationship with the sacred mother river goddess of her territory, to whom she brings gifts of thanksgiving. (My local river goddess is the Connecticut River, and my grove and I bring her gifts of flowers and fruit.) The practices described in this chapter will help to strengthen your connection with your local Land Spirits and with nature as a whole.

BÚAD AND CLES

A Forest Druid should be able to read the landscape of his home territory and understand which natural forces shape the land and its inhabitants. There are two kinds of power inherent in any landscape. The Gaelic words for these two kinds of power are *búad* and *cles*. Búad is the intrinsic or innate power that exists within the land, including natural geophysical and magnetic currents (ley lines), underground rivers and wells, huge forces like volcanic energies, and massive cleansing forces such as waterfalls and the like.

A Forest Druid should be able to "read" the contours of the topography and the vegetation like a book that reveals the hidden powers of the sacred land. For example, land that dips naturally to form a cauldron shape probably has inherent feminine energy. That land is receptive and will cradle those who go there. A glance at the surrounding, naturally occurring vegetation will confirm the reading. Are there flowering trees like cherry, elder, rowan, or crab apple in the vicinity? Are there birches or lindens nearby? These kinds of trees confirm feminine goddess energy.

Conversely, if the land is rugged with tall trees like ash, silver fir, hemlock, or oak, and if there are tall cliffs and rocky outcroppings, the evidence points to more masculine, godlike forces.

Look closely at the herbs growing in and around a landscape feature. Deep-rooted plants like dock point to grounding energy, as does the presence of yarrow. On the other hand, a preponderance of aromatic plants like thyme and bee balm points to energizing, active forces at work.

Thick barriers of raspberries, blackberries, wild rose, or furze are protective in the landscape. Ancient stone circles are often surrounded by natural fences of furze. These prickly plants are warriors who stand and defend a given area, protecting it from prying eyes and casual visitors.

A natural spring emerging from the earth or from a tree stump points to a place with inherent healing power. A swiftly running stream is energizing; a deep lake or river is meditative; a pond is an open gateway to underworld spirits. The presence of the mother ocean connects us with all beings through the waters that wash all continents and shores.

A Forest Druid can work with the inherent energies of búad to perform healing work for the land and the people. The Forest Druid can channel these forces, trusting that the energies will remain essentially constant (unless devastating forces alter the landscape).

Cles is power that is built up or depleted in a given area by the activity of humans. It is an energy that is developed in the land through deliberate planning and effort, such as the construction of a stone circle or landscape temple. It can be developed in the land when animals congregate for eons in a certain area. When humans follow the animals the power intensifies, and when ceremonies are performed, portals open that send energy down to the underworld of the fairies or up to the Star Nations.

Cles can also be developed by deliberately planting herbs to alter the energy of a place. Try planting butterfly weed and bee balm to attract butterflies and hummingbirds, which will lighten an area by bringing playful and joyful energy into the landscape. Plant deep-rooted tubers to calm an area down. Large trees will bring peace to a frenetic landscape.

SPIRITUAL PRACTICES WITH TREES

In my own practice, I like to find a natural power spot in the landscape and build up the inherent energy by offerings, rituals, and invocations. At one point in my Druidic career I worked inside a natural circle of enormous white pine trees. Later I shifted to a natural stone circle on top of a mound in the middle of an oak forest. The mound has a stream running by its base, where my grove and I make offerings of silver and tie cloots (prayer rags) to an overhanging tree. We honor oak trees with gifts of herbs, put living flowers and silver coins into the stream, and leave offerings of food on a small fairy altar nearby. In winter we leave gifts for the birds and other creatures, hanging on a fir tree.

The following meditation is a basic activity that every Forest Druid should practice regularly.

Tree Meditation

Begin by walking to a quiet spot in nature. Allow your body to relax, and focus on your feet. Feel your connection to the soil beneath you. Remember that the soil is alive and composed of countless genera-tions of ancestors—human, plant, mineral, and animal. Give thanks to the ancestors.

Send your awareness deep into the soil beneath your feet and imagine that your toes have become roots, delving deep into the soil. "See" your roots moving ever downward through layers of earth and rock and water, until they come to a luminous green light at the center of the earth. This is the emerald heart of the earth, the star within the stone. Leave your roots anchored in that green light and bring your awareness back up to your "trunk."

Feel your pulsing heart, the star in the center of your chest, and become aware of your breathing. Take a few moments to hold the green light at the center of the earth and your own heart in your awareness. Then move your awareness up to the top of your head. Visualize an eye opening at the top of your head and "see" branches emerging from your head and shoulders. Send your branches to the sky until they connect with the great star in the sky (the sun during the day, the moon at night).

Now hold all three lights—the emerald star at the center of the earth, your own pulsing human heart, and the star in the sky— simultaneously in your awareness. As you breathe begin to make a loop of breath, pulling energy down from the sky, through your heart, and down to the center of the earth as you exhale, and pulling up from the center of the earth to your heart, to the star in the sky as you inhale. Practice this circular breathing for a few minutes.

You should now feel stretched between the three worlds. You are now sharing the consciousness of trees. You are ready to walk up to a living tree and sit or stand next to it, in order to communicate with the tree spirit. Use all your senses: sight, smell, hearing, breath, and touch, to connect with the tree. Bring it your questions and prepare to hear an answer.

After about twenty minutes you can retract your roots, pull in your branches, close the eye at the top of your head, reconnect with your breathing, and utter a prayer of thanks. Caution: Do not walk away without first reversing the tree meditation. Be sure you are fully grounded before you return to regular human activities.

Bonding with Trees

Every Forest Druid should have at least one tree (or a whole grove of trees) that he or she forms a close bond with. It can be a tree that you have nurtured from seed, or one in the neighborhood that seems to call out to you. It can be a tree in the local park or in your own back yard. Give the tree gifts such as fertilizer, dried herbs, shells, coins, and cakes. Hang a birdhouse in or near the tree so it will always have company. Plant its seeds and help its babies to thrive. Bring it your prayers and songs. Hug it and let it know that it is special to you.

In ancient times altars would be set up and ribbons or wool hung from trees, to mark them as special. Hang little lights in the tree and spend the night beneath it on holy days.

MAGICAL WORKINGS WITH TREES

Make a Magical Amulet

Identify which tree has the magical qualities you need; for example, rowan (mountain ash) for protection, or willow to bring gentle healing to a life situation. Fill a small pouch or other object with roots, bark, leaves, flowers, nuts, or berries. Wear the amulet or carry it on your person.

Whenever you take anything from a tree *you must leave a gift in exchange.* In the old days apple cider, honey, or the herb vervain were the usual gifts. If you live in the Americas, sage, corn meal, and tobacco are appropriate as well (because the spirits understand those gifts).

Individual tree parts have different energies, so pick the part of the tree that most fits your magical intention. Flowers and leaves have a lightening effect and are great for uplifting your spirits and improving your mood. Twigs, cones, barks, berries, nuts, and woods will help you to focus your intent and initiate new projects. Roots will help to ground your energy and your magical intention.

Charge a Magical Object in a Tree

If you wish to magically charge a piece of jewelry, a stone, a wand, a staff, a cauldron, or any other object, first bury it in the ground for three days and nights (or one full moon cycle if it needs a lot of clearing). Then expose the object to the light of the sun and full moon for three days and nights. Once you have done so, place the object in the hollow of a tree (or in its branches if the object is large), for three full days and nights. The earth will clear it, the sun and moon will empower it, and the tree will charge it.

Another way to clear stones, crystals, and jewelry before charging them, is to put them in a secure basket with a tight lid that is weighted down with rocks, and leave them in a running stream for three days and nights.

Aspurging

Make a weak tea or sun tea of tree parts, chosen from a tree that has the qualities you desire; for example, oak or ash to contact the gods or birch to contact the goddesses. Use a leafy tree branch to sprinkle the tea on a person, place, or object. (This is a nice blessing for use in Druid rituals.)

Make a Smudge Stick

Make a smudge stick by laying fresh cedar tips and fresh sage leaves on several pieces of newspaper (making sure the tips are all pointing the same way) roll like a cigar, and bind tightly with string. Put the bundle in a dry place. After a few months, it will be dry, compact, and ready to unroll and use no longer requiring the string to hold it together. Light one end and use the smoke of the burning smudge stick to cleanse and purify an area for ritual use.

You can also shave the bark from a fragrant piece of dry cedar or juniper wood, and burn that in a clay dish or shell. The smoke from either of these smudging methods will banish negativity and prepare a ritual space for ceremony and prayer.

Make an Offering

Use tree parts to make offerings to deities and to a sacred fire. Send the smoke to the heavens as you make a prayer.

A note about Celtic deities: No Celtic deity expects you to grovel apologetically as you ask for what you need. Nor do they expect you to feel guilty (unless you have done something truly heinous!). The correct relationship to deity, from the Celtic perspective, is to see them as your relatives. This is why food offerings are made to them at feasts, and why bardic offerings such as music and poetry are made in the sacred circle.

The idea is that, as a Forest Druid, you admire the wisdom and skill of your deities and you strive to be *just like them*. An herbalist desires the skill of Airmid, a blacksmith the prowess of Goibhniu, a jeweler the mastery of Lugh, a poet the fiery inspiration of Brigid, a warrior the fearless energy of the *morrighan* (a trinity of goddesses), and so on. In ancient times, the guilds of craftsmen, warriors, brewers, and the like had their own specialized deities whom they honored. The farmers delighted in the tales of *fianna*, because these warrior-poets used their wits and skill to overcome obstacles, just as farmers must do to overcome the forces of blight, pestilence, and weather.

Celebrate a Tree Ritual

Find an old beech or apple tree, or any other tree with low hanging branches that is easy to climb. On a night when the moon is full, climb the tree alone or with your grove. Bring flutes, bells, rattles, and harps. Sing songs to the tree as the moon rises.

Bake Ritual Cakes

Add edible parts of trees to breads and cakes for use in rituals. Serve them with honey and mead during or after a ceremony.

Brew Ritual Cup Mixtures

Put a tree tea in the ritual cup or add it to other libations used for ritual. Be sure to use only nontoxic tree parts for your ritual cup. **Do not use yew.**

Strewing

Strew tree leaves and other tree parts in public places, in front of the house, in the ritual area, before a hand fasting, and so forth.

Make Ceremonial Brooms

Make a ceremonial broom using willow, ash, and birch or any other tree of power. Use it to ritually sweep a ceremonial area, to ritually sweep bad energies out of a home or other building, and so forth.

To purify a home or other space, first clean every room in the usual way: with vacuum cleaner, dust cloth, window cleaner, furniture polish, and so on. Then use the broom to "sweep" each room clean and send any lingering bad energy out the door. Next, take a bowl of salt water and sprinkle every corner, room by room. Finally, walk to every corner and all dark spaces such as closets, under the stairs, and in cubby holes, and illuminate them with a white candle. A chant should be sung while you do so.

The broom should be stored upside down (with the bristles pointing up) if a woman is the goddess of the house, and it should never be used for mundane house cleaning.

Bless the House and Barn

Hang branches of sacred trees over the cradle, in the home, in the barn, over the door. Familiarize yourself with the magical properties of trees and use appropriate ones to make tools, furniture, the cradle, or even a house.

Build a Stone Circle

Find a spot on the land that "feels right." Gather with a circle of fellow Druids and hold hands in a circle. Let go of your hands and slowly walk backward until the proper size for your circle reveals itself. Notice the space between each Druid and sense how many stones you will need by the placing of the sticks as described below.

On the next holy day, rise before dawn and stand in the center of your circle. When the sun rises, drive a stick into the ground at the perimeter of the circle, marking the exact place where the sun breaks the horizon. Do this for one full sun cycle (year) so that you know exactly where the sun rises (also where the sun sets if you want a really elegant circle) on every holy day of the year. You are now ready to place your stones. Use your *imbas* (poetic insight) to determine the size of your stones.

Make a Bell Branch

Find a suitable branch that has fallen on the ground and affix three or nine (or any multiple of three) bells to it. Use the bell branch to frighten away negativity and to attract fairies to a ceremonial area. Begin your Druid rites by walking three times *deiseal,* or "sunwise" (in a right-hand spiral, also known as clockwise) around the ritual circle, shaking the bell branch, or use the bell branch to open a Druid gathering or assembly.

Award a bell branch to a poet after a poetry competition or other Druidic contest. Give a golden branch to the most accomplished, a silver branch to the second-place winner, and a bronze branch to the third-place winner.

Open a Fairy Well

Find a spot in nature and sit quietly. Feel the energy coming toward you and going away from you in four directions. "See" these energies as fairy pathways. Set your intention that you can "travel" out along these pathways to encounter spirits, and spirits can "travel" these pathways to find you. Open your awareness to the natural forces that inhabit the space where you are sitting. Become aware of unseen presences, animal trails, the inner buzzing of the land spirits, etc.

With your finger, inscribe a circle in the grass before you and then divide it into four sections. Use your hands to "peel back" each quarter to open a "fairy well." Invite all positive spirits to emerge from the underworld. You can "dip" your hands into the well and bring up energy to "wash" your face and body. Leave the well open or close it when you are done. Give thanks.

When my grove gives thanks after "washing" in the fairy well, we are always blessed by a sign of confirmation. We have had a huge dragonfly land on our laps, and an enormous yellow and black spider drop down from the tree above us, to hang suspended over the center of our circle. We even attracted a moose who, for a few days, made a point of standing in the middle of the stone circle where we do our ceremonies.

This technique is also an excellent one for planning a magical garden. Rather than designing a garden plan from your intellect alone, take time to tune in to the natural forces and energy pathways that already exist on the land. Ask the land spirits what *they* want, and then work with them. Place a large crystal or other symbolic object in the center of your garden plot, to help you focus as you do this work.

Make a Circle of Protection

Use your finger to draw a circle of protection around yourself. Visualize the luis-rowan Ogham and chant its name softly (rowan gives protection against sorcery). You can do this with fearn-alder and tinne-holly also. Recite The Druid's Breastplate:

> *I bind myself to these;*
> *The beauty of the Stars,*
> *The Sun's life-giving ray,*
> *The whiteness of the Moon,*
> *The flash of Lightning,*
> *The whirling Wind,*
> *The stable Earth,*
> *The deep salt Sea,*
> *The strength of Stones.*

Make a Clootie Well

If you are fortunate enough to live in an area where there is a tree overhanging a spring or a well, you can establish a holy well dedicated to your patron deity. Begin by bringing offerings, such as fruits, flowers, silver coins, or jewelry, to the spirits of place. Invoke your patron or patroness and ask him or her to please come into the waters.

When anyone is afflicted or has a need they can go to the well with a small strip of cloth and a handful of silver coins, jewelry, or other gifts for the waters.* They can make their offerings, then dip the cloth into the water. Next they should touch the cloth to any part of their body, mind, or heart that is afflicted, and then tie the cloth to the overhanging tree. As the cloth rots and falls away, so will their troubles.

Make a Cairn of Blessing

Any collection of five things marks a cairn (a ritual whole). A Druid can carry on their person five small stones, or pieces of wood, acorns, or other objects, which he or she can set down anywhere to create sacred space. Similarly, when building a ritual fire the Druid can consciously lay down five sticks of wood at the base, dedicating each stick to a divine principle.

Here are some examples of sacred intentions with which five stones, sticks, or other objects can be invested:

A blessing for the sun
A blessing for the earth
A blessing for the moon
A blessing for the sacred plants
A blessing for the sacred trees
A blessing for the sacred waters
A blessing for the sacred air
A blessing for the sacred fire
A blessing for the animals
A blessing for peace
A blessing on all human hearts
A blessing on all dreams

---

*As a rule, water prefers silver.

A blessing on the spirits of place

A blessing on the gods and goddesses

A blessing on changing energies

A blessing on potential states of awareness

A blessing on all stars that are suns for planets with human life

A blessing on all planets with human life and their moons

A blessing on all dimensions of being that coexist with human life

A blessing on the fairy realms

A blessing on the spirits of the animals

A blessing on all teachers and enlightened ones from past lives and
this life

A blessing on all future teachers and enlightened ones

A blessing on the dream teachers who teach us through our dreaming

A blessing on the infinitely changing choreography of energy that
is life

MAKING TREE MEDICINES

Healing Salves

Make healing salves and balms using tree parts. I always use horse
chestnuts (*Aesculus hippocastanum*) and the green hulls of walnuts
(*Juglans* spp.) in my tree salves. The chestnuts are anti-inflammatory
and kill pain. The walnuts are antifungal and contain manganese, a
skin-healing agent.

Use a large, nonaluminum pot with a tight fitting lid for this work.
First, fill the bottom of the pot with equal portions of smashed horse
chestnuts and the green outer hulls of walnuts (you don't *have* to add
these but in my experience they are what makes a superior salve).

Then add herbs and flowers (dried or fresh) such as lavender, calendula, bee balm, plantain, pine needles, elecampagne root, and comfrey.

Pour cold-pressed organic olive oil over the herbs and nuts, one cup
at a time, keeping track of how much oil it takes to just barely cover the

plant matter. In a separate pot, melt good quality beeswax (get it from a local apiarist if at all possible so it will be fragrant and fresh).

Allow the herbs to simmer in the oil for 20 minutes (do not boil!) with the lid on. When the beeswax is also simmering you can combine the wax and oil. (Do not add cold, hard wax to the hot oil, or the salve won't gel properly.) Put in four tablespoons of melted, simmering wax for every cup of oil you used. Stir and strain into very clean glass jars. Allow to cool and set and then put on the lids.

I save old jelly and jam jars for this purpose. You won't need a preservative if everything is squeaky clean. Be sure to wash your jars in very hot soapy water before you use them. Rapid cleanup is essential after you have finished pouring the hot liquid into the jars. Wipe all tools, implements, and pots immediately with a paper towel while they are still hot, and plunge into very hot soapy water. Otherwise the wax will harden on your utensils, and it will be much harder to clean them.

Tree Baths

Make a bath or body wash from a tree whose qualities you need. Anoint yourself or someone else with the liquid or add a strong tree tea to the bath water.

Make Tree Elixirs

Gather parts from a tree whose qualities you need and soak the parts in alcohol (80 proof or higher) for a few days. Drink a few drops of the tree elixir with water or anoint yourself or an object with it. For extra magic, expose the elixir to the full moon or leave it in the hollow of a tree for three days and nights.

Tree elixirs can be added to water for baptisms and naming ceremonies, to anoint the dead, to bless a new house, to consecrate magical tools, and so forth.

To make the elixir, begin the process a few days before the full moon. You will want to keep a careful eye on your preparations—when you soak tree leaves or flowers in alcohol, it might take just a few hours or a day or two for the plant matter to start to break down. As soon as you see that happening, it is time to strain the liquid and put it into a permanent brown or blue glass container.

Roots, bark, and berries take longer to begin to break down, usually about a week to ten days. Don't leave the tree parts in the alcohol indefinitely, or all you will have is a very astringent, tannin-filled brown liquid. The best elixirs will have the color and flavor of the tree still in them, and smell fresh and alive.

Make Smoking Mixtures
Add "kinnikinnik" (red osier, red willow) to tobacco and use the mixture in the peace pipe.

CAUTION

Tobacco is a very sacred plant that was never meant to be used as a recreational drug. It should only be used with ceremony and prayer.

If possible try to find a Native American medicine person to guide you in the proper handling of sacred pipes and smoking mixtures. Their basic etiquette is to use only tobacco that is gifted to them by others. That ensures that he or she is working for the community and not for selfish purposes. The carrier also has to ritually care for the pipe every day.

A medicine pipe cannot be bought; it must be gifted to a medicine person by an elder. When praying, the pipe carrier puts a pinch of smoking mix into the pipe for each prayer or intention brought by the community. The smoke carries the intention to the divine Source of all things.

CREATE AN OGHAM ALPHABET

As I mentioned above there were many different Ogham alphabets: lists of dogs, cows, heroes, and so forth. Another Ogham alphabet was composed of plant names. The *Auraicept na N-Eces* states: "Herb *Ogham,* to wit, to take the name of whatever herb it be for the letter with which it will commence." I took that recommendation to heart and created my own Celtic Herb Ogham, as illustrated in the following table. Such an alphabet can be used by a grove of Druids to send secret communications, mark ritual tools, and so forth. (The word *lus* means "herb.")

A	*lus an airneig*	(luss un AR-nyeyk)	liverwort
B	*lus nam bansith*	(luss nuh MAN-shee)	foxglove
C	*lus a chaitheimh*	(luss uh KHA-heyv)	sweet woodruff
D	*druidh-lus*	(DROOY-luss)	mistletoe
E	*lus an ellain*	(luss un ELL-in)	herb Robert
F	*lus a fhogair*	(Luss un O-ger)	field gentian
G	*lus a ghridh*	(luss uh GHREE)	amaranth
H	*lus na hoidhche*	(luss nuh HUH-ee-hyuh)	belladonna
I	*isop*	(ISSop)	hyssop
J	(none)		
K	See C		
L	*lus an leanna*	(luss un LYEW-nuh)	hops
M	*lus marsalaidh*	(luss MAR-sa-lee)	marjoram
N	*lus na nathrach*	(luss nuh NAH-hrakh)	vipers bugloss
O	*lus nan oighreag*	(luss nun OY-rug)	cloudberry bush
P	*lus a pheubair*	(luss uh FYEH-pir)	dittany, pepperwort
Q	(none)		
R	*lus an rois*	(luss un ROSHE)	rose
S	*lus an t saoidh*	(luss un TUH-ee)	fennel
T	*lus an torranain*	(luss un TOR-run-in)	figwort
U	*uillean*	(ULL-yun)	honeysuckle
V	*(fuath) mhadaidh*	(FOO-uh VAH-tee)	aconite
Y	See I		

Celebrate the Celtic
Fire Festivals

The Fire Festivals are the most important holy days for Druids. In this chapter you will find guidelines for rituals and celebrations. Foods are an integral part of each festival, and traditional recipes are included for each observance.

BELTAINE

This festival begins on May 1 or whenever your local hawthorn tree first blooms. In Old Celtic it was called *Belo-tenia,* the fires of Belos, the Bright One. It was known as *Shenn da Boaldyn,* on the Isle of Man, as *Bealltan,* in Scotland and as *Galan-Mai,* Wales.

A Portal Between the Seasons

The ancient Celts divided the year into two seasons, summer and winter, the seasons of light and dark. The great festival of Samhain inaugurated the dark season, acting as a portal between the time of green fertility and the seeming death of the vegetation in winter. Beltaine was the other great portal, ushering in the spirits of light and life to refertilize the landscape. Both nights were regarded as potent "spirit nights," when otherworldly contact was made easier.

The outlandish costumes and tricks of the Samhain festival symbolized the forces of chaos and death roaming loose upon the land.

Similarly, at Beltaine a figure known as the Betsy or the *cadi haf* (usually a portly male with a large mustache, thinly disguised as a woman), or a Jack-in-the-Green figure covered from head to toe in ribbons, leaves, flowers, and other colorful scraps, symbolized the liminal aspects of the season when otherworldly spirits moved freely among the people.

Establishing the Date

The timing of the festival is a remnant of the Celts' ancient pastoral tradition. At Beltaine the herds were driven forth to their summer pastures, after being forced to walk between two fires of purification. At Samhain the herds were brought back to the stables and inner enclosures for their winter safekeeping.

But in a time before written calendars, newspapers, radios, televisions, and the Internet, how did the community ascertain the true date of the Beltaine feast? At least two methods have come down to us from the ancients. One was the blooming of the hawthorn tree, because this was the signal that the cold season was over and summer was indeed upon the land. It was the task of the local Druid to keep an eye on the local hawthorns to announce the first blossoms and the inauguration of the Beltaine feast.

The second method for divining the date was the observation of the skies. Beltaine marked the day when the Pleiades "disappeared into the sun"—that is, the Pleiades were no longer visible after sunset. If we were to take into account the movements of the stars in the last two thousand years, this would place astronomical Beltaine on April 26 or 27 of the current Gregorian calendar.

The Battle of Dark and Light

The significance of the Beltaine festival is preserved in the oral traditions of the Celts. Partholon, an early colonizer of Ireland who preceded the Tuatha de Danann (peoples of the goddess Danu) arrived from the otherworld on Beltaine. Again on Beltaine, the Sons of Mil (the Celts) arrived from Iberia and fought the Tuatha de Danann for possession of Ireland.

In each case, the invaders had to do battle with the existing powers in possession of the land. Partholon was forced to do battle with the Fomorians, who had held the land before him. The Fomorians were associated with chaos, darkness, blight, winter, evil, pestilence, and death. They were used as a poetic metaphor for the forces of destruction and decay.

Encoded in these stories may be an ancient mythological cycle in which strong forces muster to overcome the powers of the dark season of the year in order to gain possession of the land and her fertility. The fact that Partholon's tribe perished in an epidemic three hundred years after his invasion, and the fact that the Tuatha de Danann were eventually driven "underground" by the Celts, may be a reminder that even for victors, death is inevitable. Winter inevitably follows spring.

In the Red Book of Hegest, Gwyn and Gwyrthur waged perpetual war for the hand of Creudylad, daughter of Lludd, each one losing her and then stealing her back in endless rounds of fighting. King Arthur finally decreed that they fight at each Beltaine until the end of the world. Gwyn is champion of the Underworld of Death and Gwyrthur is a God of the Sun. Thus winter and summer, darkness and light, do battle at Beltaine for the bride who represents the flowers, grain, and fertility of the fields.

At Beltaine, Highlanders offered cakes and libations to the protective spirits of the flocks and vegetation, and also to the animal spirits more dangerous to the farmyard, such as fox, crow, and eagle. These destructive spirits were entreated not to harm the herds and fields.

Sun and Fire

At Beltaine the tribal herd was ushered between two ritual fires as it left for the surrounding hills and summer pastures. The two fires used in the Beltaine rite reinforced the idea of fire as a portal to a new season, a new state of being, and a new reality. Cures and purifications were possible as the *tuath* (the people, the community) and the herds moved through the fire portal.

It was considered very auspicious to climb to a high place to watch the sun rise on Beltaine. According to the ancient Celts the basic building blocks of creation, and hence the most potent forces for magic, transformation, and healing, were fire and water. So important was the sun in Celtic culture that moving *deiseal,* or "sun-wise" (in a right-hand spiral), was the starting point for any auspicious beginning.

As late as the nineteenth century at Barra, in the Hebrides, men would bare their heads at noon to honor the sun. Pregnant women walked three times sunwise around a church to ensure a safe delivery. At weddings the party would circumambulate the home three times sunwise before entering. A circular wedding dance was performed in many areas that revolved around the couple, sunwise. Fire was carried sunwise three times around a newborn child to protect it from abduction by fairies.

Those approaching a holy well walked three times sunwise around it before partaking of its healing waters. In Christian times sacred wells were consecrated by saying a mass at the well after which the entire congregation would move in procession sunwise around the well with lit candles. After consecration, it was forbidden to use the well water to cook food.

Wells are said to have special potency at dawn on Beltaine when the sunlight first hits the water. It is as if the fire entering the water activates the magical potency of the well. The many holy wells dedicated to Brigid are probably further evidence of this idea. Brigid is a fire goddess (later morphed into Saint Brigid), and her presence at a well provides the necessary magical mix of fire within water.

The dew on the grass on Beltaine morning, gathered just as the first rays of the sun hit, is said to have special properties, too. Young girls would once rise before dawn to bathe their faces in the dew to make them fair. May dew can be bottled for later use throughout the year.

The magical significance of the sun and the importance of moving in a sunwise direction is revealed in certain traditional Celtic practices. Coffins were turned sunwise three times before setting them into the earth. Fishing boats and boats of passage would row in a circle, sunwise, three times before setting out to sea. Ancient standing stones and dolmens were circumambulated three times sunwise to honor them.

The national dance of Brittany, a Celtic area in western France, is a *ronde,* or circular dance, which in ancient times was probably a dance in honor of the sun. Pythagoras describes a dance that was held within the circle of Stonehenge in ancient times. Given that the monument is round and solar in orientation, this too may have been a sun-honoring dance. In modern times, these circular sun dances are associated with various fairy tribes such as the Corrigans of Brittany and the Pixies of Cornwall. In more ancient times, lookouts could tell if an approaching army was friend or foe by whether they moved sunwise or *tuathail,* counterclockwise ("widdershins," "wrang-gaits") around the fort.

Sacred Trees at Beltaine

A number of traditions concerning trees at Beltaine are still observed in Celtic areas. Blackthorns should not be cut on Beltaine, or bad luck might come courtesy of the *lunantishee,* the fairies who guard these trees. Beltaine is the time to cut twigs of rowan (mountain ash) and bind them with red thread to make small solar crosses to be placed over doors and stables to keep troublemaking fairies out. These crosses are also sewn discreetly into clothing.

Hawthorn blossoms are used to decorate the outside of the home, but if they are brought into the house mischievous fairies might come in with them. Branches of hawthorn are cut the night before the festival and spirited secretly into the room of a young woman by a male admirer. She is then expected to keep company with him throughout the holiday.

The May Bush is a holly bush decorated with hawthorn blossoms or a collection of hawthorn or whitethorn branches, yellow flowers, bright ribbons, and yellow eggshells (a fertility symbol). The bush is used as a focal point for dancing. Setting up a May Bush is said to ensure abundant milk throughout the year. Candles can be placed in the bush and lit on May Eve.

The May Pole is an Anglo-Saxon custom that found its way into Celtic areas only recently. Hawthorn branches in bloom are used to decorate the top of the pole.

The Fairies at Beltaine

If one wants to see the fairies, it is a good idea to sleep under a blooming elder tree on Beltaine Eve. The fairies are said to be especially apt to steal butter on Beltaine if given a chance. If a person enters a house where butter is being churned, she has to help with the task, or there will be no butter. It is considered a good idea to leave offerings of milk for the fairies on Beltaine.

Fire must never be given away at Beltaine or the household luck will go with it. In ancient times the fires of each house and village were put out, and everyone waited until new fire was brought from the ceremonial center of Uisneach, the seat of the Archdruid and a perpetual fire in the heart of Ireland.

The most appropriate color to wear at the Beltaine feast is green. When Queen Guinevere announced to the Knights of the Round Table that she would go Maying on the fateful day of her abduction, she told them all to wear green, the color of life and rebirth. Guinevere's abductor, Melwas, was said to sleep under a green cloak, marking him as a fairy lover of otherworldly significance. The Beltaine festival was traditionally associated with trysts and sexual encounters outdoors, a method of adding sexual energy to the burgeoning vegetation of the fields and forests.

Beltaine and Children

Children added their life-giving energies to the festival by walking in procession around the village carrying a Flower Maiden, a doll adorned with flowers. Sometimes the Flower Maiden was carried by mummers wearing straw masks.

Yellow flowers such as the marsh marigold, symbolic of the sun, were used to decorate the Flower Maiden and the May Bush, and tied to the halters of horses, milk pails, doors, windowsills, and the roof. They were strewn on the path leading to the house, on and around the well, tied to cow's horns and tails, and onto churns, wagons, and coaches.

Nine Sacred Woods

Both the Beltaine and the Samhain fires were built by nine men using nine kinds of sacred wood (or just oak). The number nine is the number of change, transformation, and high magic. The identity of the nine sacred woods varied slightly from area to area, but in general these woods came from trees that held profound practical and spiritual meaning for the Celts.

Oak was the tree most often associated with the high gods across Indo-European cultures. Thor, Jupiter, the Daghda, Perkunas, Zeus, and all deities of thunder, lightning, and high places were associated with oak. Oak trees were known to draw lightning, singling them out as one of the trees known to attract celestial attention.

Oak had a durable wood that was suitable for building and made a hot fire. Its acorns fed the people, the pigs, and the deer. Its leaves and bark were used for coughs and as a wound wash. The bark was used to tan leather.

Willow wood was used to make harps, and the sound of its whispering branches inspired the poets. Its bark was a powerful febrifuge, and it helped with all the aches and pains of a strenuous life.

The hazel was associated with the Salmon of Wisdom, one of the four great totem animals of the Celtic tribes (along with eagle, boar, and stag). Its nuts symbolize the "compact wisdom" that a Druid carries in her head. Druids were said to carry hazelnuts on their person as a reminder.

Alder wood is impervious to damp and was used to make bridges and pilings. It was associated with the god Bran as a magically protective wood. Alder leaves were used in poultices to relieve feet weary from travel.

Birch trees are among the first to establish themselves in disturbed areas; hence their name, "the tree of new beginnings." Birch trees were universally associated with goddesses by Finno-Ugric cultures, Native Americans, and Indo-Europeans. Birch twigs make a soothing beverage tea, and a fungus that grows on them is useful for cancer.

The ash is another tree that "courts the flash." Where ash and oak and thorn grew together one was likely to see fairies. Ash sap was given to a newborn as its first drink by placing a green log in the fire and collecting the emerging sap with a spoon. Ash leaves were used to poultice snakebites and snakes were said to be deathly afraid of its magical leaves.

The yew was "sacred to the feast." Its wood was burned to purify an area in much the same way as Native Americans "smudge" with sage in preparation for ceremony. The best bows were made of resilient yew.

Elm was a tree known to be favored by the elves. It was said that lightning would never strike this tree. If elm leaves fell out of season, a cattle disease was in store.

Holly was a tree associated with warriors due to its hard, spiky leaves and blood-red berries. The English holly made a nice tea and the twigs were healthy for rabbits. A holly planted outside the house would protect it from storm, fire, and evil sorcery. A sprig of holly tied on the cowshed would cause the cows to thrive.

The elder tree was associated with a forest spirit known as the Elder Mother. It was considered unlucky to bring the tree into the house. Elder flowers and birch bark made a nice drink, and elder flowers were used as a tea for fevers. Elder berries were eaten and used for teas that benefited the lungs and blood. Elderflower water was used as a skin tonic and elder flowers were added to poultices and salves for skin conditions.

The apple was considered a "Tree of Immortality," associated with the otherworld. It was considered a sacrilege to cut down an apple orchard, and the last apple on each tree had to be left for the fairies. Apples and rowan berries, both high in vitamin C, were cooked and sweetened with honey to make a cure for coughs.

Pine resin was added to healing salves, and pine bark was used as a tea for fevers. Pine resin was dried, crushed and powdered, and burned as incense to purify an area.

Food Offerings at Beltaine

The following recipes are traditional foods used to help celebrate the Beltaine festival.

Beltaine Bannock

A large oatcake was baked with nine raised knobs on it. The bannock was carried out into the fields, and each knob was broken off and offered to animals that might harm the crops and herds such as crows, ravens, eagles, and foxes. These animals were petitioned to leave the flocks and fields alone. The bannock might be coated with a wash of whipped egg, milk, cream, and a bit of oat flour.

In ancient times the bannock was rolled thin and stuck to a sheepskin, which was placed on a wooden stretcher near the fire (especially a fire of rowan wood) until the bread toasted. It was considered very unlucky and an offense to the fairies for iron to touch the bannock if it was intended as a bread for ritual purposes.

⅔ cup coarsely ground oats

1 pinch salt

1 pinch baking soda

2 teaspoons melted butter or lard

1 cup hot water

A handful of ground oats for kneading

Combine the oats, salt, and soda in a bowl and stir together. Make a well in the center of the bowl with your fist. Pour in the melted butter and water and stir until a stiff batter forms. Cover a board with ground oats and empty the batter onto the board. Cover your hands with oats and knead the batter into a ball. Roll out to ½ inch thickness with a rolling pin. Sprinkle with ground oats and cook on a griddle or flat surface until the edges are curled and slightly toasted.

Caudle

A caudle was poured on the ground or into a hole in the earth as a libation. This drink has a yellow color to honor the sun.

> 5 egg yolks
> ⅔ cup white wine
> Sugar to taste
> Pinch saffron

Beat together the yolks, wine, sugar, and saffron. Heat the mixture slowly over medium heat, stirring continually, until thick and fluffy, being careful not to let it burn or scorch or stick to the pot. Serve at once, in small glasses as a drink or as a sauce for desserts.

LUGHNASAD

This festival is usually celebrated August 1 to 15, or when the first grain ripens. It is called *Lunasda, Lunasdal,* or *Lunasduinn* in Scottish Gaelic, *Laa Luanys* in Manx, *Calan Awst* in Welsh, and *Gouel an Eost* Breton.

The God of the Assembly

The Lughnasad festival occurs during the first three weeks of August and marks the celebration of the first fruits of the harvest. The feast is named after Lugh (whose name derives from Old Celtic *lugus* for "lightning, illumination"), known to the Welsh as Lleu, a god of intelligence and skill, master of every art, the perfect poet, magician, and warrior, whom the Romans equated with Mercury.

An Irish story relates that Lugh was the sole survivor of triplets, all named Lugh, making him a classic triple deity. In Indo-European tradition, triple deities are especially powerful. Lugh was associated with ravens and crows (especially in Gaul), birds known for their wisdom and prophetic powers. Ravens and crows were also associated with battlefields where they were seen to pick the eyes of dead warriors, making them fitting totems for a warrior god of exceptional prowess. Lugh had a famous spear and was a master of battle magic.

Lugh was understood to be a god who had taken human form in order to instruct the people. The ancient Celts believed that those who were great heroes on earth went to the sun after their death, and that those heroes would return to earth to aid humanity in times of need.

Lugh was associated with crafts and business in general, and was a patron of every art. He inaugurated the Lughnasad feast in honor of his foster mother Tailtiu, who was the wife of Eochaid Garb, king of the Fir Bolg (Men of the Bag). Tailtiu died of a broken heart as a result of her labor to clear the Wood of Cuan to create a plain of cultivation known as Oenach Tailten. The site later became a place of great assemblies sponsored by the High Kings of Eire.

The great Lughnasad assemblies featured horse races and other athletic competitions, poetry recitations, musical performances, the bestowal of ranks and honors, weddings, contracts, and a great display of artwork and crafts.

Rights and taxes were discussed at these intertribal gatherings. A creditor holding a brooch, a necklace, or earrings as pledges against a loan had to return them for the duration of the assembly or be fined for causing humiliation. Everyone tried to look their best.

Violence, marital discord, and the levying of debts were forbidden during the gatherings. Lughnasad marked the time when the warriors came home to help with the harvest.

The War-Mother-Fertility Goddess

The mother goddesses of Ireland were the patronesses of the great feasts. Some were local goddesses concerned with the fertility of the land and the soil, others were powerful divine mothers who had reared and nurtured the gods themselves (Tailtiu fits into the latter category).

The great trio of war-mother-fertility goddesses known as "the Morrigan" was associated with the Lughnasad feast. A triple goddess, the morrigan incarnated as three goddesses named Macha: Macha, wife of Nemed and leader of the Bolgic invasion, Macha the Red who dominated men by her wiles and physical force, and Macha, wife of Crunnchu, a farmer of Ulster who forced her to race against King Conchobar's horses though she was pregnant. Macha dutifully raced and won, and immediately gave birth to twins. Then she placed a curse on the men of Ulster for nine generations that whenever danger threatened they would become as weak as a woman in labor for five days and four nights. This is how Emhain Macha (Navan Fort) in Ulster got its name.

Markedly sexual, the Morrigan was a mistress of battle magic and shapeshifting who often appeared as a crow or raven, or as a beautiful woman dressed in splendid red raiment. She was appealed to by warriors to influence the course of battle by her magic.

An Old Celtic name for Lughnasad was Bron Trogain, "the sorrow of the earth," hinting at the seriousness with which the ancients regarded the harvesting of the earth's bounty. A god of warrior skill and a goddess of fertility and battle magic were invoked at Lughnasad because humans needed the intelligence and prophetic powers of ravens as well as divine magic, fertility, and skill to successfully bring in a crop that would feed the tribe over the long, barren winter.

Harvest Customs

In Scotland, it was the custom for farmers to circumambulate their fields with lit torches to *sain* the crops, protecting them from bad luck and evil sorcery. The first sheaf of wheat was ritually cut with great ceremony. The head of the clan would face the rising sun, cut the sheaf with a sickle, and then hold it aloft while turning on his or her heels three times sunwise.

The ear end of the grain sheaf was set on fire, which separated the grain from the straw, burned away the chaff, and hardened the grain all at once. The grain was then shaken and wiped to remove all ashes, and ground immediately into flour. It was important to grind the newly harvested grain and bake it into bread or cakes on the very same day. The cakes were then shared with the whole community.

Sacred Water at Lughnasad

The sun was at its height and the whole crop was not yet in at Lughnasad, so thunderstorms were wished for, to complete the growing cycle. It was considered very good luck to have rain on Lughnasad. Horses (associated with sacred fire in ancient thinking, much as cows were associated with sacred water) were immersed in and led through ponds and rivers as a ritual act of purification. Sacred wells, said to have particular healing virtues at this time, were visited.

Communal Activities

Today, young men and women still climb the hills looking for fruit (especially blueberries). Outdoor feasts take place, and many marriages are inspired by the events of the day, especially the more erotic activities that take place in secluded spots on the hillsides.

Interspersed with berry picking are games such as "leapfrog" and a Welsh harvest game called *rhibo,* where a young man and woman are tossed into the air on the linked arms of their compatriots, mimicking the winnowing of grain.

Groups of young men from different communities might fight with staves symbolizing the battle to bring in the harvest. Sometimes masked "monsters" and beasts threaten a figure representing Lugh, who has to triumph over them (symbolizing victory over forces that seek to damage the crops).

Garland Sunday is another traditional name for the festival, referring to the custom of wearing garlands of flowers and crowns of wheat in honor of the ancient Grain Goddess. Offerings of grain and fruit are laid at the base of local standing stones, which might also be garlanded with grains and flowers.

Men make chains of flowers and offer them to women. One woman is singled out to sit on a stone seat where flowers are offered to her as a living representative of the Grain Goddess. Flowers that have been used in the festival are later ritually buried, returning the energy of the celebration back to the land to nourish the next growing cycle.

Washing the Stones

Standing stones were venerated by ancient Celtic and pre-Celtic peoples. The stones were strategically placed to radiate energy to the land, much as acupuncture needles radiate energy to the meridians of the human body. It was felt that the sun would send energy through the stones to the soil. Special care was taken to keep the energy of the stones flowing and to strengthen the ties between the stones and the humans who depended on them for fertility.

At Lughnasad the stones are honored with food and flower offerings and with garlands of grains and flowers. The stones may be ritually washed with milk, water, and honey. At Samhain the stones are washed with a mixture of water, ashes from a sacred fire, and wine. At Imbolc the stones are again washed with milk, water, and honey. At Beltaine they are washed with milk, water, and ale or mead.

Traditional Foods at Lughnasad

To cut grain or dig potatoes before Lughnasad is considered very unlucky, but even if the harvest is not yet ripe, a small portion is gathered on the Lughnasad feast in order to make a ritual meal of "first fruits."

The usual fare at the feast is new potatoes, cabbage, fish, fowl, bacon, and fresh beef or mutton. A ritual focus for the meal is a bread pudding made from the new grain, which is gathered that day, dried by burning or in an oven, ground, and made into cake, bread, or porridge before evening.

Fresh berries served with cream and sugar are a traditional food for the Lughansad feast. Currants, gooseberries, blueberries, wild raspberries, or strawberries complete the meal. Many communities come together specifically to gather the berries. Blueberry Sunday, Heatherberry Sunday, and The Gooseberry Fair are some of the names for these gatherings.

Bread Pudding

Butter, softened to room temperature

7 slices bread

1 quart milk

3 eggs, beaten

1 cup sugar

scant tsp salt

1 cup blackberries (or blueberries, strawberries, raspberries, etc.)

1 teaspoon vanilla

Preheat oven to 325°F. Butter a 2-quart baking dish. Spread each slice of bread with butter and line the bottom and sides of the baking dish with bread, butter side up. Mix the milk, eggs, sugar, salt, berries, and vanilla together and pour over the bread. Place any extra bread slices on top and press down until submerged. Let stand for 10 minutes (longer if the bread is very dry). Bake covered for 30 minutes, then uncover and bake for 30 minutes more. For a brown upper crust, slip under the broiler for a few minutes. Serve warm with heavy cream.

SAMHAIN

Known as Halloween in modern times, this festival now takes place on October 31. However, Old Samhain was once a magical three-day interval celebrated November 9 to 11. This holy day was called *Oiche*

Shamhna, Oiche na Sprideanna, or *Sean-Shamhain* in Irish, *Samhuinn* in Scots Gaelic, *Hallow E'en* in English, *Calan Gaeaf* in Welsh, *Galen Gwaf* in Cornish, and *Kala-Goanv* in Breton.

The First Day of Winter

For the ancient Celts, the approach of Samhain meant completing the business of the agricultural year in preparation for the onset of winter. Crops of all kinds had to be safely stored, and cattle and sheep brought in from the hillsides to be quartered in the barn. Winter wheat had to be ground into flour by this date.

Turf and wood for the winter's fires had to be secured. Debts had to be recompensed, workers given their wages, rents paid. Fairs and markets were held, and communal gatherings where all contracts were settled.

Traditionally, from Samhain to Beltaine stories were told at night, around the hearth or fire. It was considered most unlucky to tell stories in the summer unless there was a very special reason (such as a wedding, an elopement, a battle, or in preparation for a voyage) because that was the season of outdoor activity.

The fianna, roving bands of free warriors with no allegiance to tribe or kin, were supported and provisioned by the Irish people from Samhain to Beltaine. (In the summer half of the year the fianna supported themselves by hunting.) In exchange the fianna policed the countryside, enforcing justice.

When the business of the old year was concluded, it was time to celebrate the three-day festival called Trinouxtion Samonii in the Coligny Calendar of the Gaulish Celts. It was a magical interval that marked the portal between the light half of the year and the dark half—the Celtic New Year.

For the Celts the day began at dusk and the year began in the dark—as all births begin, within the dark of the womb or in the moist dark of the earth. The start of the dark half of the year was a period of chaos and dissolution, breaking ground for the new cycle of growth to come. Tricks were played on unkind and unjust neighbors. Men and women exchanged clothing, a symbolic act in this magical period, showing that powers and perceptions were free to become extraordinary.

The poor wandered from door to door, seeking food and goods to help them through the winter. Families gathered to feast and entertain themselves and put out a spirit plate for any dead ancestors who might happen by.

It was important to leave a gift of blood for the land as a blessing and to ritually feed its powers. Fortunately this was not difficult, as pigs, cows, and other livestock that could not be fed and maintained through the long winter were culled before Samhain, their flesh to be salted, dried, smoked, or packed into sausages. Blood was readily available in every farmstead to be offered to the earth and the stones, and gifts of meat were made to the poor after the slaughtering.

The Fairies at Samhain

Above all, Samhain was a time of spirits: fairies, ghosts, and the ancestors. As at Beltaine, the walls between the worlds were at their thinnest, and it was easy for the beloved dead to pass over into the land of the living.

It was said that the Tuatha de Dannan appeared at Tara each Samhain. In the *Echtra Nerai,* which introduces *The Cattle Raid of Cooley* (the oldest vernacular epic in Western literature), it is related that King Aillil and Queen Medb left two recently executed criminals hanging in a tree until Samhain was safely past, because it was considered dangerous to touch a dead body when so many spirits were about. There was a grave risk that a man might be abducted by the Tuatha de Dannan and forcibly married to a fairy woman.

It was said that the fairy mounds were open at Samhain and that one could see and hear the sidhe at their feasting and drinking. The sidhe were the rulers of Samhain and had control over all the ghosts and spirits roaming the earth at that time.

The sidhe also controlled the fertility of the crops and the milk yield of cows. Throughout the year, they were propitiated with food offerings left out at night. At Samhain, offerings were left for the sidhe and for the spirits under their control, and for the spirits of the ancestors. (At Beltaine, the potent spirit night at the opposite side of the year, offerings were left for the sidhe and the dead as well.) In Celtic Brittany and in other Celtic areas, libations of milk were poured for the ancestral dead, near or on their tombs.

The last of the potato crop and the last of the grain were left outside as a gift for the fairies. It was said that on Samhain the fairies placed a blight upon all fruits left in the fields. It was forbidden to eat any unharvested produce after this time.

No blackthorn sticks (the traditional wood to make *shillelaghs*) could be cut on the eleventh of November.

Equal-armed wooden crosses, symbolic of the sun, were hung in the thatch, placed on the earth before the door, and hung in the barn to protect the cows. In Scotland these crosses were most often made of rowan, bound with red thread. Tiny rowan crosses were concealed in people's clothing as a protective charm (in some areas a cross of elder was used), a pre-Christian magical totem of protection for the wearer.

Breads and cakes for the feast were baked or toasted over a fire of rowan.

A necklace of red rowan berries was worn by Highland women as protection. Great ladies wore a necklace of amber for the same purpose.

In the Christian era, holy water was sprinkled on doors and in stables, on babies and young children as a form of protection. A bit of iron (fairies have a dread of iron) or a dead coal from the hearth were placed in the cradle. Oatmeal and salt were ceremonially rubbed on children's foreheads as a charm against evil.

A candle was lit and left burning all night in the window of a room where someone had died. Candles and lanterns were left burning all night beside graves.

Turnips were hollowed out and fantastic faces carved into them; a candle was placed inside in hopes that evil spirits would be frightened away. The spirits of Samhain were often malevolent—the Puca (hobgoblin), the Black Pig, and the Headless Ghost were frequently seen. The spirits of persons who had been wronged in life were known to haunt their offenders.

If a troop of fairies appeared, the best defense was to take some dust from your shoe and throw it at them. This would cause them to surrender any captive humans in their clutches. To prevent abduction by fairies one would carry a black-handled knife or place a bit of steel, such as a needle, somewhere in one's clothing.

So many fairies and spirits were abroad that anyone throwing out a dish of dirty water had to yell *Seachain!* ("Watch out!") so that ghosts and fairies could avoid being splashed.

A Time for Divination

Samhain was a potent time for fortune-telling and divining the future. Cakes were baked with small tokens hidden inside; the recipients of these small objects would know their fate for the year. A ring foretold marriage; a coin, wealth; a button, bachelorhood; a thimble, spinsterhood. A wooden chip meant the finder would be beaten by his or her spouse. A religious medal meant the finder was destined to become clergy.

Objects were placed under the pillow to produce a dream of one's future mate. A piece of cake, the first spoonful of colcannon (a traditional potato dish) or the last spoonful from supper, apples, a cabbage head, a spade, or nine leaves of ivy were placed in a young lady's left stocking and tied with her right garter. Before going to sleep, the young lady would eat salt herring, salty porridge, or a mixture of flour, salt, and soot to induce thirst. That night she would dream of handing her future husband a drink of water.

Nuts or beans were assigned names and placed in the fire. The one that popped and flew the farthest indicated one's future spouse.

Samhain was a powerful time for weather divination. The direction of the prevailing wind at midnight foretold the direction of the prevailing winds that winter. The winds had unique qualities. To the tenth-century Irish, the north and northeast winds meant battle or sickness. The winds from the east, southeast, and south meant abundant fruit, fish, and grain. The winds from the southwest, west and northwest meant battle and famine. The wind from the west meant the death of a king.[1]

If the moon was clearly visible at midnight, the prevailing weather that winter would be fair. If the moon was clouded over there would be much rain. If clouds raced before the moon, they foretold a winter of storms.

A stick was placed in the river to see if the water was rising or falling. High water meant winter floods or high prices for crops in the New Year.

A Time for Mischief
In keeping with the atmosphere of chaos, tricks were played on unsuspecting neighbors, probably those who had violated the rules of hospitality. A carriage might be dismantled and parts left on the roof, or an entire vegetable crop spirited away and hidden. Cabbages and turnips were pelted at doors, and chimneys blocked to flood the house with smoke.

In a more sinister vein, those desiring the aid of evil spirits would crawl through a briar that had rooted at both ends to make their petitions.

Sacred Fire and Sacred Water
Healing wells and pools were thought to be particularly potent at the Fire Festivals. At Samhain, the petitioner approached the water by circumambulating it three times sunwise and then silvering it with coins. As he or she drank the water a wish or need was held in mind. Afterward, a small token such as a hairpin was left near the water, or a small strip of cloth might be tied to a branch of a nearby tree. These actions were a way of casting off the troubles to be left behind. Everything had to be done in silence, before sunrise. On no account

were these cloths, pins, or other objects to be touched, lest the ill luck they carried be transferred to another person.

As with all the Fire Festivals, bonfires were a central aspect of the celebration. In ancient times a great central fire was lit by Druids at Tlaghtga (near Tara), the burial place of the daughter of Mogh Ruith, the Druid. Herself a great sorceress, Tlaghtga became conflated with the Land Goddess to whom the fire was dedicated. The fire was made with nine sacred woods: willow, hazel, alder, birch, rowan, yew, ash, elm, and oak. All household flames were extinguished, and runners carried torches back to the provinces, bearing fresh flames from the goddess's pyre. Thus, as at Beltaine, the kingdoms and tribes were spiritually united through the medium of sacred fire.

The Deities of Samhain

The Horned God Cernunnos was said to lead his wild hunt through the skies at Samhain, gathering in wandering spirits to bring them home to the underworld.

On the Isle of Lewis, offerings of ale were made to the sea god Shony, in hopes that he would cause rich crops of seaweed to wash onto the shore for use as food and compost for the fields. Throughout Scotland, NicNevin (daughter of Nemain), an aspect of the Morrigan, was honored, and the Cailleach, in her guise as the harsh Land Goddess of Winter.

Preparing for the Feast

Apples and nuts (especially hazelnuts) were sacred foods of the Samhain feast. Hazels were sacred to the Goddess because of the "milk" found in the green nut. Children born in autumn were fed the milk of the nuts mixed with honey to strengthen them.

Apples were sacred because they grew in Avalloch (Avalon), the Celtic Land of the Dead. An apple branch or a single apple could magically transport one to the Otherworld. Apples were associated with immortality, possibly because those who ate them remained healthy and lived long lives.

Children and youths with their faces painted or wearing masks went door-to-door asking for apples, nuts, bread, cake, butter, milk, cheese, or eggs, anything to help them make a party. The procession was led by a mysterious figure wrapped in a white sheet and having a mare's head. This figure was known as the White Mare, or "hobby horse," and may have been a symbol of the Land Goddess to whom offerings were due.

Games were played that featured apples, such as bobbing for them from a vat of water. The water was first "silvered" by tossing in a few silver coins, the traditional offering of peace to water and waves. Water is the medium through which the ancestors can be contacted, adding further symbolism to the sport.

Another apple game featured a stick tied to the end of a rope with an apple stuck onto one end of the stick and a lit candle affixed to the other. As the rope was swung in a circle the object was to catch the apple in one's teeth. (For younger children a potato was substituted for the lit candle, in the interest of safety.)

Traditional Foods at Samhain

A place was set at the table for the use of the beloved dead, and offerings of food and drink were placed there. It was forbidden for any mortal to touch or consume this food.

Traditional foods were eaten, especially foods with nine ingredients. Nine is the number of death and of transformation, and of the nine maidens who guard the Cauldron of Inspiration in the depths of Annwn, the Celtic underworld of the dead. See A Time for Divination above.

Here are some foods appropriate to the Samhain Feast, each consists of nine ingredients.

Stwmp Naw Rhyw

Mashed potato, carrot, turnip, peas, parsnips, leeks, pepper, salt, and milk.

Vegetable Pancakes

Flour, milk, baking powder, salt, grated cheese, sautéed vegetables (such as zucchini and onions), and basil and marjoram, served with sour cream on the side.

Fruit Crepes

Filled with a filling of mixed fruits, especially apples. Horn-shaped cookies, cakes, and breads. Apple pies and pastries. Hazelnuts.

IMBOLC

The festival of Imbolc (in the bag, in the belly), or Oimelc (ewe milk) in Scotland, is celebrated on February 1 and 2, or when the ewes begin to lactate. It is also called *La Fheile Bride* in Ireland, because it is also the festival of the goddess Brigid or Bride, patroness of the flocks, herds, and motherhood. The observance is called *Gwyl Mair Dechraur Gwanwyn* in Wales, *Laa'l Breeshey* in the Isle of Man, and *Goel Kantolyon* Brittany. The English name for the festival was once Candlemas, which eventually evolved into the Groundhog Day festival of modern times.

The Feast Day of Brigid

Saint Brigid is one of the best known and most venerated of Celtic saints. She has been given many titles: The Lady of the Isles, Bride of the Mantle, Gentle Shepherdess, Guardian of the Cattle, Protector of the Newborn, Nursemaid to the Sick, Midwife of Mary, and Mary of the Gael. Saint Brigid was said to have been reared on the milk of a white cow with red ears, the typical colorations of a Celtic Otherworld beast. She was said to possess a girdle that could heal all disease.

But long before Brigid the saint there was another Brigid, one whose identity and feast day were gradually subsumed by the later historical figure, a goddess who was known as Brigid in Ireland, Bride in Scotland, and Brigantia in Britain. Daughter of the Daghda, she was a triple goddess, said to always appear as three sisters, each named Brigid. Her spheres of influence were poetry, smithcraft, and healing. She was the patroness of the Druids and bards. The Brigantes, a British Celtic tribe, honored Brigantia as The High One and Mother of the Gods. She was the most prominent pan-Celtic female deity.

Brighid was especially associated with healing wells and springs, and with sacred fire. As Brigantia she was especially concerned with the flocks and herds and with the produce of the earth. These spheres were later taken up by Saint Brigid of Kildare, patroness of numerous holy wells, whose fire temple was tended by nine maidens until the Pope declared it heretical and shut it down. (The perpetual fire of Brigid has recently been relit by nuns in Ireland, and Pagans and Christians across the globe are once again tending fires in her name.)

Brigid's sacred bird was the oystercatcher, also called *giolla bride* (Irish for Brigid's servant) and *brideun* (Scots Gaelic, meaning Brigid's bird), which was said to guide people who were under her protection. Her mother was Boann, Cow Goddess of the White Moon and Goddess of the Boyne River in Ireland, making cows her sacred animals. She was also associated with the white mare, the serpent, and red-eared, white-bodied hounds who guide travelers to the otherworld.

Imbolc marks the midpoint of the dark half of the year. It also marks the beginning of the lactation of the ewes, an all-important milk festival of the ancients. The name of the festival may derive from *m(b)lig*, "milk," or the Old Celtic *ouimelko,* "ewes' milk."

Along with the streams of new milk, Imbolc marks the time when other streams of life are reinvigorated in the land—forest animals begin their mating rituals and serpents begin to stir in their lairs. Farmers test the soil to see if it is thawed enough for the first plowings, and snowdrops spring up in the spots where Brigid's feet have trod.

At this time the Hag of Winter, the Cailleach, who has ruled since Samhain, visits the Well of Youth. At dawn on the day of the festival she drinks from the Well of Youth and her face is transformed from haggard old age to the serene and youthful face of Brigid. For this reason, Brigid is sometimes called The Maiden of the Rising Sun.

The Cailleach carries a Druid wand of great power, a white rod, or slachdan, made of birch, willow, bramble, or broom. With its magic powers she controls the elements and the weather. Brigid carries a white rod too; but, whereas the Cailleach's rod brings storms and harsh weather, Brigid's brings warm winds and new life.

It was said that where Brigid walked over the waters or touched them with her finger the ice melted, and that the land turned green where she spread her mantle upon it or when she breathed upon the hills. Families would leave a mantle or a cloth outdoors on the eve of the festival to be blessed by the sun and by Brigid on Imbolc morn. The mantle was later used to cover the sick, and the cloth would be cut into strips to be tied onto a sick person or animal throughout the remaining year.

Purification by Fire and Water

Imbolc celebrates the rekindling of the fires in the earth that give life and movement to plants and animals. Seeds burst open, sap rises, and animals begin their mating rites. The fire in the sun begins to wax noticeably. Imbolc marks the time when it is no longer necessary to carry a candle to do the early morning chores. Candles are left burning on windowsills all night to mark the seasonal passage.

Brigid's blessings are invoked on the forge and on the tools of the smith, and also on agricultural implements and the plow, the product of the smith's transformative art. Smithcraft is potent magic, the ability to fashion metallic ore into bronze or iron, and is directly under the sanction of Brigid.

To this day in Ireland there are numerous holy wells dedicated to

Brigid. The ancient Celts marked the beginning of each agricultural cycle by purifying themselves with water. The feet, hands, and head were ritually washed and who better to bless the waters than Brigid herself? Fire and water were seen as the building blocks of creation, the basic foundations for all transformative magic. By invoking a fire goddess in the waters the stage was set for growth and change.

The Solar Cross of the Goddess

At Imbolc, equal-armed solar crosses were plaited from rushes to bring luck to the home. In the Western Isles of Scotland the women dressed a doll, named her Brigid, and placed her in a reed basket. On Imbolc Eve, at sunset, they circled the house three times sunwise, carrying the basket, and then moved from house to house carrying Brigid's crosses and lit candles to every home in the village.

In parts of Ireland the eldest daughter of the house gathered rushes and brought them home, where she was formally welcomed by the family as a representative of Brigid. The girl would then go through the house, blessing the home, the food and drink within it, and especially the hearth.

A solar cross-shaped bread was placed on top of the rushes to be eaten later, or crumbs from the cross-shaped bread were strewn on the rushes. The whole family participated in the making of *crosoga,* equal-armed crosses to be hung in the home and placed in windows. Rushes might be left by the fire overnight, covered by a white cloth, as a "Bride's Bed." The Goddess was invited to sleep there overnight, thus empowering the rushes with her healing strength.

Any left over rushes were used for healing work throughout the year. They could be tied to the horns of cattle as protection or fastened to the handle of the churn to prevent hexing of the milk. They could also be tied around an ailing limb or placed around the neck of one who was ill.

A *crios bride,* a hoop of straw with four solar crosses tied to it, was carried from home to home. Men would step through it and women would lower it over their heads and step through it three times to mark a ritual "rebirth."

In some areas a *brideog*, a straw doll wearing child's clothing, would be carried from house to house by young girls who sang and recited prayers at every door, where they were given small gifts in exchange. Often the girls would meet at the last house for a party with music and dancing.

Sometimes a single woman was chosen to carry a solar cross from door to door. She was understood to be the representative of Brigid, bringing blessings to each household. In Munster and Connacht the procession was composed entirely of men, dressed in white skirts and with conical straw masks over their heads. (I actually witnessed this rite in Ulster when a group of men appeared suddenly, dressed in white robes and with plaited straw masks, uttering poetry.)

To Make a Brigid's Cross

Collect reeds from a nearby bog or pond and soak them overnight in water to make them pliable. The length of your cross will be about the length of one cut reed, so try to collect a bundle of reeds that is the length of the size cross you want (usually 12 to 15 inches).

1. Take two of the reeds and place them one over the other to make a cross shape.
2. Fold one of the reeds back on itself to loop it around the other one.
3. Take a fresh reed and fold it around the second one, parallel to the first.
4. Bend a fourth reed over the third to make a cross again.
5. Bend a fifth reed around the fourth parallel to the single strand.

6. Keep folding reeds around the previous one until the central square is about two inches in width.

7. Bind each of the arms with a tied reed or with natural wool. Hang the cross in the window or elsewhere in the home or barn.

Snakes and Hedgehogs

> *Moch maduinn Bhride, thig an nimhir as*
> *an toll;*
> *Cha bhoin mise ris an nimhir, Cha bhoin an*
> *nimhir rium.*
>
> Early on Bride's morn, the serpent will come from
> the hollow;
> I will not molest the serpent, nor will the serpent
> molest me.
>
> TRADITIONAL

In Scottish tradition a snake was said to emerge from its mound on Oimelc, its motions and behavior determining the remaining days of frost. If the snake became active, a thaw was imminent. If it returned to its nest, a month more of winter was to be expected.

The serpent is an ancient symbol of the powers of the earth and of the Spirit that motivates the forces of growth, decay, and transformation. As the serpent sheds its skin, it illustrates the eternal powers of renewal inherent in the land. Snakes are also a symbol of healing. Pictish stone carvings often depict sacred snakes.

In Ireland it was the hedgehog who made an Imbolc appearance, and in the modern United States it is the groundhog who carries on the tradition.

Traditional Foods at Imbolc

To celebrate the lactation of the ewes, butter is a traditional addition to any Imbolc dish. Cake, bread, butter, or porridge are placed in the window and left as an offering for Brigid's white cow, with whom she travels. The next morning these foods, blessed by Brigid, are eaten by the household or shared with the needy. Straw or fresh rushes are left on the doorstep overnight as well, in hopes that the Goddess will stop there and bless the home. Butter or oil left out on Imbolc Eve is saved to make healing salves and ointments later in the season.

The blackberry is an herb sacred to Brigid. Its leaves are used to poultice wounds and burns and its roots are made into a tea to cure diarrhea. Crawling under a blackberry bush was once regarded as a potent charm against rheumatism, boils, and blackheads. The whole plant was valued as a charm against disease. Blackberry pies, jams, jellies, and wines can be added to the feast in Brigid's honor.

In Scotland a *bonnach bride* or bannock of Bride was made at Imbolc, a *bonnach Bealltain* at Beltaine, a *bonnach Lunastain* at Lughnasad, and a *bonnach Samthain* at Samhain. In each case a large cake was baked for the family and smaller cakes for each family member. The family walked out into the fields to eat the cakes, throwing a piece over each shoulder and offering it to dangerous spirits who might harm the fields and flocks such as wolf, fox, eagle, hawk, martin, and raven. The cakes and breads used in this way featured hidden fruits and nuts.

In Brittany the ubiquitous crepe is the traditional festival dish. Here is a potato dish from Ireland that can be served at Imbolc or on any of the major Fire Festivals.

Colcannon

Chop and shred a white cabbage and cook until tender. Steam 8 medium potatoes and pass through a food mill, or boil until soft and mash in a hot pan. Chop a bunch of scallions and simmer lightly in 1½ cups milk for 5 minutes. Beat the scallions into the mashed potatoes until smooth and fluffy. Fold in the cabbage. Add salt and pepper to taste. Serve with a large lump of butter melting on top and a glass of cold milk. (This dish is also traditional at Samhain.)

Dandelions are particularly associated with Brigid and so are sacred to this Feast Day.

Dandelion Salad

In Ireland, dandelions, with their yellow solar flowers and their milky white sap, first bloom at the time of Brigid's festival, and their greens make a healthful early spring dish. The roots are medicine for the liver and the flowers are used to make a yellow wine.

Soak the new greens and freshly grated roots for 20 minutes in cold water with 2 tablespoons vinegar added to remove possible parasites. Rinse thoroughly and toss lightly with lemon juice, olive oil, and sea salt. Try adding slivered onions, grated carrot, baby lettuce, violet leaves and flowers, or spinach. Top with grated garlic or nutmeg, or grated lemon peel for variety. Add dandelion greens to soups or boil the greens like spinach.

The following is a rich dessert cake that is expensive but well worth the effort.

Porter Cake

Melt 1 cup butter and 1 cup brown sugar in 1 cup porter (a type of dark ale) in a saucepan. Add 6 cups total of mixed fruit (equal portions of currants, raisins, slivered almonds, and about half as much mixed candied peel) and simmer for 10 minutes. Allow to cool completely and add 4 cups sieved flour, ½ teaspoon baking soda, 1 teaspoon grated lemon zest, and 1 teaspoon allspice. Beat 3 eggs and fold in with a wooden spoon.

Pour into a greased 9-inch cake pan and bake in a preheated oven at 325°F for about 1½ hours. Test with a skewer and remove when the skewer comes out clean. Allow cake to cool in the tin.

Boxty Cakes

½ pound hot cooked potatoes
½ pound grated raw potatoes
2 cups flour
1 teaspoon baking soda
1½ cups buttermilk
Butter for frying
Salt and pepper

Drain, peel, and mash the hot potatoes. Stir in the raw, grated potatoes, flour, and baking soda. Add salt and pepper to taste. Mix with enough buttermilk to make a stiff batter. Shape into 3-inch patties about ¼-inch thick and fry on hot greased griddle until crispy and golden on both sides. (Makes 12 cakes.)

Oatcakes

2 cups uncooked, old-fashioned rolled oats (not instant)
1¼ cups buttermilk
2½ cups sifted bread flour
1 teaspoon baking soda
½ teaspoon baking powder
1 teaspoon salt
Vegetable oil spray

A day ahead, combine the oats and buttermilk in a small bowl. Blend thoroughly, cover, and refrigerate overnight. The next day, preheat the oven to 350°F. Remove the oat mixture from the refrigerator. Combine the bread flour, baking soda, baking powder, and salt in a large bowl. Slowly add the oat mixture and stir with a wooden spoon 20 to 30 times, or until you have a smooth dough. Grease a baking sheet with the oil spray. Turn the dough onto the baking sheet, and use your hands to form a round, cake-shaped loaf about 1-inch thick. Use a sharp knife or pizza cutter to cut the dough into 4 quarters. Move the quarters apart slightly, but keep them in the original round shape. Bake until the cakes are light golden brown and firm to the touch, 30 to 35 minutes. Cool slightly on a rack, and serve with butter and jam or preserves. Makes 1 loaf (in quarters).[2]

Traditional Bannocks and Breads for the Fire Festivals

You can easily make your own homemade butter to go with the breads. Place whole heavy cream (not low fat) in a jar with a tight lid and shake vigorously for about twenty minutes.

Welsh Speckled Bread (Bara Brith)
  1 pound flour
  1 pound mixed dried fruit
  2 tablespoons warm orange marmalade
  1 egg, beaten
  6 ounces brown sugar
  ½ pint warm, strained tea
  1 teaspoon allspice

Place fruit and sugar in mixing bowl and soak overnight in the strained tea. Sift the flour and spice and warm the marmalade. Add flour, marmalade, and beaten egg to soaked fruit. Mix well and pour the mixture into a greased loaf tin. Bake for 1½ hours at 350°F. Cool on wire rack. Serve sliced with butter.

Irish Barm Brack
From *From Celtic Hearths* by Deborah Krasner
  3 pounds flour
  2 ounces yeast

2 teaspoons salt

1½ pints milk

4 ounces butter

4 ounces sugar

1 pound sultanas

4 ounces currants and raisins, mixed

4 ounces mixed peel (such as candied orange or lemon peels)

1 teaspoon allspice

Sift together all the dry ingredients except the sugar into a bowl. Mix the yeast with 1 tsp sugar and half the milk. Sprinkle a little flour on top, and leave in a warm place for 10 minutes. Mix in flour, add remaining liquid, and mix thoroughly. Knead into a ball and turn onto a floured surface. Knead for 15 minutes, or until the dough no longer feels sticky. Punch down, and flatten into a large round. Place butter, sugar, and dried fruit in the middle, and work these ingredients into the dough by kneading it until they are evenly distributed. Return the dough to greased bowl, let rise for another 30 minutes. Divide in half, and shape to fit loaf tins. Cover and leave to rise until dough reaches top of tins. Brush with milk and bake for about 50 minutes at 400°F or until hollow. Serve sliced with butter.

Welsh Oatcakes (Bara Ceirch)

2 cups rolled oats

2 tablespoons unsalted butter

½ teaspoon salt

⅓ cup hot water

Preheat oven to 350°F. Take 1½ cups oats and grind in a quern until it becomes coarse meal (use a food processor if you don't have a quern). Cut in the butter and salt until the mix resembles coarse meal. Add the water and work in until you can make a ball. Sprinkle some oats on a board. Flatten the ball of dough and roll out to a thickness of ⅛ inch, sprinkling a few oats on top to prevent sticking. Place on oiled or air-bake nonstick cookie sheet and cut into cracker-sized shapes. Bake until edges are crisp and brown, 20 to 25 minutes. Makes about 25 pieces, depending on size. Serve with honey, butter, and cheese.

For additional breads see http://cathf.addr.com/recipe1.htm

Ogham Divination

Every Forest Druid needs to have a set of Ogham divination tools. These can be a set of twenty sticks with one Ogham letter inscribed or burned into each stick, or stones with an Ogham letter painted on each small pebble, or small ceramic discs with a single Ogham letter glazed onto each one. (When making your set of Ogham divination tools, please be sure to put a dot or other symbol at the top of each letter. Otherwise, you will never know which way is up and the letters will be impossible to read.)

DRUID METHODS
FOR USING THE OGHAMS

There are a variety of ways Druids can use the Ogham Tree Alphabet for divination. This chapter describes some of those methods. The divinatory meanings associated with each of the tree letters can be found in the next chapter.

Divination Using One Ogham Tree
The simplest divination technique is to reach into a bag with all of the Ogham letters in it and pull out one. Meditate on the qualities of the tree you have picked and apply this information toward answering your question.

Divination of Past, Present, and Future

A slightly more involved method is to draw three tree letters: one for the past, one for the present, and one for the future. Use the three to understand your situation.

Here is an example:

First Ogham drawn—Blackthorn

Second Ogham drawn—Birch

Third Ogham drawn—Oak

One possible interpretation of this (depending on the question asked) is that you have come through a difficult or painful patch in the recent past as shown by the presence of Blackthorn. In the present the powers of Birch are with you, indicating a new beginning and a clear direction. Oak is telling you that your feet will be firmly on the ground and your head in the skies in the near future; a nicely balanced forecast of enduring success.

Ogham as a Tool of Blessing

Three Oghams can be selected and buried near the front door or in the center of a ritual area to bless it with positive energies and protection.

Making an Ogham Cairn

Next in complexity is the Ogham cairn, composed of five Ogham trees. After grounding and centering yourself, hold your question in mind and place one randomly drawn letter in the north, the direction of battle. This tree will illuminate your struggle and tell you what forces you will be fighting to overcome.

Next, place a letter in the east, which will illuminate your path to prosperity. This letter represents your physical well-being, work, and possessions.

Then place a letter in the south, the direction of the creative arts and feelings. This tree will give you guidance with your creative life.

The next letter should be placed in the west, the direction of mind, intellect, and thoughts. It will illuminate and inspire your mental work and efforts.

Finally, place a letter in the center, the position of self-mastery. It will tell you what you need to do in order to act with authority in the situation you are pondering.

Other letters can be pulled and read. For example, you could pull one to illuminate your spiritual path and another to divine the will of the gods in the matter at hand.

Doing Ogham Readings for Others

Have the querent hold the Ogham sticks or stones in his or her hands and focus on a question. Then ask the querent to hand the sticks or stones back to you while continuing to focus on the question (which does not have to be stated out loud).

Scatter the stones or sticks before the two of you, taking note of which letters lie close to each other, which are closest to you, and which are further away. The closest letters are more significant than those that are at a distance. (Keep in mind that the meaning or import of a tree can be shaded by the tree that is next to it.)

The process is repeated three times. The first time, the purpose of the reading is to determine the present state of the querent. The second reading is to divine the future fate of the querent, and to make a prediction for the coming year (or another span of time). The third reading is to determine what the querent can do to influence his or her own fate in the situation.

If the querent's questions are not addressed or answered it means that there is something more important that he or she needs to know. Advise the querent to be prepared for a message from the gods concerning this matter.

Drum Divination

I have a shaman's drum on which I have painted the Ogham letters in a circle around the edge. I have a small bag of dried apple seeds that I use to do drum divination. I hold the drum flat in a horizontal position and place a small mound of about ten or fifteen apple seeds in the center. Then I tap softly on the skin of the drum with my drumstick. Eventually, the apple seeds begin to pop out of the mound and land on certain letters. I continue until I have enough letters to do a reading (maybe three to five).

Divination with Living Trees

A very nice technique is to do the Tree Meditation described on pages 152–53 and while you are in that altered state of awareness, walk through the forest with your eyes half-lidded, using slow, careful steps. At some point one particular tree will attract your attention. Determine the species and meditate on its qualities. This becomes your divination for the day.

All blessings on your work with the trees!

Divinatory Meanings

BIRCH—*BEITH*

Insight: Birch reminds us to act cleanly in a situation, to avoid distractions and to get the job done. She also reminds us to honor the eternal feminine principle.

Divinatory Meaning: If birch has entered your awareness today, you are being asked to "clean up your act." Perhaps you need to focus enough to finish a project, organize a paper, spruce up the house and yard, get the bills paid, or come to a final decision about some long put-off issue. Alternatively, birch may be inviting you to honor your vulnerability and your feminine, nurturing qualities, or those qualities as they exist in someone you know, or in women and men in general.

Affirmation: O Lady Birch, I honor you and respect you. Show me the straight path of wisdom. Lead me safely through dark forests and bring me home to the Eternal Clear Light.

ROWAN—*LUIS*

Insight: Rowan reminds us to strengthen our personal protection and our spiritual shields.

Divinatory Meaning: If rowan has been brought to your awareness today, you are being reminded to strengthen your shields. As a spiritual warrior you may be facing challenges to your strength, your patience, or your integrity. Use the protective aura of rowan to repel all forces that threaten your inner peace, while allowing in only those influences that brighten and uplift your spirit.

Affirmation: O Red Lady Rowan, Enchantress of Old, I place myself in your circle of light, that it may shield me from all harm.

ALDER—*FEARN*

Insight: Alder reminds us to build bridges in the face of conflict, rather than allowing ourselves to be storm-tossed on the seas of passion.

Divinatory Meaning: Alder is a tree of protection, especially from the painful excesses of watery emotion. Use the protective power of alder to withstand tidal waves of fear and anger and storms of doubt in yourself and in others. If alder has come into your awareness today it may be that you need a raft to float you gently over a sea of troubled feelings.

Affirmation: O Alder of the waters, strengthen me today. Show me the way to direct my passion into clear channels of focused activity, that I may bring change and healing to my situation.

WILLOW—*SAILLE*

Insight: Willow reminds us to adjust to circumstances by bending with the flow and by speaking and treading softly.

Divinatory Meaning: If willow has come into your awareness today, there is some aspect of your life that needs to soften. Perhaps you are being hard on yourself or on someone else. Willow asks that we whisper rather than shout, and teaches us to bend gracefully with circumstances. Willow reminds us to keep our awareness of Spirit, even as we negotiate the tasks of daily life, and to be ever aware of the inherent beauty of existence.

Affirmation: O Willow tree, great Lady of the Moon, show me the way to make my feelings flow, that I may reach out to others with Your gentle healing touch.

ASH—*NUIN*

Insight: Ash gives us the courage and strength of the sun as we face the trials of life.

Divinatory Meaning: If ash has been brought to your awareness today, you are being called to examine some aspect of your life in which action needs to be taken. Perhaps a habit needs to be broken or a relationship needs adjustment. It could be that some change is needed in your creative life, your work life, or your spiritual path. Ash will give you the courage and determination to persevere in the contests life brings. Ash is a solar tree, bringing courage and strength of will, along with the wisdom to bend like a mighty bow when compromise is called for.

Affirmation: O Ash of power, Ash of the Sun's light, lend me your strength today. Bring me vitality in Spirit, body, and mind!

HAWTHORN—*HUATH*

Insight: Hawthorn reminds us that love can be beautiful, and to beware its hidden thorns.

Divinatory Meaning: If hawthorn has been brought to your awareness today, you may need to look into matters of the heart. Like the hawthorn tree in flower, love is sometimes delightfully joyful. Long and steady relationships bear fruit that sustain us through life's cold and difficult passages. But beware the thorns hidden among the fruits and flowers. It has been said that a true lover's heart is always half broken, and that we tend to hurt those we love best.

Affirmation: O Hawthorn tree, harbinger of summer's light and of lovers' joyful unions, may I be wise in the ways of love. Help me to celebrate love's fruitful blossoms even as I make light of its thorns.

OAK—*DAIR*

Insight: Oak reminds us to stay centered and balanced, with our roots in the ground and our head in the spiritual skies.

Divinatory Meaning: The oak tree is a symbol of balance; its mighty branches reach to the heavens and attract lightning while its roots dig deep into the soil. If stout oak has come to your awareness today, you are being reminded to seek balance in your life. Perhaps a spiritual path or some other obsession has kept your head in the clouds too long. Or is it time to pay attention to your earthbound concerns? Has your mundane existence taken over, leaving you feeling tired, trapped, and frustrated? It may be time to poke your head in the clouds to gain a fresh perspective.

Affirmation: O mighty Oak, luminous Being of strength and of Fire, like you I gaze fearlessly at the eternal Divine while staying grounded in mind, body, and Spirit.

HOLLY—*TINNE*

Insight: Holly reminds us to sharpen our wits and strengthen our resolve as we face life's spiritual battles.

Divinatory Meaning: If holly has come to your awareness today, you are being offered assistance in life's trials. As a spiritual warrior you may feel abandoned from time to time, as if you have been left to face life's battles alone. Holly reminds you to take heart from your plant allies, who are always with you, if you but take the time to remember.

Affirmation: Spirit of the Holly, I call on you now. Give me the courage to face life's trials with strength, determination, and certitude.

HAZEL—*COLL*

Insight: Hazel reminds us to seek for the source of things, the origins of a situation or problem, and the ultimate Source of all being.

Divinatory Meaning: If hazel has come to your awareness today, you are being reminded to seek the deepest roots of something. It may be a recurring life situation or a habit that seems hard to shake. Only by swimming backwards in time to the origin of the problem will you be able face it head on and come to the necessary realizations. It is by facing feelings directly that they can be felt, integrated, and transformed.

Affirmation: O Hazel of Wisdom, thank you for your presence here today. Lead me, like the salmon, to the deepest source of inspiration and joy.

APPLE—*QUERT*

Insight: Apple reminds us to cultivate joy and optimism in every situation, in this life and the next.

Divinatory Meaning: If apple has come to your awareness today, you are being reminded to meditate on the sweetness that life has to offer. If you are feeling bitter about something, remember that Mother Nature is always renewing herself, and that growth and evolution are her goal in everything she does. Learn to see your situation as a gift, moving you ever closer to your destiny.

Affirmation: O Apple, whose fruit is of love and of the Spirit, I, like you, am sheltering and nurturing to all who come near.

VINE—*MUIN*

Insight: Vine reminds us that work is a form of prayer, and that by making an effort we benefit all of sacred creation.

Divinatory Meaning: If vine has entered your awareness today, you are being advised that effort is called for. There may be a project or a relationship that needs care and attention, or you may be putting too much effort into something that would better be dropped. Vine reminds us that life requires noble sacrifice, and that all lives must ultimately give their life force for the good of the whole.

Affirmation: O Vine, lend me your strength and endurance, that I may serve all beings with my breath and my blood, even as I have been served by the generations before me.

IVY—*GORT*

Insight: Ivy reminds us that nature provides enough for all. She makes large grassy fields for kings, to hold gatherings, to race upon, and to nourish their horses, and ivy to feed the widow's herd. When the grasses stop blooming, she gives ivy blossoms to the bees.

Divinatory Meaning: If ivy has entered your awareness today, you are being reminded that all things have their place in sacred creation. Everything is unfolding as it should and there are no mistakes. See what sweetness and wisdom you can gather from your experiences, to bring back to the people.

Affirmation: O Ivy who blooms in the chill Autumn wind, show me the way to gather the light of my Higher Self and share it with all Beings.

REED—*NGETAL*

Insight: Reed gives strength to the physician and is an attribute of Brigid, patroness of all healers.

Divinatory Meaning: If reed has come into your awareness today, you are being asked to focus on your own healing or on someone else's. Know that the strength and guidance of Brigid is with you. Like the arrows that were once made of reed stalks, let Brigid's fiery arrow guide your hands, heart, and intuition to any person, place, or thing that needs healing energy.

Affirmation: O Reed, may I, like you, be a hollow channel for the healing fire of Brigid to flow, wherever it is needed, in myself or in others.

BLACKTHORN—*STRAIF*

Insight: Blackthorn enables us to walk within a circle of protection but beware its thorns.

Divinatory Meaning: If blackthorn has entered your awareness today, it is a sign that a struggle is approaching or that a struggle may have recently passed. Either way, it is a life and death matter for your body, your mind, or your spirit. Use the protective energy of blackthorn to strengthen your personal shields and to fearlessly face your trials.

Affirmation: O Blackthorn, I may dread the fight but I *KNOW* I am protected in body, mind, and Spirit.

ELDER—*RUIS*

Insight: Elder reminds us to honor the mother principle of the universe and to work selflessly for the betterment of all beings.

Divinatory Meaning: If elder has entered your awareness today, you are being reminded to honor the mother principle that exists in the universe. The Great Mother regards all of creation as her children, from the smallest dancing atom to the great exploding stars. Look into the eyes of the next being you encounter and see that creature through her eyes, as your divine child, to be cherished and cared for.

Affirmation: O Elder Mother, teach me to care for your children, ever remembering that I, too, am a child of the Goddess.

SILVER FIR—*AILM*

Insight: Silver fir reminds us to cleanse our minds of all that is inessential, and to focus on who we were before we were born and who we will remain after we leave this planet.

Divinatory Meaning: If silver fir has come into your awareness today, you are being reminded to look at the big picture of your life's situation. Which aspects are *truly* urgent and demanding of your attention, and which are simply distractions, unimportant in the greater scheme of things? What is your soul's purpose, which you have carried here from before you were born and will take with you when you leave the earth plane? What really matters in the great scheme of things?

Affirmation: O Silver Fir whose origins are in the stars, we, like you, are star stuff, destined for eternity.

FURZE—*ONN*

Insight: If furze has come into your awareness today, you are being advised that something dear to you needs a wall of protection.

Divinatory Meaning: Furze is a shield for things that are precious. It may be your spiritual path that is threatened by the doubt of others, or a relationship that needs to be surrounded by a hedge of attention and care. Does your heart need guarding? Is there a person, place, or thing that needs extra loving and care? Is that person yourself? Use the warrior shield of furze to block out negativity, so that your most tender and exalted feelings may flourish. Let furze bestow a protective aura of courage that has all the strength of the sun.

Affirmation: O Furze of the golden blossoms, give me courage. I call upon the Sacred Warrior Spirit within me to protect all that I hold dear.

HEATHER—*ÚR*

Insight: If heather has come into your awareness today, there is sweetness to be gathered.

Divinatory Meaning: Heather is a favorite of the bees. Use your "bee wisdom" to learn a lesson today. What gift has the universe brought? Amplify it, celebrate it in word, song, or picture, and bring it back to your tribe. *Know* that this is your lucky day.

Affirmation: O Heather, thank you for your sweetness, thank you for the joy you bring to my Spirit! I am sharing it with everyone I meet.

ASPEN—*EDAD*

Insight: Aspen reminds us to strengthen our communication with the ancestors, the spirits, and the gods and godesses.

Divinatory Meaning: Throughout the ages, aspen has been thought of as a tree of communication with the gods and goddesses and spirits, especially the spirits of the dead. Its trembling leaves are said to whisper messages to the winds, carrying them to the otherworld. If aspen has come to your awareness today, you are being reminded to strengthen your communication with spiritual realms. Have the everyday concerns and distractions of life pulled you away from your daily communion with the sacred? Has your relationship with your patron deity lapsed or gone unattended? Another meaning may be that something has passed, or is passing, out of your life. Give thanks for all that has been, and prepare to welcome change. Take a moment from your day to offer up a prayer of thanks, or to make an offering of sweet smoke or flowers.

Affirmation: Trembling Aspen! Like you I stand in awe of the Divine as it manifests within and without creation, and I am offering up a prayer of thanks.

YEW—*IDAD*

Insight: Yew reminds us that all nature grows in cycles, and that our creative talents and self-healing powers are constantly renewed.

Divinatory Meaning: If yew has been brought to your awareness today, you are being asked to examine some aspect of your life that has been allowed to stagnate and wither. Is there a talent or skill that you have been neglecting? Are you allowing an all-consuming passion for something to steal time and energy from other important areas of your life? Perhaps you have neglected your body, or your diet and exercise program. Or is there some demon of sickness, fear, or loss of faith that is preventing you from expressing your full potential? It is time to focus on the ancient self-healing powers of your body and spirit.

Affirmation: O Yew of resurrection, I welcome you into my life today. I am using your example to reanimate my hidden talents, my unrecognized potential, and my self-healing power.

Appendix One

SELECTED GAELIC PRONUNCIATION GUIDE

aball	AH-vol
Abhalloch	AH-vul-lukh
Adamnan	ATH-uv-nawn
adéitche	ATH-eyj-huh
Aed Sláin	EETH SLAWN
Aengus	EYNG-uss AWG
áes dána	EESS DAWN-uh
aicme	ACK-muh
Aicme na bhForfiodh	AK-muh nuh VOR-fyugh [modern]
Aillinn	AL-lin
Airgthech	ARG-thyekh
airlise	AR-lish-uh
Airmid	AR-veth
airmitnech túaithe	AR-vij-nyekh TOOY-thyuh
aitenn	ATSH-un
Aithirne	ATH-eer-nyuh
Amargen	AV-ur-ghyen
Annwfn	AHN-noovn
ánruth	AWN-ruth
antrenn	AN-tryehn
armogam	AR-uh-MO-ghum
Audacht Morainn	UTH-akht VOR-in
Auraicept na N-Eces	UR-uh-kyept nuh NYEY-guss
Baile	BAL-yuh

Baile in Scáil	BAL-yuh in SKAWL
ban-druí	BON-DREE
Banfili	BON-il-uh
banliaig túaithe	BON-lee-agh TOO-uh-thuh
bansáer	BON-SEER
bardd teulu	BARTH TEY-lee
bech	BYEKH
Bechbretha	BYEKH-vreth-uh
Beithi	BETH-uh
Bellovaci	Bel-lo-WAH-kee
Beltaine	BYAL-tin-yuh
Berecyntia	Beh-reh-KIN-tyah
Bethu Brigte	BETH-uh BREEGH-juh
Bforfiodh	VOR-fyugh
biadogam	BLOTH-o-ghum
bíle	BIL-uh
bile Tortan	BIL-uh TOHR-tun
bile Uisnigh	BIL-uh USH-neegh
Bláth	BLAWTH
boaire	BOE-ar-yuh
Boann	BOE-un
boogam	BOE-o-ghum
Bran	BRAHN
Brehon [English]	BREH-ohn
Bretha Comaithchesa	BRETH-uh KOV-ath-khyess-uh
Bricia	BREEK-yah
Bricriu	BRIK-ryuh
Bricta	BRIK-tah
Brigit	BREEGH-ij
Brigindu	Brig-IN-doo
Brigantia	Brig-AHNT-yah
Brigid	Breej
Brixia	BRIKH-syah
Brocóit	BRO-gawj
búad	BOO-uth

buide	BWITH-uh
Caer Ibormeith	KWEER IH-vor-veth
caill crínmón	KAL KREEN-vawn
Cailleach	KAL-lyukh
Cailte	KWEEL-tyuh
Cain Iarraith	KWEEN EE-ur-uth
Cáin Lánamna	KWEEN LAWN-uv-nuh
cairn [English]	CARE-n
camáin	KOM-mawn
Carmina Gadelica	Kar-NEE-nah Gah-DEH-lee-kah
carn	KAHRN
Cath	KAHTH
ceirt	KEHRCH
celtar	KYEL-tur
ceó druidechta	KYOE DRITH-ekh-tuh
Cerridwen	Kehr-RID-wen
cert	KYEHRT
Cesarn	KYEH-sarn
cétal	KYEY-dal
cleis	KLESH
cles	KLYESS
clíab	KLEE-uv
cloot [English]	Kloot
clootie [English]	Klootee
cluiche cainte	KLIH-hyuh KAN-chuh
Conall	KON-al
cóe	KWEE
colcannon [English]	Kohl-can-un
Coll	KOLL
colpthach	KOLP-thukh
Connacht	KON-nukht
Connla	KON-luh
conogam	KON-o-ghum
Corc	KOHRK

corcra	KOHRK-ruh
Cormac	KOHR-mok
Corrán	KOR-rawn
crann	KRAWN
crann fulachta fiannsa	KRAWN FUL-ukh-tuh FEE-awn-suh
crannogam	KRAWN-o-ghum
Craob Daithi	KRWEEV DAH-thee
Craobh a b'áirde de 'n abhall thu	KRUH-uv uh BAR-juh jun AH-vul oo
crimfes	KRIV-fesh
Críth Gablach	KREETH GAV-lukh
crithach	KRITH-ukh
cromán tige bantrebthaige	KROM-awn TEE-ghuh Bon-TRYEV-thih-ghuh
Cúan hua Lothcháin	KOO-an HOO-uh LOTH-khawn
Cúchulainn	KOO KHUL-in
Cuileann	KWIL-yun
cuilenn	[Old/Middle Irish form of above]
cuim	KWIRN
Culdub	KOOL-duv
Cumhal	KOO-vul
Cumhal mac Airt	KOO-vul mok AHRCH
currach	KUR-rukh
Da Derga	DAH DYEHR-guh [or THEHR-guh]
daenogam	DWEEN-o-ghum
Daghda	DAGH-thuh
dairt	DARCH
Dálán	DAWL-awn
damogam	DARN-o-ghum
Danann	DON-un
danogam	DAWN-o-ghum
Danu	DON-uh
Daoine Maithe	DWEEN-yuh MAH-huh
datán	DOT-awn
Dathi	DAH-thee
Dathogam	DAH-tho-ghum

Daur	DUR
daurmess	DUR-mess
dearg	JAR-ug
derg	DYEHRG
Diancecht	DEE-un KYEKHT
Dichetal do Chennaib	DEE-khyed-ul duh KHYEN-nuv
Dindsenchas	DEEN-HEN-khus
dinnogam	DEEN-yo-ghum
díthir Dé	Deetheer Deh
donndraigen	DON-dra-ghyun
Draighean	DRY-un or DREEN
dris	DRISH
Druí	DREE
Drunemeton	Droo-NEH-meh-ton
dub	DUV
Eadha	AA or AA-uh [modern]
echtrai	EKHT-ruh
ed uath	ETH OO-uth
Edad	ETH-uth
Eire, Eiriu	EY-ryuh
Emain Ablach	EV-in AV-lukh
Emhain Abhlach	A-win AW-lukh
Enogam	EYN-o-ghum
Eo Mugna	YO [or O] MOOGH-nuh
Eochaid Airgthech	YO-khith [or O-khith] ARG-thyekh
Esus	EYSS-oos
Fál	FAWL
Fé	FEH
(f)é at uath	FEH ud OO-uth
(f)é a tuth	FEH uh TUTH
fe-fiada	FEH FEE-uh-thuh
Fearn	FYEHRN
Febal	FYEV-ul

Feradach	FEHR-uth-ukh
Fiachra	FEE-ukh-ruh
Fian	FEE-un
fianna	FEE-un-uh
Fid	FEETH
Fidlann	FITH-lawn
Fid na nDruad	FITH nun ROO-uth
fidogam	FITH-o-ghum
fidchell	FITH-khyell
Fili	FIL-uh
find	FIN
finn cumhal	FIN KHOO-vul
Finn mac Cumhaill	FIN mok KOO-vil [modern KOO-il]
Finnégeas	FIN-YEY-guss
Fis	FEESH
fled	FLYETH
flesc idaith	FLYESK ITH-ith
fodla fedo	FOTH-luh FETH-uh
Forfeda	FOR-feth-uh
Forraidh	FOR-ree
Fothadh Airgthech	FOTH-uth ARG-thyekh
fróech	FRWEEKH
Fúamnach	FOO-uv-nukh
fuidir	FWITH-ir
fulacht	FUL-akht
fulacht fian	FUL-akht FEE-un
gétal	GYEY-dul
glám dícenn	GLAWV DEE-khyen
glas	GLAHSS
gleslige	GLYESS-lee-ghuh
gorm	GOHRM
Gort	GOHRT
gwanu	GWAN-ee
Hebrides [English]	HE-bre-deez

Huath	HOO-uth
Ibar	EEV-ur
Idad	ITH-uth
Imbas	IM-muss
Imbas Forosnai	IM-muss FOR-oss-nee
Imbolc	IM-molk
Immrama	IM-rawv-uh
Ined erc	IN-uth EHRK
Kil Dara = Cill Dara	KEEL DAH-ruh [Irish] or Kildare [English]
Labhraidh Loingseach	LAV-rith LING-shukh
lachtnae	LAKHT-nuh
Leabhar na h-Uidhre	LYOAR nuh HWEE-ruh [modern]
liaig	LEE-ugh
linnogam	LIN-yo-ghum
loarg	LO-arg
Loegaire	LWEE-ghur-yuh
lónchrúachait	LAWN-khroo-uh-khuh
Lubhdan	LUV-thawn
Lugaid	LOO-ghith
Lughnasad	LOOGH-nas-suth or LOO-nuh-suh [modern]
lunantishee [English]	LOO-nant-shee
lusogam	LUSS-o-ghum
Mabinogion	Mah-bee-NOG-yon
Mac Cuilin	MOK KWIL-in
Mac Cuill	MOK KWIL
Mac Ibar	MOK EEV-ur
Mac ind Oc	MOK in AWG
Maccslechta	MOK-hlyekh-tuh
Maedhbh	METH-uv
Maeldúin	MWEEL-DOON
Maeve [English]	MAVE
Maige Tuired	MOGH TUR-eth
maínech ferta	MWEEN-yukh FYER-tuh

Magh Meall	MOY MYAL
Maidhi Meascorach	MAH-yuh MASS-kor-ukh
Manannán	MON-un-awn
Mannanán Mac Lir	M. MOK LEER
Matholwch	Mah-THOL-ookh
Miach	MEE-ukh
mid	MITH
midach	MITH-ukh
mídiuit	MEE-thee-udj
mil	MIL
Modarn	MOTH-urn
mruigfer	MRWEEGH-fer
mucogam	MUK-o-ghum
muimme	MWIM-uh
Muirbretha	MWIR-vreth-uh
mwn	MOON
náu	NAW
nemed	NEH-veth
Nuadu	NOO-uh-thuh
Ochtach	OKH-tukh
Octriuil	OK-tryool
Ogam n-eathrach	O-um NYAKHT-ṛul\kh
Ogham	O-ghum [medieval]; O-um [modern]
Ogham usceach	O-um USH-kyugh
Oimelc	EE-myelg
Oisín	USH-een
ollam	OL-luv
Ollarba	OL-lar-buh
omthann	OV-thawn
onnaid	ON-nith
Oscar	OSS-kar
Osogam	OSS-o-ghum
Parisi	Pah-REE-see

pencerdd	PEN-kehrth
quert	*See* cert
quillenn	*See* cuilenn
Roid	RWITH
Rosmerta	Ross-MEHR-tah
rus	RUSS
Samhain	SAV-in [medieval]; SOW-in [modern]
Sanas Cormac	SAH-nuss KOHR-mik
Scál	SKAWL
Segais	SHEH-ghish
Séis	SHEYSH
senachie [English]	Shan-ah-hee
Senchus Mór	SHEN-khuss MAWR
séta	SHEY-duh
Shee [English]	Sh-ee
shillelaghs [English]	Shil-ley-lee
sidhe	SHEE-thuh [medieval]; SHEE [modern]
siúr na gcnó gcuill	SHYOOR nug NAW GWIL
slachdan [Scottish]	SLAKH-kun
sraiph	SRAYV
straif	SRAYF
Suidigud Tige Midchúarda	SITH-i-ghuth TYEE-ghuh MITH-khoo-ur-tuh
taghairm	TAA-rum
taibhsear	TAV-sher
Tailltiu	TAL-tyuh
Táin	TAWN
Táin Bó Cúailnge	TAWN BOE KOO-ul-nguh
Taran	TAH-rahn
Taranis	Tah-RAH-niss
tarbh feis	TAH-ruv-eysh
Tarvostrigaranus	TAHR-woss Tree-gah-RAH-noss
teagasc ríogh	CHAG-usk REE
Tech Midchúarta	TYEKH MITH-khoo-ur-tuh

Técosca Cormaic	TYEH-goss-kuh KOHR-mik
Teinm Laegda	TYEHN-um LEEGH-thuh
teithe	TYETH-uh
tellach	TYEL-lukh
Temar [Temair]	TYEH-vir [medieval]; CHOW-ir (or TAA-wir) [modern]
Tír Tairngire	TYEER TARNG-ir-uh
Tlaghtga	TLAKHT-ghuh
Tochmarc Etaíne	TOKH-vurk Eh-DEEN-yuh
Tom-na-h-Iubhraich	TAWM nuh HYOOW-rikh
torc	TOHRK
Tortu	TOHR-tuh
Trian	TREE-un
Trom	TROM
Truagh	TROO-ugh
truagh an mhuc	TROO-ugh (or TROO-uh) uh VUK
túath	TOO-uth [medieval]; TOO-ah [modern]
Tuatha de Danann	TOO-uh-thuh DYEH DON-un [medieval]; TOO-uh-huh JEH Don-un [modern]
ubhal	UV-al, OO-ul [modern]
Uibh Maccuais	UV Mok-KOO-ish
Uinnius	IN-nyusS
Uirgriu	UR-gryuh
Uisneach	USH-nyukh
ulaidh	UL-ee
Úr	OOR
Uraicecht Na Ríar	UR-i-kyekht nuh REE-ur

Appendix Two

PRONUNCIATION GUIDE
FOR THE WORD OGHAMS

Briatharogam	BREE-uh-thur-O-ghum; BREE-hur-O-um [modern]
Briatharogam Morainn mic Moín	VOR-in VIK VWEEN
Briatharogam Mic ind Oic	VIK in NYAWG
Briatharogam Con Culainn	KOO khULL-in
Birch—Beith	BETH
Feocus foltchain	FYO-guss FOLT-khween
Glasium cnis	GLASH-uv KNISH
Maise malach	MASH-uh MAWL-ukh
Rowan—Luis	LUSH
Lí súla	LEE SOOL-uh
Cara ceathra	KAH-ruh KYETH-ruh
Luth cethrae	LOOTH KYETH-ruh
Alder—Fearn	FYEHRN
Airinach fian	AR-in-ukh FEE-un
Comet lachta	KOV-ed LAKH-tuh
Din cridi	DEEN KRITH-uh
Willow—Saille	SAL-yuh
Li naimbi	LEE NAM-me
Luth bech	LOOTH BYEKH
Tosach mela	TOSS-ukh MYEL-uh

Ash—Nion NEEN
Cosdad sida KOST-uth SHEE-thuh
Bag ban BAWGH BON
Bag maise BAWGH MAH-uh

Hawthorn—Huath HOO-ath
Comdal cuan KOV-thawl KOO-un
Banad gnuise BAWN-uth GNOO-shuh
Annsam aidche AWN-suv ATH-hyuh

Oak—Dair DAR
Ardam dossaib ARD-uv DOS-suv
Gres sair GRYEYS SEER
Slechtam soire SHLYEKHT-uv SEER-uh

Holly—Tinne TIN-nyuh
Trian roith TREE-un ROTH
Smir guaile SMIHR GOO-uh-lyuh
Trian n-airm TREE-un NAR-um

Hazel—Coll KOLL
Cainiu fedaib KWEE-nyuh FETH-uv
Ithcar cnocar ITH-kur KNOG-ur
Caincar fid KWEEN-gur FITH
Carae bloesc Kah-ruh BLWEESK
Milsem fedo MIL-shuv FETH-uh

Apple—Qert KYEHRT
Clithar mbaiscaill KLITH-ur MWEESH-kil
Brig an duine BREEGH un DUN-yuh
Digu fethail .i. Cumdaig DEE-ghuh FETH-il, KUV-theegh

Vine—Muin MWIN
Tresim fedma TRESH-uv FETH-muh
Arusc n-airlig AR-usk NAR-leegh
Conair gotha .i. Tre muin KON-ur GOTH-uh TREH VWIN

Ivy—Gort GOHRT
Milsiu féraib MIL-shuh FYEYR-uv

Glaiseb gelta	GLASH-uv GYEL-tuh
Med n-erc	METH NEHRK
Sasad ile	SAWS-uth IL-yuh

Reed—Ngetal	NGYEH-dul
Luth legha	LOOTH LYEGH-uh
Etiud midach	EJ-yuth MITH-ukh
Tosach n-echto	TOSS-ukh NYEYKH-tuh

Blackthorn—Straif	STRAF
Tressam ruamnat	TRESS-uv ROO-uv-nud
Aire srabae	AR-yuh SRAW-vuh
Morad run	MAWR-uth ROON
Saigid nel	SEYE-ghith NYEYL

Elder—Ruis	RUSH
Tindem ruccae	TIN-nyuv RUK-kuh
Ruamnae dreach	ROO-uv-nuh DRYEKH
Bruth fergae	BROOTH FYERG-uh

Silver Fir—Ailm	AL-um or AL-uv
Ardam iachta	ARD-uv EE-ukh-tuh
Tosach fregra	TOSS-ukh FRYEG-ruh
Tosach garmae	TOSS-ukh GAR-muh

Furze—Onn	UHN
Congnamaid ech	KONG-nav-uth EKH
Fetham soire	FYEYTH-uv SEER-uh
Luth fiann	LOOTH FEE-un

Heather—Úr	OOR
Uaraib adbaib	OO-ur-uv AHTH-vuv
Silad cland	SHEEL-uth KLAWN
Forbbaid ambi	FORB-uth AM-mee

Aspen—Edad	ETH-ath
Flesc idaith	FLESK ITH-uth
Fe	FEH

Fe a tuth	FEH uh TUTH
Fe at uath	FEH ud OO-uth
Yew—Idad	ITH-ath
Sinem fedaib	SHIN-uv FETH-uv
Cainem sen	KWEEN-uv SHEN
Aildem ais	AL-lyuv EESH
Luth lobair	LOOTH LOV-ir

Notes

Introduction

1. Personal conversation.
2. Please see The Magical Arts of the Forest Druids chapter for instructions on how to make salves.
3. Please see my book *A Druid's Herbal for the Sacred Earth Year* for more on the topic of Druids.
4. O'Boyle, *Ogam*, 20.
5. Ibid., 9.
6. Ibid., 13.
7. Ibid.
8. Mac Coitir, *Irish Trees*, 32.
9. O'Boyle, 14.
10. Ibid.
11. Ibid., 15.
12. Meroney, "Early Irish Letter Names," 27.
13. Ibid., 33.
14. Ibid., 29.
15. Ibid., 33.
16. Ibid., 30.
17. Ibid.
18. Ibid., 31.
19. Ibid., 34.

Part One:
The Ogham Tree Alphabet

1. O'Boyle, *Ogam*, 9.
2. Ibid., 10–11.
3. Mac Coitir, *Irish Trees*, 175.
4. O'Boyle, 11.
5. Ibid., 56.
6. Calder, *Auraicept na N-Eces*.
7. Kelly, *A Guide to Early Irish Law*, 186–87.
8. Kelly, *Early Irish Farming*, 409.
9. Ibid.
10. Caitlín and John Matthews, *Encyclopedia of Celtic Wisdom*, 28–29.
11. Ibid., 29.

Birch—*Beith*

1. O'Boyle, *Ogam*, 13.
2. Mac Coitir, *Irish Trees*, 161–62.
3. Hopman, Tree Medicine, Tree Magic class, www.greyschool.com.
4. Mac Coitir, 22.
5. Ibid., 25.
6. Hopman, Tree Medicine, Tree Magic class.

7. Ibid.
8. Moerman, "Medicinal Plants," *Medicinal Plants of Native America 1,* 92–93.
9. Ibid.
10. Ibid.
11. Ibid.
12. Ibid.
13. Ibid.
14. Roth, *Betula pendula,* Plants for a Future. www.pfaf.org/database/plants. Accessed February 20, 2007.
15. Moerman, 92–93.
16. Lust, *The Herb Book,* 119.
17. Ibid.
18. Ibid.
19. Hopman, Tree Medicine, Tree Magic class.
20. Ibid.

ROWAN—*LUIS*

1. O'Boyle, *Ogam,* 15–16.
2. Mac Coitir, *Irish Trees,* 160–61.
3. Ibid., 164.
4. Hopman, *Tree Medicine, Tree Magic,* 84.
5. Hopman, Tree Medicine, Tree Magic class.
6. Ibid.
7. Mac Coitir, *Irish Trees,* 28.
8. Ibid., 29.
9. Ibid.
10. Ibid., 30.
11. Ibid.
12. Ibid.
13. Hopman, Tree Medicine, Tree Magic class.
14. Mac Coitir, *Irish Trees,* 31.
15. Lust, *The Herb Book,* 339.

16. Please see my book *Tree Medicine, Tree Magic* for a recipe to make rowan berry jam.
17. Hopman, *Tree Medicine, Tree Magic,* 82.
18. Ibid.
19. Erichsen-Brown, *Herbal and Other Uses of North American Plants,* 88.
20. Ibid., 89.
21. Ibid.
22. Ibid.
23. Beith, *Healing Threads,* 27.

ALDER—*FEARN*

1. O'Boyle, *Ogam,* 15–16.
2. Mac Coitir, *Irish Trees,* 161–62.
3. Hopman, Tree Medicine, Tree Magic class.
4. Ibid.
5. Ibid.
6. Mac Coitir, 34–36.
7. Lust, *The Herb Book,* 122.
8. Ibid.
9. Moerman, "Medicinal Plants," 29.
10. Ibid.
11. Mac Coitir, 34.
12. Ibid., 38.
13. Ibid.

WILLOW—SAILLE

1. For more on Druids, please see my book *A Druid's Herbal for the Sacred Earth Year.*
2. O'Boyle, *Ogam,* 18.
3. Ibid., 28.
4. See O'Boyle for examples of Ogham scales and musical notation.
5. Rees, *Celtic Heritage,* 113.
6. Ibid., 127.

7. Ibid., 181.

8. Mac Coitir, *Irish Trees,* 43.

9. Ibid., 43–44.

10. Ibid., 162.

11. "The Tragic Death of Fergus mac Leide," The Celtic Literature Collective. www.ancienttexts.org/library/celtic/texts/fergusmacleide.html. Accessed February 27, 2007.

12. Mac Coitir, 43.

13. Hopman, Tree Medicine, Tree Magic class.

14. Bride (Scotland) is the same goddess as Brigid (Ireland) and Brigantia (England). She is the summer face of the Cailleach, the powerful creator goddess and Hag of Winter.

15. Mac Coitir, 42.

16. Ibid., 45.

17. Hopman, Tree Medicine, Tree Magic class.

18. Lust, *The Herb Book,* 402.

19. Ibid., 403.

20. Moerman, "Medicinal Plants," 426.

21. Ibid., 427

22. Ibid.

23. Ibid., 427–28

24. Ross, *Pagan Celtic Britain,* 279.

25. Ibid., 291, 296.

26. Ibid., 285.

ASH—NION

1. Rees, *Celtic Heritage,* 123.

2. Ibid., 120.

3. Kelly, *Early Irish Farming,* 388.

4. Hopman, Tree Medicine, Tree Magic class.

5. Ibid.

6. Ibid.

7. Ibid.

8. Ibid.

9. Ibid.

10. Ibid.

11. Meroney, "Early Irish Letter Names," 28.

12. Ibid.

13. Kelly, *Early Irish Farming,* 449.

14. Ibid.

15. Ibid., 451.

16. Lust, *The Herb Book,* 119.

17. Moerman, "Medicinal Plants," 190.

18. Ibid., 190–91.

19. Ibid., 190.

20. Mac Coitir, *Irish Trees,* 123.

21. Ibid., 124.

22. Ibid.

23. Ibid., 126.

24. Ibid.

HAWTHORN—HUATH

1. Kelly, *Early Irish Law,* 44.

2. Ibid.

3. Joyce, *Social History,* 242–43.

4. Ibid., 243.

5. For examples of this, see the various Finn stories in "Imbas Forosnai" by Nora Chadwick, in *Scottish Gaelic Studies,* vol. 4, part 2. Oxford University Press, 1935.

6. Ibid.

7. P. W. Joyce, *A Social History of Ancient Ireland, 1,* 244.

8. Kelly, *A Guide to Early Irish Law,* 137–38.

9. Ibid., 138.

10. Ibid., 138–39.

11. Ibid., 51.

12. Bretnach, *Uraicecht Na Ríar,* 115.

13. Ibid., 140.

14. Meroney, "Early Irish Letter Names," 28.

15. Lust, *The Herb Book*, 215.

16. Moerman, "Medicinal Plants," 139.

17. Ibid., 139–40.

18. Ibid., 140.

19. Hopman, Tree Medicine, Tree Magic class.

20. Ibid.

21. Ibid.

22. Aburrow, *Auguries and Omens*, 190–91.

OAK—*DAIR*

1. Kelly, *Early Irish Farming*, 381.

2. Ibid., 380.

3. Ibid., 381–82.

4. Ibid., 386–87.

5. Ibid., 84.

6. Ibid., 83.

7. Meroney, "Early Irish Letter Names," 29.

8. Mac Coitir, *Irish Trees*, 162.

9. Hopman, *Tree Medicine, Tree Magic*, 22–23.

10. Ibid., 23.

11. Ibid.

12. Lust, *The Herb Book*, 295–96.

13. Moerman, "Medicinal Plants," 389.

14. Ibid.

15. Ibid., 390.

16. Ibid.

17. Ibid., 390–91.

18. Ibid., 391.

19. Hopman, Tree Medicine, Tree Magic class.

20. Ibid.

21. Ibid.

22. Ibid.

23. For a full discussion on the Druid's use of mistletoe and its medical uses, please see my book *A Druid's Herbal for the Sacred Earth Year.*

24. Hopman, Tree Medicine, Tree Magic class.

25. Ibid.

HOLLY—*TINNE*

1. O'Boyle, *Ogam*, 15.

2. Meroney, "Early Irish Letter Names," 29.

3. Kelly, *Early Irish Farming*, 380.

4. Ibid., 382.

5. Ibid., 46–47.

6. Ibid., 497.

7. Ibid., 337.

8. Ibid., 379.

9. Hopman, Tree Medicine, Tree Magic class.

10. "The Tragic Death of Fergus mac Leide," The Celtic Literature Collective. www.ancienttexts.org/ library/celtic/ctexts/fergusmacleide .html. Accessed February 27, 2007.

11. Mac Coitir, *Irish Trees*, 161–62.

12. Lust, *The Herb Book*, 227.

13. Moerman, "Medicinal Plants," 231.

14. Ibid., 232.

15. Lust, 228–29.

16. Moerman, 232.

17. Lust, 228.

18. Ibid., 229.

19. Hopman, Tree Medicine, Tree Magic class.

20. Ibid.

HAZEL—COLL

1. Kelly, *Audacht Morainn*, xiv.

2. Ibid., 7.

3. Kelly, *Early Irish Farming*, 306.

4. Ibid., 382.

5. Ibid., 84.

6. Ibid., 84n.

7. Ibid., 576.

8. Mac Coitir, *Irish Trees*, 161–62.

9. Hopman, *Tree Medicine, Tree Magic*, 66.

10. Ibid., 66.

11. Erichsen-Brown, *Herbal and Other Uses of North American Plants*, 176–77.

12. Ibid., 177.

13. Mac Coitir, 75.

14. Ibid.

15. Ibid., 77.

16. Hopman, Tree Medicine, Tree Magic class.

17. Mac Coitir, 79.

18. Hopman, Tree Medicine, Tree Magic class.

19. Ibid.

APPLE—QUERT

1. Meroney, "Early Irish Letter Names," 29.

2. Kelly, *Early Irish Farming*, 383.

3. Ibid., 259–60.

4. Ibid., 304.

5. Ibid., 368.

6. Meroney, 29–30.

7. O'Boyle, *Ogam*, 15.

8. Hopman, *Tree Medicine, Tree Magic*, 89–90.

9. Moerman, "Medicinal Plants," 387.

10. Ibid., 387–88.

11. Ibid., 388.

12. Ibid.

13. "The Tragic Death of Fergus mac Leide," The Celtic Literature Collective. www.ancienttexts.org/library/celtic/ctexts/fergusmacleide.html. Accessed February 27, 2007.

14. Hopman, Tree Medicine, Tree Magic class.

15. Ibid.

16. Ibid.

17. Ibid.

18. Cross and Slover, *Ancient Irish Tales*, 588–89.

19. Mac Coitir, *Irish Trees*, 84–85.

20. Squire, *Celtic Myth and Legend*, 135–36.

VINE—MUIN

1. Meroney, "Early Irish Letter Names," 30.

2. Green, *The Celtic World*, 165.

3. Ibid., 231–33.

4. Ibid., 28.

5. Ibid., 29.

6. Kelly, *Early Irish Farming*, 262–63.

7. Ibid., 319.

8. Ibid., 320.

9. Ibid., 321.

10. Ibid., 322.

11. Ibid., 357.

12. Ibid., 358.

13. Ibid.

14. Ibid.

15. Culpeper, *Culpeper's Color Herbal,* 196.

16. Ibid., 196.

17. Grieve, *A Modern Herbal,* 832–33.

18. Moerman, "Medicinal Plants," 516.

19. Ibid., 517.

20. Ibid., 518.

21. See note 19 above.

22. O'Boyle, *Ogam,* 15–16.

23. Meroney, 30.

24. Calder, John, ed. and trans., *Auraicept na N-Eces (The Scholars' Primer),* John Grant, Edinburgh, 1917.

25. Lincoln, *Death, War and Sacrifice,* 170–71.

26. Ibid.

27. Ibid., 169.

IVY—*GORT*

1. Kelly, *Early Irish Farming,* 46.

2. Ibid., 491.

3. Ibid., 384.

4. Ibid., 381.

5. Ibid., 367.

6. Ibid., 368.

7. Ibid., 369.

8. Ibid., 369–70.

9. Ibid., 371–72.

10. Ibid., 419–20.

11. Ibid., 424–25.

12. Ibid., 425–26.

13. Ibid., 426.

14. Mac Coitir, *Irish Trees,* 161–62.

15. Hopman, *Druid's Herbal,* 60.

16. Ibid., 97.

17. Lust, *The Herb Book,* 183.

18. Kelly, *A Guide to Early Irish Law,* 60.

19. For information on modern Druid orders, please visit the Order of the White Oak (Ord na Darach Gile) at www.whiteoakdruids.org.

20. Hopman, *Druid's Herbal,* 94.

21. Ibid., 60, 171.

REED—*NGETAL*

1. Mac Coitir, *Irish Trees,* 169.

2. Meroney, "Early Irish Letter Names," 30.

3. Kelly, *A Guide To Early Irish Law,* 57–58.

4. Ibid., 58–59.

5. Ibid., 77.

6. Markale, *The Druids,* 32.

7. Kelly, *Early Irish Farming,* 216.

8. Carmichael, *Carmina Gadelica,* 398–99.

9. Markale, 71.

10. Kelly, *Early Irish Farming,* 384.

11. Meroney, 31.

12. (Cav.) Trin. ex Steud., *Phragmites australis,* Plants for a Future. www.pfaf.org/database/plants. Accessed March 13, 2007.

13. Ibid.

14. Ibid.

15. Ibid.

16. Ibid.

17. Moerman, "Medicinal Plants," 335.

18. Hopman, "The Virtual Shrine of Brighid."

19. For more information on Imbolc customs and the history of Brigid, please visit The Virtual Shrine of Brigid at www.celticheritage.co.uk/virtualshrine.

BLACKTHORN—*STRAIF*

1. Calder, John, ed. and trans., *Auraicept na n-Eces* (*The Scholars' Primer*), John Grant, Edinburgh, 1917.
2. Meroney, "Early Irish Letter Names."
3. Riley, M. E., *Clothing of the Ancient Celts/Dyes,* Indiana State University http://mama.indstate.edu/users/ morgan/Dyes1.htm. Accessed March 15, 2007.
4. L., *Prunus spinosa*—L., Sloe, Plants for a Future. www.pfaf.org/database/ plants. Accessed March 15, 2007.
5. Kelly, *Early Irish Farming,* 263.
6. Ibid., 263–64.
7. Ibid., 267.
8. Ibid., 267–68.
9. Grierson, *The Colour Cauldron.*
10. Kelly, *Early Irish Farming,* 374–75.
11. Ibid., 394.
12. Mac Coitir, *Irish Trees,* 161, 163.
13. Blackthorn as a dye herb: www.spar .co.uk/rooted-in-the-community. Accessed March 15, 2007.
14. "The Tragic Death of Fergus mac Leide," The Celtic Literature Collective. www.ancienttexts.org/ library/celtic/ctexts/fergusmacleide .html. Accessed February 27, 2007.
15. L., *Prunus spinosa*—L., Sloe, Plants for a Future. www.pfaf.org/database/ plants.Accessed March 15, 2007.
16. Lust, *The Herb Book,* 314.
17. Beith, *Healing Threads,* 205.
18. Lust, 314.
19. Moerman, "Medicinal Plants," 371.
20. Ibid.
21. L., *Prunus spinosa*—L., Sloe, Plants for a Future. www.pfaf.org/database/ plants. Accessed March 15, 2007.
22. Erichsen-Brown, *Herbal and Other Uses of North American Plants,* 164–65.
23. Mac Coitir, *Irish Trees,* 102.
24. Ibid., 103.
25. Fairy—Fae—Fay, The Witches Way—Fairy Information www. witchesway.net/links/fairy.
26. Mac Coitir, 105.

ELDER—*RUIS*

1. Meroney, "Early Irish Letter Names," 32.
2. Kelly, *A Guide to Early Irish Law,* 81.
3. Ibid., 82.
4. Ibid., 83.
5. Ibid.
6. Ibid., 84.
7. Ibid., 85–86.
8. Ibid., 87.
9. Ibid.
10. Ibid., 91.
11. Ibid., 88.
12. Ibid., 95–96.
13. Kelly, *Early Irish Farming,* 351.
14. Rees, *Celtic Heritage,* 241–43.
15. Ibid., 215.
16. Mac Coitir, *Irish Trees,* 161, 163.
17. Beith, *Healing Threads,* 215.
18. Lust, *The Herb Book,* 178.
19. Ibid., 179.
20. Ibid., 180.
21. Ibid., 180–81.
22. Moerman, "Medicinal Plants," 435–37.

23. Ibid., 438.

24. Hopman, Tree Medicine, Tree Magic class.

25. Ibid.

26. McNeill, *The Silver Bough*, 79.

SILVER FIR—*AILM*

1. Kelly, *Early Irish Farming*, 383.

2. Mill., *Abies alba*—Mill., Silver Fir, Plants for a Future. www.pfaf.org/database/plants. Accessed March 20, 2007.

3. Kelly, *Early Irish Farming*, 499.

4. Ibid., 54–55.

5. Rees, *Celtic Heritage*, 314.

6. Ibid., 316.

7. Ibid., 319–22.

8. Mac Coitir, *Irish Trees*, 162–63.

9. Calder, John, ed. and trans., *Auraicept na N-Eces.*

10. Mill., *Abies alba*—Mill., Silver Fir, Plants for a Future. www.pfaf .org/database/plants. Accessed March 20, 2007.

11. Moerman, "Medicinal Plants," 1–2.

12. Ibid., 2–3.

13. Ibid., 3.

14. Hopman, Tree Medicine, Tree Magic class.

15. Evans-Wentz, *The Fairy Faith in Celtic Countries*, 427–28.

16. Ibid., 435.

FURZE—*ONN*

1. Meroney, "Early Irish Letter Names," 33.

2. Kelly, *Early Irish Farming*, 381.

3. Ibid., 395.

4. L., *Ulex europaeus*—L. Gorse, Plants for a Future. www.pfaf.org/database/plants. Accessed March 22, 2007.

5. Grieve, *A Modern Herbal*, 367.

6. Mac Coitir, *Irish Trees*, 96–97.

7. Ibid., 161, 163.

8. Meroney, 33.

9. L., *Ulex europaeus*—L. Gorse, Plants for a Future. www.pfaf.org/database/plants. Accessed March 22, 2007.

10. *The Scottish Field Magazine*, 1967, http://193.62.154.38/cgi-bin/nph-readbtree.pl/usedata/max vals=10/firstval=1?SPECIES_XREF=Ulex+europaeus. Accessed March 22, 2007.

11. Grieve, 368.

12. Mac Coitir, 94–95.

HEATHER—*ÚR*

1. Kelly, *Early Irish Farming*, Dublin 381, 395.

2. (L.) Hull., *Calluna vulgaris*—(L.) Hull. Heather, Plants for a Future. www.pfaf.org/database/plants. Accessed March 26, 2007.

3. Ibid.

4. Ibid.

5. Ibid.

6. Ibid.

7. Ibid.

8. Kelly, *Early Irish Farming*, 108–9.

9. Ibid., 110–11.

10. Ibid., 111–12.

11. Ibid., 113–14.

12. Mac Coitir, *Irish Trees*, 92.

13. Ibid., 162–63.

14. (L.) Hull., *Calluna vulgaris*—(L.) Hull. Heather, Plants for a

Future. www.pfaf.org/database/ plants. Accessed March 26, 2007.

15. Ibid.

16. Lust, *The Herb Book*, 215–16.

17. For information on modern Druid orders, please visit the Order of the White Oak (Ord na Darach Gile) at www.whiteoakdruids.org.

18. Hopman, *A Druid's Herbal*, 4.

19. (L.) Hull., *Calluna vulgaris*— (L.) Hull. Heather, Plants for a Future. www.pfaf.org/database/. Accessed March 26, 2007.

ASPEN—*EDAD*

1. Meroney, "Early Irish Letter Names," 34.

2. Green, *The Celtic World*, 492–95.

3. Ibid., 496–97.

4. Ibid., 497–98.

5. Ibid., 499–500.

6. Ibid., 501.

7. Ibid.

8. Ibid., 505–6.

9. Ibid., 506–9.

10. Rees, *Celtic Heritage*, 188–89.

11. Evans-Wentz, *The Fairy Faith in Celtic Countries*, 33, 74–75.

12. Ibid., 52–53.

13. Ibid., 46–47.

14. Ibid., 49–50.

15. Ibid., 155.

16. Meroney, "Early Irish Letter Names," 34–35.

17. Lust, *The Herb Book*, 318.

18. Ibid., 319.

19. Moerman, "Medicinal Plants," 362.

20. Ibid.

21. Ibid.

22. Ibid., 363.

23. Ibid.

24. Ibid., 363–64.

25. Ibid., 364.

26. Ibid., 365–66.

27. Ibid., 366.

28. Hopman, Tree Medicine, Tree Magic class.

29. Ibid.

30. Mac Coitir, *Irish Trees*, 136–37.

YEW—*IDAD*

1. Rees and Rees, *Celtic Heritage*, 120.

2. Ross, *Pagan Celtic Britain*, 38.

3. Matthews, *Taliesin*, 222.

4. McNeill, *The Silver Bough*, 80.

5. "The Tragic Death of Fergus mac Leide," The Celtic Literature Collective. www.ancienttexts.org/ library/celtic/ctexts/fergusmacleide .html. Accessed February 27, 2007.

6. Mac Coitir, *Irish Trees*, 145.

7. Kelly, *Early Irish Farming*, 380, 383.

8. Ibid., 487.

9. Ibid., 183–84.

10. Ibid., 214.

11. Meroney, "Early Irish Letter Names," 35.

12. Mac Coitir, 162–63.

13. Jaffe, "Killing the Cure," 16.

14. Ibid., 17–18.

15. *Nutt., Taxus brevifolia*—Nutt. Pacific Yew, Plants for a Future. www.pfaf.org/database/plants. Accessed April 1, 2007.

16. L., *Taxus baccata*—L. Yew, Plants for a Future. www.pfaf.org/database/ plants. Accessed April 1, 2007.

17. Moerman, "Medicinal Plants," 477.

18. Ibid., 477–78.

19. Hopman, unpublished essay on yew, 1996.

DRUID MAGIC

1. Joyce, *A Social History of Ancient Ireland,* 240.

2. Ibid., 241–42.

3. Ibid., 242.

4. Matthews, *The Encyclopedia of Celtic Wisdom,* 243.

5. Joyce, 246–47.

6. Ibid., 248.

7. Please see my book *Priestess of the Forest: A Druid Journey,* published by Llewellyn Publishers, Saint Paul, Minn., 2008, for an idea of what Druid rituals may have looked like.

MAGICAL TOOLS OF THE DRUIDS

1. Rees, *Celtic Heritage,* 29.

2. Ibid., 47.

3. Ibid., 193, 313.

4. Ibid., 48.

5. Ibid., 313.

6. Ibid., 271.

7. Ibid., 311–12.

8. Ibid., 312–13.

9. Ibid., 310.

10. Ibid., 315.

11. Bretnach, *Uraicecht Na Ríar,* 94.

CELEBRATE THE CELTIC FIRE FESTIVALS

1. *Hibernica Minora,* Kuno Meyer, trans., *Anecdota Oxoniensia,* Oxford, 1894, and in the Early Christian text "Saltair na Rann," Canto 1, quatrains 12 to 24.

2. Feast of St. Brigid, Fish Eaters, www.fisheaters.com. Accessed March 15, 2007.

BIBLIOGRAPHY

Aburrow, Yvonne. *Auguries and Omens: The Magical Lore of Birds.* Newbury, Berkshire, England: Capall Bann, 1996.

Adams, Barbara Means. *Prayers of Smoke: Renewing Makaha Tribal Tradition.* Berkeley, Calif.: Celestial Arts, 1990.

Baker, Margaret. *Discovering the Folklore of Plants.* Aylesbury, Bucks, U.K.: Shire Publications, 1975.

Beith, Mary. *Healing Threads.* Edinburgh: Polygon, 1995.

Bretnach, Liam, ed. *Uraicecht Na Riar.* Dublin: Dublin Institute for Advanced Studies, 1987.

Brunaux, Jean Louis. *The Celtic Gauls: Gods, Rites and Sanctuaries.* London: Seaby, 1988.

Calder, George, ed. and trans. Book of Ballymote: *Auraicept na N-Eces (The Scholars' Primer).* Edinburgh: John Grant, 1917.

Carmichael, Alexander. *Carmina Gadelica: Hymns and Incantations.* Hudson, N.Y.: Lindisfarne Press, 1992.

Cross, Tom P., and Harris Slover Clark, eds. *Ancient Irish Tales.* New York: Barnes and Noble Books, 1996.

Culpeper, Nicholas. *Culpeper's Color Herbal.* New York: Sterling Publishing, 1983.

Cunliffe, Barry. *The Celtic World.* New York: St. Martin's Press, 1993.

Cunningham, Scott. *Encyclopedia of Magical Herbs.* St. Paul, Minn.: Llewellyn Publications, 1986.

Danaher, Kevin. *The Year in Ireland.* Cork: The Mercier Press, 1972.

Ellis, Peter Berresford. *Celtic Women.* Grand Rapids, Mich.: Wm. B. Erdman's Publishing, 1996.

Erichsen-Brown, Charlotte. *Herbal and Other Uses of North American Plants.* New York: Dover Publications, 1989.

Evans-Wentz, W. Y. *The Fairy Faith in Celtic Countries.* New York: Citadel Press, 1990.

Farrar, Janet and Stewart. *The Witch's Goddess.* Custer, Wash.: Phoenix Publishing, 1987.

Frazier, James G. *The Golden Bough: The Roots of Religion and Folklore.* New York: Avenel Books, 1981.

Friedrich, Paul. *Proto-Indo-European Trees.* Chicago: University of Chicago Press, 1970.

Green, Miranda J. *The Celtic World.* London: Routledge, 1995.

———. *The World of the Druids.* London: Thames and Hudson, 1997.

Grierson, Su. *The Colour Cauldron.* Self-published, 1986. ISBN 0951013211.

Grieve, M. *A Modern Herbal.* New York: Dover Publications, 1971.

Hoagland, Kathleen. *1,000 Years of Irish Poetry: The Gaelic and the Anglo-Irish Poets from Pagan Times to the Present.* Old Greenwich, Conn.: The Devin-Adair Company, 1981.

Hopman, Ellen Evert. *A Druid's Herbal for the Sacred Earth Year.* Rochester, Vt.: Destiny Books, 1995.

———. *Tree Medicine, Tree Magic.* Custer, Wash.: Phoenix Publishers, 1991.

———. Tree Medicine, Tree Magic. Class for the Grey School of Wizardry, 2005–2007. www.greyschool.com.

Jaffe, Mark. "Killing the Cure." *Philadelphia Inquirer,* February 23, 1992.

Joyce, P. W. *A Social History of Ancient Ireland,* vol. 1. London: Longmans, Green, 1903.

Kelly, Fergus. Audacht Morainn. Dublin: The Dublin Institute for Advanced Studies, 1976.

———. *A Guide to Early Irish Law.* Dublin: Dublin Institute for Advanced Studies, 1991.

———. *Early Irish Farming.* Dublin: Dublin Institute for Advanced Studies.

Kondratiev, Alexei. *The Apple Branch.* Cork: The Collins Press, 1998.

Krasner, Deborah. *From Celtic Hearths.* New York: Viking Studio Books, 1991.

Lincoln, Bruce. *Death, War and Sacrifice.* Chicago: University of Chicago Press, 1991.

Little, Elbert L. *The Audubon Society Field Guide to North American Trees.* New York: Knopf, 1980.

Lust, John. *The Herb Book.* New York: Bantam Books, 1974.

Mac Coitir, Niall. *Irish Trees.* Cork: The Collins Press, 2003.

Markale, Jean. *The Druids.* Rochester, Vt.: Inner Traditions, 1999.

Matthews, Caitlin and John. *The Encyclopedia of Celtic Wisdom.* Rockport, Mass.: Element Books, 1994.

Matthews, John. *Taliesin: Shamanism and the Bardic Mysteries in Britain and Ireland.* London: The Aquarian Press, 1991.

———. *The Druid Sourcebook.* London: Blanford Press, 1996.

McNeill, F. Marian. *The Silver Bough,* vol. 1. Glasgow: William Maclellan, 1977.

Meroney, Howard. "Early Irish Letter Names." *Speculum* 24, no. 1 (Jan. 1949).

Meyer, Kuno, trans. *Hibernica Minora, Anecdota Oxoniensia.* Oxford, 1894.

———. *Selections from Ancient Irish Poetry.* London: Constable, 1959.

Moerman, Daniel E. *Medicinal Plants of Native America.* University of Michigan Museum of Anthropology Technical Reports, Number 19, 1986.

Mooney, James. *History, Myths and Sacred Formulas of the Cherokees.* Asheville, N.C.: Bright Mountain Books, 1992.

Naddair, Kaledon. *Keltic Folk and Faerie Tales.* London: Century Hutchinson, 1987.

O'Boyle, Sean. *Ogam: The Poet's Secret.* Dublin: Gilbert Dalton, 1980.

Rees, Alwyn and Brinley. *Celtic Heritage.* New York: Thames and Hudson, 1989.

Ross, Anne. *Pagan Celtic Britain.* New York: Columbia University Press, 1967.

Saintine, X. B. *The Myths of the Rhine.* Rutland, Vt.: Charles E. Tuttle, 1967 (reprint of the 1875 edition).

Squire, Charles. *Celtic Myth and Legend.* Van Nuys, Calif.: Newcastle, 1975.

Stone, Merlin. *Ancient Mirrors of Womanhood.* Boston: Beacon Press, 1984.

About the Author

Ellen Evert Hopman is a Druid priestess, master herbalist, and lay homeopath who holds an M.Ed. in mental health counseling. She is a founding member and cochief of the Order of the White Oak (Ord na Darach Gile), serves on the Grey Council of Mages and Sages, and is a professor of Wortcunning at the Grey School of Wizardry. She is the author of *A Druid's Herbal for the Sacred Earth Year; Walking the World in Wonder: A Children's Herbal; Tree Medicine, Tree Magic; Being a Pagan* (with Lawrence Bond); and a novel *Priestess of the Forest: A Druid Journey*. She lives in an oak forest in Western Massachusetts. See a complete list of her books, videos, and audiotapes at

www.celticheritage.co.uk/EllenEvertHopman

Index

Abies genus. *See* silver fir
abortifacients, 58, 140
acorns, 61
Aengus Og, 71
Aillinn, 136
airlise, 85
Aithirne, 50
Alaska bog willow, 37
alder, 14, 171–72, 204
  herbal uses of, 30–31
  history of, 29–30
  spiritual aspects of, 31–32
Alnus genus. *See* alder
altars, 131
American hazelnut, 60
American holly, 64
American mountain ash, 25
American white ash, 45
American wild plum, 100
American yew, 140
amulets, 154
anaphrodisiacs, 37
anemia, 82
Annals of Ulster, 48
antibiotics, 114
antiseptics, 114
Apache, 94
apple, 14, 172–73, 206–207

herbal uses of, 74–76
  history of, 73–74
  spiritual aspects of, 76–78
Arthen, Leona, 98
arthritis, 64, 126
Arundo genus. *See* reed
ash, 14, 172, 204–5
  herbal uses of, 45–46
  history of, 41–45
  spiritual aspects of, 46–47
Ash of Tortu, 42, 47
Ash of Uisneach, 42, 47
aspen, 210
  herbal uses of, 132–34
  history of, 128–32
  spiritual aspects of, 135
aspirin, 36–37
aspurging, 155
asthma, 107, 139
Attis, 116
Audacht Morainn, 67–68

back pain, 133
Baile, 136
Baile in Scáil, 4–5
Ballymote, Book of, 3, 14
Balm of Gilead, 132
balsam fir, 115

balsam poplar, 133
Balts, 59
bards, 48
battle, 41, 145–46
Battle of the Trees, 32
beaked hazelnut, 69
Beauvais, Vincent de, 96
beer, 90
bees, 88–89, 124, 126–27
Bella Coola, 75, 115, 133, 134, 140
Bell Branch, 148, 149, 158
Beltaine, 22, 24, 53, 71, 120–21, 165–74
Bethu Brigte, 73–74
Betula genus. *See* birch
birch, 14, 17–18, 172, 203
    herbal uses, 18–21
    spiritual aspects of, 22
birds, 24
black alder, 30
black ash, 46
black cottonwood, 133, 134
black elder, 106–7
Blackfeet, 116
black hawthorn, 53
black oak, 57
blackthorn, 208
    herbal uses of, 99–100
    history of, 96–99
    spiritual aspects of, 100–101
black willow, 37
blood disorders, 52
blood pressure, 52, 126
bloody urine, 57
boaire, 34
Boann, 94
Bole of Ross, 42
Book of Leinster, 5
Book of the Dun Cow, 16
Bough of Dathi, 42

Bran, 78, 112–13, 147, 148–49
Brehon Laws, 14–16, 86
Bretha Comaithchesa, 14, 55, 68
bride dolls, 36
Brigid, 36, 94–95
Brigid, Saint, 73–74, 95, 187–89
bronchitis, 93, 107, 115, 133, 139–40
brooms, 157
búad, 150–52
bull feasts, 145
burial traditions, 15–16, 128–30

cairn of blessing, 160–61
Calluna genus. *See* heather
cancer, 138–39
Carmina Gadelica, 91–92, 141
Carnea, 53
Carter, Mary, 135
Catawba, 64
cattle, 24
Cattle Raid of Cooley, The, 4, 46–47
Cauldron of Rebirth, 147–48
Celtic Heritage, 34
Celts, 60–61, 80–81
Center, 41
Cernunnos, 185
Cesarn, 5
chaga, 19
chariot making, 62–63
Charlemagne, 116–17
Chehalis, 115, 140
Cherokee, 19–20, 37–38, 45–46, 53,
    57–58, 64, 76, 82, 83, 115, 134
cherrybark oak, 58
cherry birch, 19
Cheyenne, 37, 100
Chickasaw, 109
childbirth, 27, 105
children, 102–6, 170–71

Chippewa, 19, 69, 83, 100, 109, 115, 133, 134, 140

Choctaw, 83, 109

cholera, 93

class, 33–34, 86

cles, 150–52

clootie walls, 159–60

coastal plain willow, 38

coast live oak, 57

Cocidius, 32

colds, 63–64, 107, 115, 126, 133

colic, 26

Connacht, 41

cooking pits, 63

Corc, 5

Cormac Mac Airt, 78, 148

Corylus genus. *See* hazel

cottonwood, 133

coughs, 26, 38, 63–64, 107, 115, 126, 133

Cowlitz, 46, 140

crab apple, 75

crack willow, 38

cramps, 31

Crane Posture, 144–45

cranes, 39–40

Crataegus genus. *See* hawthorn

Cree, 26

Creek, 109

cremation, 129–30

croup, 26

Cúchulainn, 4, 130

Culdub, 49

Culpeper, Nicholas, 69

Cumhal, 105–6

cup mixtures, 156

cystitis, 126

Dálán, 4

dandruff, 57

Danu, 23

daoine maithe, 12, 130

Dearg, 39

death candles, 131

Death of King Fergus, The, 35

Delaware, 45–46, 58, 83, 109, 133–34

Delos, 54

dentifrice, 30, 82

Diarmid, 22

diarrhea, 25–26, 37, 53, 58, 74, 83, 99, 119

dichetal do chennaib, 48–49

digestion, 132

diphtheria, 26, 31

divination, 183–84, 199–211

dorw, 60

douches, 87

dowsing, 71

Druids and Druidism, 5–7, 144–46

divination and, 199–211

magical tools of, 147–49

practices with trees, 152–63

reading the land, 150–52

training of, 33

Durotriges, 128

dwarf elder, 108

dyes, 96–97, 120, 123

dysentery, 58

east, 41

elder, 208–9

herbal uses of, 106–9

history of, 102–6

spiritual aspects of, 109–11

Elder Mother, 109–10, 172

elixirs, 162–63

elm, 172

emetics, 38, 64

emphysema, 69

English oak, 57
English yew, 139–40
Eo Mugna, 42
epilepsy, 139–40
Eskimo, 37
Esus, Lord Master, 39
European ash, 25, 45
eyes, 75, 115

fainting, 38
fairies, 24, 53, 109, 130, 170, 181–83
fairy wells, 158–59
feasts, 81–82
Feradach, King, 5
festivals
    Beltaine, 22, 24, 53, 71, 120–21,
        165–74
    Imbolc, 187–96
    Lughnasad, 38, 174–79
    Samhain, 120, 179–87
fevers, 26, 37, 57, 74, 94, 99, 107, 132
Fiachra, 15–16
fian, 86–87
filid, 48
Finn and the Man in the Tree, 49
Finn mac Cumhaill, 5, 39, 70–71, 106,
    130
fire, 63, 184–85, 189–90
Fire Temple, 95
Fjorgyn, 59
flax, 43
flue, 63–64
fodder, 62, 85
Fomorians, 167
foster children, 102–6
Fox, 45–46, 100, 109
fox grape, 83
Fraxinus genus. *See* ash
Fremont cottonwood, 134

Frigga, 22
fulacht fian, 63
furze, 14, 209
    herbal uses of, 119–20
    history of, 118–19
    spiritual aspects of, 120–21

gentry, 130
gingerroot, 21
Gitksan, 75–76, 115, 134
goat willow, 37
goiters, 57
gonorrhea, 116
Goodding's willow, 38
gout, 45, 64, 82, 126
Grainne, 22
grapes, 82
graves, 15–16, 128–30
gray birch, 20
Greeks, 59, 135, 141–42
Green Man, 54
Grierson, Su, 98
ground hemlock, 140
Gullett, Christopher, 110
Gwern, 32

hair growth, 37
harps, 34–35, 149
hawthorn, 48–51, 205
    herbal uses of, 51–53
    spiritual aspects of, 52–54
Haxey Hood, 35
hazel, 14, 171, 206
    herbal uses of, 69–70
    history of, 67–69
    spiritual aspects of, 70–71
hazel alder, 31
heartburn, 75
heart conditions, 51–52

heartleaf willow, 38
heath, 14
heather, 209–10
  herbal uses of, 125–26
  history of, 122–25
  spiritual aspects of, 126–27
Hecate, 141–42
Hedera genus. *See* ivy
hedgehogs, 192–93
Heliades, 135
herbal basics
Hercules, 135
Herne the Hunter, 61
Heron's Stance, 144–45
hiccups, 139–40
hoarseness, 37
holly, 172, 206
  herbal uses of, 63–64
  history of, 61–62
  spiritual aspects of, 65–66
home, 41
horse chestnuts, 161
hospitality, 80–81
Houma, 38, 58
house blessing, 157

Ilex genus. *See* holly
imbas forosnai, 48–49
Imbolc, 187–96
immune system, 25
indigestion, 139–40
infusions, 9
inheritance, 102
insomnia, 52
internal injuries, 30
intestinal flora, 75
Iona, 137
iron, 27
Iron Age, 129

Iroquois, 19, 38, 46, 58, 64, 83, 115, 133, 134, 140
Isles of the Blessed, 130–31
Ithunn, 77
ivy, 14, 62, 207
  herbal uses of, 87–88
  history of, 85–87
  spiritual aspects of, 88–89

Janus, 53
jaundice, 45
Jupiter, 59

Karok, 140
Kawaiisu, 134
kidneys, 69, 99, 119
kinnikinnik, 133–34, 163
Klallam, 134, 140
Koasati, 64
Kwakiutl, 53, 115–16

land ownership, 15, 85–86
large-toothed aspen, 134
laxatives, 25, 74, 99
Leinster, 41
liaig, 90–91
lice, 30
littletree willow, 37
liver, 99, 125
Lleu, 60
Loki, 77
loso fedo, 122
low birch, 20
Lubhdan, 35
Lughnasad, 38, 174–79
lunantishees, 130

Macha, 176
Maeldúin, 113

Maeve, Queen, 46–47
Mahuna, 57–58
Makah, 76
Malus genus. *See* apple
Manannán, 39, 78, 113
marriage ceremonies, 54
Marston, John, 135
Martin, Saint, 117
mattresses, 123
May Day. *See* Beltaine
mead, 90, 124–25
Meath, 41
Medicinal Plants of Native America,
    58
meditation, tree, 152–53
Menominee, 58, 83, 115
merchants, 86
Mercury, 39
Merlin's Oak, 117
Meroney, Howard, 73, 83
Meskwaki, 69
MicMac, 31, 38, 46, 109, 115, 133
Moerman, Daniel, 58
Mohawk, 70
Mohegan, 31, 83, 100, 109
Montagnais, 26, 31
Montana, 133, 134
mountain ash. *See* rowan
mouth sores, 37
Munster, 41
mushrooms, 71
music, 41

narrowleaf cottonwood, 133
Native Americans, 19
    alder and, 31
    apple and, 75–76
    ash and, 45–46
    aspen and, 133–34

blackthorn and, 100
elder and, 109
grapes and, 82–83
hawthorn and, 53
hazel and, 69–70
holly and, 64
oak and, 57–58
reed and, 94
rowan and, 26–27
silver fir and, 115–16
willow and, 37–38
yew and, 140
nemed, 33–34
Niall of the Nine Hostages, 15–16
north, 41
northern pin oak, 58

oak, 14, 171, 205–6
    herbal uses of, 56–58
    history of, 55–56
    spiritual aspects of, 59–61
Oak Brides, 59
offerings, 131, 156, 173–74
Ogham, 163–64
    Brehon Laws and, 14–16
    for divination, 199–211
    legacy of, 3–4
    magical uses of, 4–5
    as musical notation, 33
    use of, 13–14
Ogma, 17
Oisín, 39
Ojibwa, 26, 38, 53, 58, 69–70, 100, 115,
    133, 134
Okanagan, 134
Ollarba, Battle, 16
Omaha, 100
Oregon ash, 46
Oregon crab apple, 75

Oscar, 135
Osiris, 116

Pacific yew, 138–39, 140
Paiute, 94, 133
paper birch, 20
Parjanyah, 59
Patrick, Saint, 145–46
peachleaf willow, 37
pencerdd, 34
Penobscot, 31, 46
Perkunas, 59
Persephone, 135
Perun, 59
physicians, 90–91
pigs, 56, 68
piles, 56–57
pleurisy, 26
Pliny, 43
pneumonia, 26
Poetic Grades of Early Irish Law, The, 51
poets, 34, 48
Populus genus. *See* aspen
Poseidonios, 80
Potawatomi, 26–27, 140
poultices, 9
prosperity, 41
protection circles, 159
Prunus genus. *See* blackthorn
purple willow, 37
pussy willow, 38

quaking aspen, 132, 134
Quercus genus. *See* oak
Quinault, 134, 140

recipes, 173–74, 179, 187, 193–98
red alder, 31

red elder, 108
red oak, 57
reed, 208
    herbal uses of, 93–94
    history of, 90–92
    spiritual aspects of, 94–95
Rees, Alwyn, 34
Rees, Brinley, 34
rheumatism, 45, 64, 75, 109, 126, 134,
    139–40
ritual cakes, 156
river birch, 19–20
Rosmerta, 39
Ross, Anne, 39
rowan, 203–4
    herbal uses of, 25–27
    history of, 23–25
    spiritual aspects of, 27–28

sacred wood, 171–73
sage willow, 38
salicylic acid, 36–37
Salishan, 134
Salix genus. *See* willow
salves, 9, 161–62
Sambucus genus. *See* elder
Samhain, 120, 179–87
Samish, 76
Sanas Cormaic, 5, 71
sassafras, 21
satire, 49–51
saunas, 18
scabies, 30
Scál, 5
scarlet hawthorn, 53
scurvy, 25
shillelagh, 101
Shoshone, 133

sickles, 147

Sikani, 134

silver branches, 148–49

silver fir, 209

   herbal uses of, 114–16

   history of, 112–14

   spiritual aspects of, 116–17

skin rashes, 64

slavery, 104–5

sloe, 14

smoking mixtures. See kinnikinnik

smooth alder, 31

smudge sticks, 155

snakes, 192

solar crosses, 190–92

Songs of the Forest Trees, 29, 34, 137

soporific sponge, 87

Sorbus genus. See ash

sore throats, 26, 30, 37, 58, 74, 99

south, 41

Southern Carriers, 133

Spanish oak, 58

spring tonics, 21

Squaxin, 134

standing stones, 178

stomach problems, 38, 115, 133

stone circles, 157–58

stones, Ogham and, 13

strewing, 157

summer grape, 82–83

sunburn, 87

swamp white oak, 58

sweet apple, 76

sweet crab apple, 75

taghairm, 145

Taliesin, 32, 105

Tara, 41

Taran, 65

Taranis, 65

taxol, 138–39

Taxus genus. See yew

tea, 63

teinm laegda, 48–49

tellach, 15

Teutons, 59

Thompson Indians, 134

Thor, 59, 65

Thurneysen, Rudolf, 6

Tina, 65

tonsillitis, 37

tree baths, 162

Tree Medicine, Tree Magic, 1

tree medicines, 161–63

trembling, 38

Tuatha de Danann, 23

tuberculosis, 115

Twelfth Night, 77

Uisneach, 41

Ulster, 41

varicose veins, 57

venereal diseases, 133, 134

Vernostonus, 32

vine, 14, 207

   herbal uses of, 82–83

   history of, 79–82

   spiritual aspects of, 83–84

Vitis genus. See vine

vomiting, 31

Voyage of Bran, Son of Febal, The, 78

Wall, Monroe, 138

walnuts, 161

water, 184–85, 189–90

weather forecasting, 43

weaving, 44

weeping willow, 38

west, 41

white birch, 19

white fairy horse, 31–32

white oak, 57–58

white poplar, 133

whitethorn, 14

white willow, 37

wild apple, 73

willow, 14, 171, 204

   herbal uses of, 36–38

   history of, 33–36

   spiritual aspects of, 38–40

wine, 79–80, 123

winterberry holly, 64

woad, 43

Wooing of Etaine, The, 4

wool, 43

worms, 134

wounds, 30, 37, 134

yaupon holly, 64

yerba maté, 64

yew, 172, 210–11

   herbal uses of, 138–40

   history of, 136–38

   spiritual aspects of, 140–42

Yggdrasil, 42

Yokia, 46

Yule logs, 42

Zeus, 42